GOING IT ALONE?

For Megan, Nina and Stella

Going it Alone?
Lone Motherhood in Late Modernity

MARTINA KLETT-DAVIES
London School of Economics, UK

Routledge
Taylor & Francis Group
LONDON AND NEW YORK

First published 2007 by Ashgate Publishing

2 Park Square, Milton Park, Abingdon, Oxon, OX14 4RN
711 Third Avenue, New York, NY 10017, USA

Routledge is an imprint of the Taylor & Francis Group, an informa business

First issued in paperback 2016

British Library Cataloguing in Publication Data
Klett-Davies, Martina
Going it alone? : lone motherhood in later modernity
1. Single mothers – Cross-cultural studies 2. Single mothers – Great Britain 3. Single mothers – Germany
306.8'7432

Library of Congress Cataloging-in-Publication Data
Klett-Davis, Martina.
Going it alone? : lone motherhood in late modernity / by Martina Klett-Davies.
p. cm.
Includes bibliographical references and index.
ISBN-13: 978-0-7546-4388-3 1. Single mothers--Great Britain--Social conditions. 2. Single mothers--Germany--Social conditions. 3. Single mothers--Great Britain--Economic conditions. 4. Single mothers--Germany--Economic conditions. I. Title.
HQ759.915.K63 2007
306.874'320941--dc22

2006031577

ISBN 13: 978-0-7546-4388-3 (hbk)
ISBN 13: 978-1-138-26678-0 (pbk)

Contents

List of Figures

List of Tables

Acknowledgements

Going it alone? I wish to thank the Economic and Social Research Council for providing the financial backing for the research that was the foundation for this book. Their Fellowship funding enabled me to write this book. I owe sincere gratitude to my mentor Diane Perrons and to Professor Bridget Hutter, both at the London School of Economics, for their unfailing support and stimulating suggesting. Their guidance provided the academic foundation for developing this book.

I am especially grateful to all the 70 interviewees for giving their time so generously to this project. I cannot name them individually because it was felt necessary to maintain their confidentiality. Their accounts form the core of this book and I hope they think this study is a worthy representation of their lives.

A number of colleagues and friends have helped me in various stages throughout this project. Special mention must go to Joan O'Mahony and Jim Ottaway for their challenging and inspiring comments at different stages of this work. I would also like to thank Ursula Arens, Anne Boller, Diana Colinese, Rachel Condry, Hazel Johnstone, Victoria Hands, Stephanie Schreiber, Olivia Silverwood-Cope and Sarah Spittle for their suggestions and encouragement.

My most heartfelt thanks go to my three daughters Megan, Nina and Stella – for being the happy little people they are – may they become pioneers. I have left the most important person to the end. I will forever be indebted to David Davies. He supported me and believed in me at all times during the ups and downs of this major piece of work. I could not have done it without them and I did not go it alone.

Chapter 1

Introduction

This book is about how women negotiate lone motherhood in Britain and Germany within late modernity. The western industrialized world has been experiencing dramatic changes in family structures since the 1970s. The nuclear family consisting of a father, mother and their child or children is declining; divorce and cohabitation rates are increasing rapidly (Giddens 1997, 148); women are having their children at a much later age and having fewer children than ever before (Gonzáles López and Solsona Pairó 2000, 60). But the most striking change in family composition has been the escalating number of lone parent families. This is a growing female life form, since the mother heads most lone parent households. I am going to use the term 'lone' mother rather than 'single' or 'solo' mother as the majority of women defined themselves as a lone mother in my interviews in Britain. In Germany, they refer to themselves as Alleinerziehende (alone-educators). For the purpose of this study a lone mother is defined as a mother who lives alone with her child.

The number of lone mothers has almost tripled since the early 1970s to 20 per cent in Germany and 25 per cent in Britain in 2004. Never-married mothers are now the most common type of single mothers with dependent children (Haskey 2002, Statistisches Bundesamt 2006). Although the paid employment rate has been gradually increasing for married mothers, this cannot be said for lone mothers whose employment rate tends to be lower in both countries. German lone mothers are more likely to be in paid employment than their counterparts in Britain (63% and 54% respectively in 2002). Lone mothers in Britain are twice as likely to receive Income Support than lone mothers in Germany (49% and 25% respectively) (Evans et al 2003; Statistisches Bundesamt 2006).

The book draws on interviews with 70 lone mothers who live on state benefits, are unmarried and live in inner city areas in Berlin and London. It aims to explore how these mothers negotiate their lives within two different welfare states with their own public discourses. By listening to lone mothers' experiences we can learn how mothers create meaning and make sense of their situation and of the social policies that effect their lives. In the chapters that follow, I will explain the complexity and diversity of lone mothers' lives and demonstrate the extent of their heterogeneity. State-dependent lone mothering is contradictory. It can be promising as well as threatening. This study focuses on these contradictions and on the way in which lone mothers try to manage choices and constraints. Their strategies are interwoven with how they position themselves as carers, dependants or as paid workers in the German and British welfare states.

Lone mothers are often presented as a homogeneous group, sharing similar disadvantages and existing as a group distinct from other women and from two-parent households. This conflation facilitates the social construction of lone motherhood as a social problem. This book will show that lone mothers are by no means all alike. Even if they are in receipt of state benefits and are not in paid employment they are not poor and deprived in identical ways. Mothers who are going it alone – vary in their 'loneness'. They vary in their degrees of feeling lonely and being alone. Some might have extensive networks of family or friends, while others might be less well connected but do not circumstances as 'lonely'. Some mothers 'go it alone' more so than others. Some have initiative and are self-realized. They use the situation to make it suit their needs and wishes and value the time spent out of paid employment. They go it alone because they lead a life contrary to current policies in the UK and Germany, which prioritize paid work. The book will recognize difference and diversity amongst lone mothers while simultaneously identifying the common problems that lone mothers face in contemporary Germany and Britain.

Lone motherhood is at the cutting edge between Gemeinschaft and Gesellschaft, between the public and the private sphere, and between individual interests and the interests of the system. My research investigates the tension between the public and the private sphere; between paid employment, the welfare state, childcare and state benefit dependency related to the public sphere and to mothering in the private sphere. An example of this tension can be found in the way in which welfare state policies facilitate state-dependent lone mothers while at the same time regulating them (see chapter 4). The book examines how lone mothers themselves experience, construct and negotiate within these divisions under circumstances that may be both constraining and enabling. For some, state-dependent lone motherhood can be a liberating experience, a feminist project. Without falling into the trap of voluntarism and relativism by essentialising women as nurturers, the welfare state may be empowering and an aid to women's self-development and self-fulfilment. Second Wave feminism tended to regard women's financial independence through paid work as a major factor for their emancipation as it no longer confines women to the private patriarchy in the home (Becker-Schmidt 1987). However, there has been increasing recognition that paid employment may not be the way to gender equality and that women themselves value and prioritize their childrearing activities (Brannen 1994, 85; Ribbens 1994, 2).

It can be argued that working women may have escaped a private patriarchy but they have entered a public patriarchy, with its masculine model of employment that also devalues unpaid work (Schön 1989, 13). I would also argue that in capitalism and post-industrialism, full employment has become a utopian thought and paid employment has become highly flexible (Beck 1998a, 13; Bowring 1999, 69). Hypothetically then, the welfare state instead of paid work may be a great contributing factor in women's emancipation because it enables women not only to escape private patriarchy but also parts of public patriarchy, such as the masculine model of employment and gendered inequality in the work place (see chapter 11). Admittedly, the welfare state does not primarily facilitate emancipation as financial support is minimal (see chapter 4). Therefore, my approach sits uncomfortably between the theory of patriarchy, that argues that the welfare state is an instrument for the oppression of women, and the empowerment hypothesis that argues that the welfare state may improve women's lives and is enabling too (Mädje and Neusüß 1994a; Walby 1990).

In Britain, lone motherhood research has a social policy focus restricted to lone mothers' structural constraints. This may be because there are so many unmarried young mothers from a working-class background who have no educational qualifications or work experience and are state-dependent (see chapter 2). Such an approach appears to have influenced Giddens's social theory, which it could be argued reduces and simplifies lone motherhood. It divides lone parents into two groups depending on their economic resources: into the growing minority of 'single mothers by choice' and into the majority of 'single mothers in poverty' (Giddens 1997, 154). The first group consists of women who choose to become lone mothers – who set out to have a child without the support of a spouse or partner. These are 'normally those who possess sufficient resources to manage satisfactorily as a single-parent household.' (Giddens 1997, 154). The second group is characterized by indicators of poverty and social deprivation. Giddens (1991, 6) argues that 'modernity produces difference, exclusion and marginalization'. Clearly, class divisions and gender inequalities result in different access to forms of self-actualization and empowerment. However, it is implied that women with financial resources have the *freedom to* while poor women have *freedom from* only as poor women's lives are dominated by constraints that may make them despair and unable to plan their life while well-off women have choices that add to their self-enrichment.

This book argues that to define material resources alone as the divider between lone mothers' choices and constraints reduces lone mothers' lives to an economic equation. Hypothetically, a well-off mother may feel trapped and stays in a marriage for economic reasons while a poor mother may be better off financially after a separation because she is in control of the money. This approach not only perceives lives as overly determined by structural constraints; it is also over simplistic because it overlooks issues such as the social construction of choices and constraints and of norms and values, such as the concept of mothering and paid employment. In fact, I would argue that poor lone mothers are able to enrich their lives and to negotiate their life satisfactorily despite scarce financial resources. This research implies that mothers can individualize themselves within their different constraints of different social backgrounds. This means that lone mothers, independently of their social background, can create opportunities and shape their self-identity.

The concept of individualization has advanced to the orienteering concept of my research and is an integral part of late modernity (Beck 1992, Beck and Beck-Gernsheim 1990, 1993, 1994, 1995, 1996, 2002). It has been suggested that individualization is the most influential societal theory of the present (Junge 2002). I find the concept of individualization useful because it puts the individual in the centre of society. It incorporates an individual's agency; the powers as well as the obligations individuals have to create their biography, to construct their own lives and relationships albeit in circumstances they have not always chosen. The concept is particularly helpful because it appreciates the fluidity and diversity of family life. It allows for a multidimensional approach that does not just focus on paid work or poverty. It does not look at the family in isolation and as a fixed concept but as a part of a growing diversity in family life, which mirrors and has an impact on other shifts and changes in wider society.

Late modernity is the type of social organization that has been produced by modernization, a product of the political and industrial revolution (Cheal 1991, 26). Where classic modernity was characterized by class-based societies that shaped people's lives as destiny, in late modernity, individuals are left to shape their own destinies. The family has become a fluid and changing concept that is viewed in the context of all the other changes that are occurring under late modernity (Beck and Beck-Gernsheim 1995).

To Beck and Beck-Gernsheim (2002, 151), late modern society is characterized by a process called reflexive modernization, because the modernization process is becoming reflexive by being reproduced and pushed forward in scientific and public discourses about the problems it generates. It is essentially an acceleration and radicalization of the development of core institutional features of modern society, which are capitalism, industrialism, state administration and military power. Reflexive modernization throws all basic social principles into flux in that it undermines modern society as simple modernization has undermined the traditional society. Part of this process is *social reflexivity*. This implies that individuals have their lives no longer set out for them and their lives are no longer governed by traditional assumptions and expectations but are constantly faced with choices. The establishment of identity increasingly becomes a life project of reflexive subjects. Reflexive modernity maintains that there are new rules for political and social systems that sociologists should set out to explain (Beck, Bonß and Lau 2003, 2-8). This is different from post-modernity theorists who mark the emergence of a wholly new historical epoch (see chapter 3).

The concept of individualization is based on the idea that, consequent to industrialization and urbanization, a liberation from traditional values such as tradition, religion or the state followed. The main causes of individualization are increased social rights, women's emancipation and the educational revolution in the 1960s and 1970s. Categories such as class and social status, gender roles and family are supposed to have become increasingly fragile and replaced with new demands and constraints such as the job market, the welfare state and institutions and regulations. This means that there are more choices and negotiations about available lifestyles. While individualization should not be confused with self-fulfilment, the individual becomes focused on his or her own growth and self-development. This is because individualization emphasizes the need to make choices in a world that no longer has universal certainties and fixed models of life. An individual striving for fulfilment sets the traditional family under pressure, especially as it is no longer predetermined but has to be negotiated (see chapter 3). The concept has high explanatory value because it allows for a wider range of possibilities and contradictions of how state-dependent lone mothers actively negotiate their choices and constraints in creating their biography and self-identity.

Identity is defined as people's source of meaning and experience (Berger and Luckmann 1991, 210). It is also who or what a person is as well as the characteristics determining this (Oxford Dictionary 2006). According to Giddens (1991, 2) the self is not a passive entity and self-identity is a reflexively organized endeavour. The concept of individualization too acknowledges that as part of the reflexive project the self continuously revises biographical narratives. In my study, some mothers viewed their situation as an opportunity to construct their biographies actively in non-traditional ways. Other mothers experienced state dependency and lone motherhood as an individual misfortune because ideally they would have liked to conform to the traditional nuclear family.[1] Because individualization is a process, it enables us to locate lone mothers at different points of this continuum and it therefore aides the identification of patterns of diversity. The only question is in how far negotiations continue to be contextualized within class and ethnicity.

Lone mothers' lives are not just constrained by external structures and norms that are fixed rules of conduct. This study emphasizes the powers as well as the obligation individuals have to create their biography. Some of those I have interviewed perceived state benefits as a legitimate source of income for looking after their child full-time, or as a 'citizen's income' or a 'carers allowance'. These lone mothers felt empowered because they were able to make state benefits suit their needs. I have defined this group as pioneers because they have 'escaped' a form of social control by giving it a new meaning. Their attitude might prove most successful in coping with the stigma attached with state dependence (see chapter 7). Full-time mothering may also be a liberalising experience because it offers a connectedness with existential holistic life processes (Schön 1989, 29). For others, the transition to motherhood offered a new sense of cohesion and direction (Baily 1999, 351). Motherhood therefore operates as a narrative pivot in the construction of a reflexive biography and is an opportunity for renewed narrative movement (see chapter 5).

I specifically chose lone mothers who are not in paid employment because they are in a 'precarious' situation or at least are perceived to be by various political and academic discourses. This book, which has gender at its centre, and aims to further our understanding of lone mothers and to develop the concept of individualization. To explore whether and to what extent the concept of individualization has explanatory value for lone motherhood, three research questions were developed:

1. How do lone mothers negotiate their lives as mothers and as dependants?

2. Can state-dependent lone motherhood be experienced as a liberating experience?

3. To what extent can the thesis of individualization explain the experience of state-dependent lone mothers?

My research set out to investigate whether lone motherhood is the result of a demise of tradition and to consider how far lone mothers are driven by the search for self-development and self-fulfilment. Viewing individualization as a process, enables us to locate lone mothers at different points of a continuum therefore allowing for patterns of diversity.

1 The *Oxford Dictionary* (2006) defines a nuclear family as a 'couple and their dependent children, regarded as a basic social unit.'

The study

Public and academic discourses on lone motherhood are not just based on lone mothers' characteristics; they are also culturally and historically embedded in their respective welfare states and academic traditions. Comparative research is useful because lone motherhood in one country can be looked at from a new angle by using the questions raised in the other country. Comparative research is also valuable because it not only enables the study of patterns of diversity that are embedded in the different welfare states but it also is analyses patterns that are not nation-bound but transcend these structures (Keränen 1997).

My qualitative research has been based on ideas of grounded theory. The advantages of this approach is that it lends itself to a multi-dimensional and holistic approach (Glaser and Strauss 1967, Bryman and Burgess 1994, Sayer 1992, Stanley and Wise 1993). Grounded theory is a very useful framework since it maintains openness and scepticism and enables the researcher to challenge assumptions, question even the mundane, and to think analytically rather than descriptively about data (Whyte 1984, 250). It uses a combination of inductive and deductive thinking to systematize and solidify connections and moves constantly between asking questions and making comparisons. The approach of grounded theory is interrelated with feminist epistemology and the theory of feeling, belief and experientially based knowledge (Stanley and Wise 1993). This perceives academic research knowledge to be embedded within gendered cultural contexts (Ramazanaglou 1989). Feminist epistemology has revitalized social science methodology by incorporating anthropological and feminist concepts and by addressing the power relationship between theory and experience (Stanley and Wise 1993, 161-162). Both approaches enable us to chart the parameters of discourse rather than draw firm conclusions about factors influencing the situations of lone mothers in Britain and Germany.

Seventy in-depth interviews were conducted over a period of three years (summer 1996 to summer 1998). My study acknowledges that lone mothers carry a multitude of identities but focused on 'situated identities', such as state dependency, relationships, paid employment and mothering. The interviews are based on the 'life-history' approach that collects information about mothers' past, present and future. This is close to how people 'naturally' think of their lives and it is more holistic because it does not narrow the interview to predetermined topics (Ribbens 1994, 38). Further research will show to what extent this study is representative of state-dependent lone motherhood in general. Nonetheless, common patterns can be found to exist in London and Berlin as well as practices and patterns that transcend national social policies and political cultures. The type categories in particular may be employed as a platform for more theoretical prepositions about lone motherhood.

Choice of locality

For this study, the urban centres of Berlin and London were chosen because they are areas with a high proportion of lone mothers. According to the concept of individualization 'new' lifestyles may be more pronounced in urban centres (Beck and Beck-Gernsheim 1990). Studies show that lone mothers tend to move to larger cities because they fear prejudice and discrimination and anticipate increased labour market opportunities, relative anonymity and more open-minded attitudes (Drauschke and Stolzenburg 1994a).

The research was not only concentrated on London, East and West Berlin but also on inner city areas or boroughs with the countries' highest proportion of lone mothers. In particular, the focus was on one inner-city neighbourhood in each city because in order to understand how lone mothers negotiate their lives their neighbourhoods need to be understood. Neighbourhoods tend to have their own gendered value system and expectations and belief systems which depend on historical and regionally developed processes (Duncan 2000, 18). Moreover, lone mothers' opportunities for finding work need to be seen in the context of the local labour market and local facilities such as public and private childcare, commercial facilities and infrastructure.

The neighbourhoods selected as a reference point were in East Berlin (Katzenhain), in West Berlin (Hundedorf) and in London (Northington). I conducted exactly half of the interviews in Germany with single lone mothers in West Berlin and the other half in former East Berlin because the situation and the discourse of lone mothers was quite different before reunification and remains so (see chapter 4).

On first sight, West Berlins' Hundedorf distinguishes itself from East Berlins' Katzenhain because it is much larger and there are affluent parts as well as Berlin's largest council estates such as the 'Märkisches Viertel' built in 1964. Many of the interviewees lived in high rises or in council flats built just before or after the Second World War. However, none of the estates were as run down or as unsafe as many estates in London. It was unique to the Katzenhain borough that its state benefit council officers come from social rather than administrative professions (for example nursery school teachers). This has had a great effect on how positively lone mothers have perceived their experiences with the council. Most of the interviewees in Katzenhain live in four storey purpose built blocks built in the middle of last century and some of them were partly or fully renovated after reunification in 1990.

The number of lone mothers in the inner London boroughs is high and it is particularly high in the borough of Northington (Haskey 1993). Lone mothers tend to live in areas with high unemployment and Northington is typical for this as it has a higher than average unemployment rate and is also the second poorest area in Britain (Northington Council 1996). Moreover, Northington has more council housing than private sector housing (Hasluck et al 1996).

Finding lone mothers

In finding mothers that would agree to be interviewed every attempt has been made to avoid the emphasis on 'likeminded' lone mothers. Several methods were tried with varying success rates. I advertised in local classified newspapers and was given new leads through 'snowballing'. I was most successful when approaching lone mothers in person at the Friedrichshain and Hundedorf state benefit departments of the two borough councils. I introduced myself to each lone mother who was a personal caller in the waiting corridors of the benefit offices during office hours. Here, lone mothers could enquire about and receive their benefits.

In London, I found most lone mothers when I placed myself in front of post offices on Monday and Tuesday mornings in Northington. These were the days, when state-dependent lone mothers cashed in their Income Support or Child Benefit cheque books. I handed out my letter in which I explained my research. Many women, who I asked in person, perceived me as non-threatening and wanted to help.

The structure of the book

While this first chapter introduces the research issue, the second chapter describes common themes in the analysis of the position of lone mothers in political and academic discourses. It is argued that academic discourses influence and are a reflection of how lone mothers are positioned in society in East and West Germany and Britain. I suggest that the representation of lone mothers is different in both countries due to their specific welfare states' ideologies and culture. This may be further interrelated with lone mothers' different socio-demographic characteristics.

Chapter three discusses the concept of individualization and to what extent it can explain the experience of state-dependent lone mothers. It seems a good orienteering concept as it recognizes the individual's obligation to create one's own biography and leaves room to discover patterns of diversity in lone motherhood. Nonetheless, it may overemphasize the demise of tradition and ignore old structural constraints such as class.

The fourth chapter analyses the development of the German and the British welfare states. Modern Germany was born from two countries: the Berlin Wall was demolished in 1989 but economic and social walls continue to exist. Reunification had a profound impact on the life courses of East German women who grew up under a different set of gender values. These gender values continue to influence women's lives. Therefore, at least two national trends in Germany have to be considered. Nonetheless, common patterns in the way in which lone mothers negotiate their lives can be found in Britain and in East and West Germany. This knowledge is particularly useful as Germany and Britain are converging in the common European market and the European Union. This chapter is concerned with two levels of welfare state analysis. The first part explores the ideological and historical developments of the welfare state concerning lone mothers. The second part focuses on the analysis of specific state benefits available to lone mothers when the fieldwork took place.

The remaining chapters discuss the research data. The interview data enables me to chart the parameters of discourse rather than draw firm conclusions about factors influencing the situations of lone mothers in Britain and Germany.

Chapter five focuses on lone mothers' social identities and positioning vis-à-vis the labour market and analyses the construction of 'good' mothering. Most mothers were in paid employment prior to having children and some had worked after having children. The first part of this chapter identifies key barriers for paid employment. The second part explores the concept of mothering and mothers' identities as mothers. It shows the limited influence of the welfare state regarding the paid employment/caring dilemma. This is partly because social policies tend to be based on a rational-economic model, which is based on neo-classical assumptions (Edwards and Duncan

1996). Folbre (1994) has already critiqued neo-classical assumptions for failing to insert non-economic features such as altruism into a theory of the economics of the family. The social construction of good mothering or 'gendered moral rationalities' is also an important influencing factor in the paid employment/caring dilemma. Gendered moral rationalities are social negotiated understandings about the proper relationship between good mothering and paid work (Duncan and Pfau-Effinger 2000, 7). Here, norms have been replaced by morals that leave room for debate over the right course of action.

The main theme of this research was to find out how lone mothers negotiated their lives with respect to relationships, motherhood, paid work and state dependency. Distinct patterns arose out of the data and these and the subsequent chapters demonstrate the way in which the data informed the creation of three type categories (see chapter 6). The 'pioneer', 'coper' and the 'struggler' types are based on lone mothers' coping strategies, identity and confidence. Pioneers were an 'ideal fit' with the concept of individualization (see chapter 7). Copers viewed their situation as temporary and improvable (see chapter 8). A couple of strugglers felt overwhelmed by constraints and perceived themselves to have no choices (see chapter 9). Chapter ten shows that there are also 'borderliners'. These are women that have characteristics of two different categories.

Chapter eleven summarizes the research findings and cross-national explanations and discusses the research questions: How do lone mothers negotiate their lives as mothers and as dependants? Can state-dependent lone motherhood be experienced as a liberating experience? And to what extent can the thesis of individualization explain the experience of state-dependent lone mothers? This chapter also gives some social policy indications for increasing lone mothers' choices. Recommendations with regards to paid employment, education and state benefits derived from specific suggestions made by interviewees and from conclusions I draw from the findings. I suggest that classifying lone mothers according to their relationship to the labour market ignores their social construction of good mothering.

Chapter 2

Explaining Lone Motherhood – Academic and Political Discourses in Britain and Germany

This chapter focuses on the dominant academic and political debates about lone motherhood in Britain and Germany. These debates are particularly relevant as they make sense of social relationships whilst reflecting and influencing how lone mothers are positioned in society. Moreover, the dominance of a particular discourse in a national context may affect how the situation of lone motherhood is understood within each country.

Lone mothers are particularly vulnerable in economic terms and stand out among the poverty-prone population. For this reason, the category has caught the attention of researchers studying family lifestyles for being, on the one hand, a social 'risk group' and on the other, a 'marker of social change'. The first part of this chapter organizes the presentation of lone mothers in Britain and Germany into three main discourses; the 'alternative lifestyle', the 'social problem' and the 'social threat' discourses. Duncan and Edwards (1999) proposed a similar scheme, which allows us to systematize the public-political, and the scientific debate on lone parents. In Germany, the alternative lifestyle discourse welcomes lone motherhood essentially as an irreversible result of modernization with one strand viewing lone mothers as a way to escape patriarchy. The social problem discourse, prevalent in both Germany and Britain, accepts the fact that lone motherhood is part of modern society and aims to improve the lives of lone mothers through social policy. The third discourse, specific to Britain and to the US, is the social threat discourse, which promotes the nuclear family.

The representation of lone mothers in Britain

A sense of optimism about the family was prevalent in Britain and in Germany after the Second World War. In the 1950s and 1960s, in Germany, as in Britain, family sociology was theoretically embedded in Parsons's (1971) structural functionalism that gave importance to the evaluation of families in relation to society. During industrialization the family changed, from consisting of several working generations, to the nuclear family which consists of a male breadwinner and a female homemaker who cares for the children. Other functions, such as the care for the elderly, were taken over by alternative systems. Structural functionalism argues that the nuclear family is 'functional' because it creates the status quo necessary to meet the demands of industrialization. This implies that other family forms such as lone motherhood are 'dysfunctional' and threaten social cohesion, or are at least theoretically residual (Cheal 1991, 34).

The family of the 1950s has hitherto been perceived as a benchmark of the pre-industrialization family. Interestingly, this is a great misconception as the family of the 1950s actually presents a historical exception (Burkhart 1998, 125; Smart and Neale 1999, 28).[1] Structural functionalism suffers another major flaw, this time of 'gender blindness', by not acknowledging the unequal gendered power relationships and hierarchies between family members.

In the 1970s, relationships within the family became a legitimate area of sociological analysis for the first time (Finch 1989; Kameraman and Kahn 1988). In the 1970s and 1980s several strands of second wave feminism viewed the nuclear family and motherhood as an indicator for the oppression of women (Abbott and Wallace 1997, 153; Barrett and McIntosh 1991; Ferri and Smith 1996; Oakley 1974). This idea that there could be such a thing as a core site of oppression was later rejected, as the meaning of 'the family' is not consistent for all women (Smart and Neale 1999, 3). Instead of developing the idea of a new type of family and motherhood as a feminist project, different strands of feminisms analysed and criticized the nuclear family and motherhood, as well as lone motherhood. By the end of the 1980s, while the Conservative Party was in government under John Major, lone mothers, particularly those who received state benefits and who were single, became a symbol for low morals and high public expenditure in the political and public discourse.

The social threat discourse

In the late eighties and the beginning of the 1990s, under the Tory government, lone mothers featured prominently in social exclusion debates. The definitions of 'social exclusion' vary according to the Party in government, but for lone mothers they were defined in both, relational and economic terms (Stewart 2000, 10). The term social exclusion creates outsiders and thus arises from the need to set boundaries. Under the Tory government lone mothers were portrayed as economically undeserving and morally wrong.

The social threat discourse is concerned with three issues in particular. It deals with lone mothers' perceived unwillingness to work and the subsequent costs to the state. Similarly it cites lone mothers' perceived infidelity and moral irresponsibility. Academic versions of this discourse were popular in the 1990s, right until the Labour government came to power in 1997 (Dennis and Erdos 1992; Morgan 1995). In Britain and US, the socio-economic theorist Charles Murray reintroduced a media-friendly definition of the term 'underclass' with its signs of illegitimacy, violent crime and unemployment (Murray 1990). The underclass discourse identifies the cause of social exclusion with the moral and cultural characteristics of those who are

---

1 According to Burkhart (1998:125) the 1950s experienced a catch-up effect that is a marriage and family boom because both had been interrupted and postponed by WWII and the years after.

excluded. The excluded, the so-called underclass, are presented as culturally distinct from the mainstream.

The social threat discourse is in favour of the traditional nuclear family, with its obligations and socially binding moral codes that ensure the wider stability of society. According to Murray (1994), the lack of a male providing partner, the absence of a male role model for children, the absence of paid employment and state benefit dependency lead to juvenile crime. Here, children are reproducing the underclass and unmarried lone mothers on state benefits must then produce the underclass and can be viewed as a social threat. Conversely, the affluent, qualified and working lone mother is not (Murray 1994).

The social threat discourse also masks inequality, focussing on the individual's agency and overlooking structural constraints. It presumes that people are driven by a moral self-interest, a key feature of Libertarianism. Duncan and Edwards (1999, 36) argue that this discourse views lone mothers as actively choosing to receive state benefits because entering paid employment or marriage is considered uneconomical. This 'rational choice' assumption led the neo-conservative wing of the British Conservative Party in government (1979-1997) to see cutting state benefits as a way to reinstall the traditional nuclear family and an incentive to enter paid work. Here, paid work is viewed as a means of social discipline (Duncan and Edwards 1999, 30). In the mid 1990s a 'Back To Basics' campaign stressed a 'return to family values' and castigated the role of the welfare state in providing housing and benefits and hence encouraging lone motherhood. Nonetheless, it was the Labour government that removed the extra allowances available to lone parents, such as the One Parent Benefit in 1998.

The social problem discourse

The main difference between the social threat and the social problem discourses is their distinctive emphasis on agency and structure. In social problem discourses, lone mothers are positioned as victims of external circumstances who are in need of more support, not less. Mostly, lone mothers are presented as a social problem, which is a result of their and their children's relative deprivation (Ely 1999, 188; Giddens 1997, 155). Nonetheless, the concern about lone mothers' poverty is mixed with concern about levels of public expenditure, anti-social behaviour of unattached young men and the fate of lone mothers' children (Millar and Ridge 2001).

The Labour Party's election victory in 1997 marked a shift from viewing lone mothers within the social threat discourse to viewing mothers as a social problem, because of the associations of child poverty with a lone parent family. Contrary to the underclass discourse that assumed lone mothers were unwilling to work, the Labour government referred to research, which showed that lone mothers want to work but there are barriers such as lack of childcare and the poverty trap. Since 1997, the Labour Party has made a concerted effort to improve lone mothers' labour market opportunities but the success of in-work-benefits and welfare-to-work programmes has been limited (see chapter 4). This social problem discourse undermines the legitimacy of non-participation in paid work and can therefore be criticized for its inability to address the question of unpaid work in society (see chapter 11).

Britain, unlike Germany, has a strong social policy tradition, which is integral to much academic lone motherhood research in the 1990s. This research focuses on the development and evaluation of social policies that are thought to influence lone mothers to enter employment. Examples are the improvement of lone mothers' educational and vocational qualifications, tax incentives and public childcare (Bradshaw et al 1998; Bryson et al 1997; Ford 1998; Harrop and Moss 1995; Joshi 1990, McKay and Marsh 1994; Millar 1994).

Since New Labour took over in 1997, a large number of policy-based studies have been conducted into the new design of core elements in British social policy. New Labour promotes the concept of work activation under the 'New Deal for lone parents' trademark and in-depth studies are available for those programmes (for example Evans et al 2002; Evans et al 2004). In Germany, social programmes have rarely been the subjects of evaluation (Erler 2004).

The representation of lone mothers in Germany

In Germany, lone mothers have not been viewed as a social threat at all. Hence German research, in contrast to most research in Anglo-American countries, does not primarily focus on the problem areas of lone motherhood, such as costs to the welfare state, poverty and teenage pregnancies (Klett-Davies 2005). Nonetheless, a couple of economic researchers are concerned with the question of how the labour market participation of lone mothers can be increased. Their work, based on economic modelling, assumes that lone mothers make rational economic choices to maximize financial and personal gain. It is suggested that better schooling and training, improved childcare facilities and a different benefit system, would increase the probability of lone mothers entering paid work (Staat and Wagenhals 1993 and 1994). In Britain, these models have long been criticized by sociologists for ignoring that mothers are involved in wider social negotiations of how they should operate, as mothers, solely responsible for their children (Duncan and Pfau-Effinger 2000, 1). In other words, mothers may decide not to take up work because they feel morally obliged to care for their children themselves (Barlow et al 2002, 113) (see chapter 4).

In West Germany, the role of lone mothers with very young children is perceived as a full-time carer, based on the psychological attachment theory that the first years are the most important in a child's life (Mählmann 1998, 66). Experts such as paediatricians, psychologists and powerful charitable networks encourage mothers with young children to stay at home. These gendered values are surprisingly persistent and are valid across all social classes. In West Germany, mothering and being out of paid employment is highly valued even by feminists. An example is the 1987 'mother manifesto' (Müttermanifest) of the Green Party in parliament, which appealed for the re-evaluation and remuneration of full-time mothering. In comparison to other European countries, the employment rate of mothers with young children and with qualifications at graduate level is lowest in West Germany (Sackmann 2000, 246). The behaviour that is regarded most appropriately for women in West Germany is an employment break of several years for home-based childcare and part-time work during the phase of active motherhood (Pfau-Effinger and Geissler 2002, 79) (see chapter 4). This public perception is reinforced by the political discussion of a declining fertility rate in Germany.

Social problem discourse

The dominant popular discourse of lone motherhood in Germany is that lone mothers are poor, overworked and to be pitied. This may be a legacy from the 1960s when most single parents were widows of soldiers that died in the Second World War (Erler 2004). This more sympathetic attitude entails patronising patriarchal elements. In the past, lone motherhood has been perceived as merely a temporary 'emergency' solution. The women were to be shown pity and their children supported (Schülein 1994). The government periodically discusses how Income Support recipients can be encouraged to take up paid work. Lone mothers are not included in this debate as their working capability is regarded as limited. Also, in comparison to state-dependent lone mothers - who tend to be white and to have German citizenship - asylum seekers are made much more responsible for high state benefit expenditure. They now compose a significant part of state benefit recipients partly because asylum seekers are legally prevented from working (Leisering and Leibfried 1999, 226).

The rhetoric around lone mothers in Germany's social policy is different from that in Britain. The German government does not provide a welfare-to-work programme specifically designed for lone mothers. Lone mothers are included in policies for mothers in general and this makes Germany a more sympathetic place for lone mothers to live. Despite the high costs of reunification, a long-lasting recession and economic restructuring, the Red-Green Coalition German government (in power until 2005) actually expanded family policies while unemployment benefits and pensions were cut (Seeleib-Kaiser 2004). For example, current parental leave arrangements allow parents on Childrearing Benefits to work up to 30 hours a week. Lone mothers only lose their 'immunity' status from blame when children are no longer dependent, or when they enter a partnership with a man, who, in public and political perception, should maintain the family (Schülein and Simsa 1994). This reinforces the dominant image of traditional breadwinner/female part-time worker model.

Alternative lifestyle discourse

The 'lifestyle choice' discourse puts lone mothers into a more 'autonomous' and positive position than the social problem discourse. The lifestyle discourse can partly be explained by the fact that lone motherhood research in Germany tends to be conducted within the discipline of sociology. Reflecting this is a body of research that examines the well-being or the alternative lifestyle of lone motherhood rather than its assumed negative effects (Drauschke and Stolzenburg 1994b; Frise and Stahlberg 1992; Napp-Peters 1983 and 1987; Nave-Herz 1992a, 1992b and 1994; Niepel 1994a and 1994b). More recently, research has been exploring arrangements of how single parents relate to their own children and their social network (Hoff 2001; Kosmann et al 2003; Vetter et al 2002).

Seeing lone motherhood as an alternative lifestyle cannot be confused with 'single motherhood by choice' (women consciously becoming pregnant and choosing motherhood without a partner); nevertheless, within this discourse, it is no longer assumed that lone parenthood is just an emergency and short-term arrangement. It has also been found that once lone parents, and especially lone mothers, discover the advantages of this family form they may wish to prolong it (Mädje and Neusüß 1994a and 1994b; Nave-Herz and Krüger 1992). Lone motherhood has been 'normalized', as just another family type, that is a result of social change.

The German discourse has begun to follow the British discourse that concentrates on lone mothers' precarious economic situation albeit within the alternative lifestyle discourse that emphasizes their heterogeneity (Andreß 2001; Kosman et al 2003; Ott 2001). In one study from Thuringa, one third of the lone mothers interviewed were satisfied with their situation while two thirds face problems such as unsatisfactory job situation, problematic family situation, childcare problems and social isolation (Brand and Hammer 2002). Schneider et al (2001) detect clear differences between routes into lone motherhood, their labour market integration and their material parameters. The thesis of 'differentiation' is now used when talking about lone motherhood in Germany. This encompasses the material aspects of lone mothers' situation in relation to 'social change'.

Escaping patriarchy discourse

In opposition to both the social problem and alternative lifestyle discourses, a radical feminist view of lone motherhood plays a peripheral role in the relevant research work and public debate in Germany. However, this approach laid the groundwork for normalising single parenting and furthered the integration of biographical decision-making into lone motherhood research. Here, lone motherhood is connected with the liberation from private, as well as public, patriarchy. This view accepts the economic and social disadvantages faced by lone mothers but mainly focuses on the positive aspects for children, and the liberating effects for the mother (Gutschmidt 1994 and 1997; Mädje and Neusüß 1994b; Meyer and Schulze 1989).

According to Heiliger (1993 and 1994) children with lone mothers receive more time, care and love, and they are more independent, less aggressive, and sometimes especially talented. In this discourse women are no longer willing to subordinate themselves in relationships with men. Women's lives have become more independent and their expectations of men have changed. Most of the women can no longer imagine participating in a traditional division of labour but men who share their expectations, however, seem to be difficult to find. For lone mothers, economic dependence is no longer a barrier to escaping patriarchy, even if it means receiving state benefits. Therefore, in this discourse these state benefits are viewed positively and as enabling (Mädje and Neusüß 1994b). Heiliger's research in particular gives an indication of the confidence of lone mothers in Germany.

I have also found women who view lone motherhood within this escaping patriarchy discourse in both, Britain and Germany. However, this discourse is hardly recognized by British academic research and is only on the periphery in German research.

Socio-demographic characteristics of lone mothers in Britain and Germany

This section compares and contrasts socio-demographic characteristics between lone mothers in Britain and Germany that may partly explain the different political and academic discourses. The major points are that in Britain, lone mothers are not only more likely to be never-married and have fewer educational qualifications, but they are also younger and tend to have more children. In 2000 in Britain, twice as many lone mothers were under 25 years of age than in Germany (12% and 6% respectively) (Evans et al 2003; Statistisches Bundesamt 2006).

Table 2.1 indicates that the number of lone parent families in Britain remains higher than in Germany because of the lower number of lone parents in West Germany. Historically, in East Germany, parenthood was not as much connected with marriage or co-habitation as in West Germany (see chapter 4). Interestingly, while the number of lone parents is still on the increase in Germany, in Britain, we can actually speak of a slight decline or of a plateau that has been reached.

Table 2.1 Proportion of lone parent families of all families with dependent children in percent, 1990–2004

	West Germany	East Germany	United Germany	Great Britain
1990	13*	21*	15	19**
1996	16	20	17	21
2000	17	22	18	26
2004	19	25	20	25

Source: General Household Survey (2006), Mikrozensus (Statistisches Bundesamt 2006)
* Until 1996, the Mikrozensus included co-habiting parents into the lone parent category.
** Britain's figure is for 1991.

German lone mothers are more likely to be in paid employment than their British counterparts (63% and 54% respectively in 2002) (Evans et al 2003; Statistisches Bundesamt 2006). Nonetheless, Figure 2.1 illustrates that the lone mothers' employment rate in unified Germany is stagnating. This is mainly due to high unemployment connected to the economic recession and restructuring (see chapter 4). In Britain, the lone mothers' employment rate is still slightly on the increase, most likely due to policy reforms and low unemployment (see chapter 4).

Nonetheless, in Germany, lone mothers are more likely to work *full-time* than in Britain (65% and 40% respectively). German lone mothers are also more likely to be in full-time employment than their married counterparts (65% and 48% respectively) (Evans et al 2002; Statistisches Bundesamt 2006). On one hand, part-time work may well offer flexible hours of work, which enables lone mothers to combine employment and domestic responsibilities. On the other hand however, part-time employment does not secure financial independence and tends to be badly paid and insecure. It is highly 'flexibilized' and is characterized by short-term contracts and few hours (Daune-Richard 1998, 221; Rubery 1998,140).

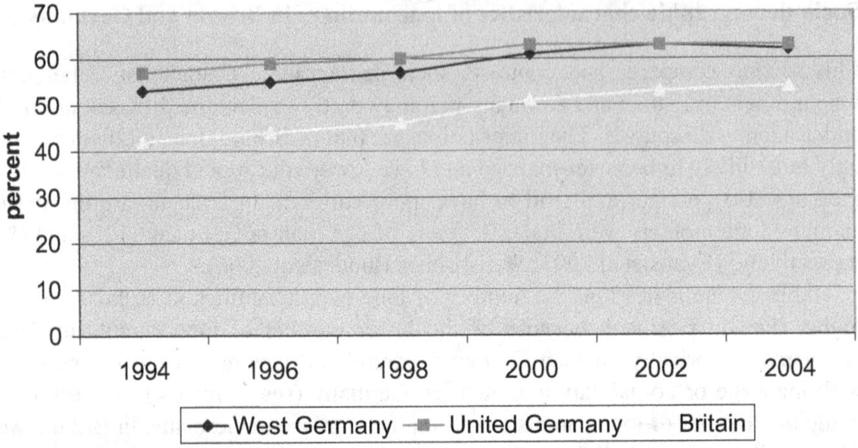

Figure 2.1 Employment rates of lone mothers with dependent children, 1994–2004

Britain has seen a large increase in the number of lone mothers who draw state benefits but the number is slowly declining. In 1995, the proportion that received Income Support was 63 per cent but the number decreased to 49 per cent by 2002. This is partly due to policy changes and to lone mothers' transfer to Jobseeker Allowance or disability benefits (Evans et al 2003). In Germany, only 25 per cent received Income Support in 2002, up from 22 per cent in 1996. However, lone parents in former East Germany are more dependent on Income Support than lone parents in West Germany (27% and 16% per cent) (Statistisches Bundesamt 2006). This increase of state dependency and related child poverty has generated interest by the academic community, just like in Britain (Kosmann et al 2003; Strohmeier and Kersting 2003).

Lone mothers in Germany may not receive state benefits for as long as British lone mothers. Although in both countries, women who continue to have more children and have no educational qualifications, tend to remain on state benefits for longer (Evans et al 2003; Kosman et al 2003, 10). A British study, that interviewed lone parents in 1991 and again ten years later, ascertained that there is a strong long-term continuity in benefit receipt. More than half (54%) of those on Income Support in 1991 and who subsequently remained alone in 2001, remained on Income Support (Marsh and Vegeris 2004, 4).

In Britain, the social problem discourse may be influenced by lone mothers' 'non-conformist' characteristics. First, they are more likely to have more than one child than their married counterparts and lone mothers in Germany. According to Eurostat data, almost three quarters of unmarried lone parents in Germany have one child only (71%), in comparison to only 44 per cent in Britain (Lehmann and Wirtz 2004). Secondly, in contrast to German lone mothers, British lone mothers continue to have more children alone and this may partly explain why there are less likely to be in paid employment and reliant on state benefits instead. Although German lone mothers are older, they have fewer children and do not have more children alone. Unmarried mothers have even fewer children.

Another factor related to state benefit dependency is education. In Britain, there are many educationally 'under-achieving' lone mothers in contrast to their married counterparts (Bryson et al 1997, 17). In contrast, lone mothers in Germany are more likely to have basic educational qualifications than married mothers (Wagner 1999). Low educational qualifications may explain why lone mothers in Britain are more likely to work in low-paid unskilled and semi-skilled manual jobs or in personnel services, such as cleaning, catering, hairdressing and related occupations. In comparison, lone mothers in Germany seem to be more likely to work in the public and in skilled jobs in the service sector (Rowlingson and McKay 1998, 47).

Unmarried lone mothers are more likely to be state-benefit-dependent and Britain has a higher proportion of unmarried mothers compared to Germany. In 2000, 41 lone mothers in Britain were unmarried as supposed to 37 per cent in Germany (Haskey 2002; Statistisches Bundesamt 2006). British never-married lone mothers tend to be from a working-class background, be much younger than other lone mothers and coupled mothers and they are least likely to be in paid work (Rowlingson and McKay 2005).

Another reason for the different discourse in Britain and Germany is that teenage pregnancies are very rare in Germany in contrast to Britain (Office of National Statistics 2001). Britain has the highest rate of teenage motherhood compared with other European Union countries. In Britain, teenagers from disadvantaged backgrounds may progress more quickly into motherhood because a child is viewed as a provider of an identity and a purpose in life. Researchers found that job prospects and material position of teenage lone mothers were unlikely to have been improved by delaying child bearing (Phoenix 1994; Rowlingson and McKay 1998, 197).

Conclusion

This chapter has given an overview over the different public and academic discourses of lone motherhood in Germany and Britain. It has illustrated the social problem discourse, the alternative discourse and the escaping patriarchy discourse in Germany and the social threat and social problem discourse in Britain.

In contrast to the social threat debate in the US, ethnicity has neither figured prominently in the discussion about lone parents and state benefits in Britain nor in Germany. This is most probably the result of the relative racial homogeneity of Britain and Germany's lone motherhood population. In Britain, black lone mothers constitute less than five per cent of all lone mothers' households although women from West Indian backgrounds are the single most likely ethnic group to be in lone motherhood. This group is five times more likely than white or Asian women to become lone mothers, and especially never-married lone mothers (Rowlingson and McKay 1998). Nonetheless, they cannot feed the social problem debate because studies show that they tend to be in paid work, especially in full-time work although it is slowly decreasing among Black mothers under the age of 25 (Reynolds 2002, 71).[2]

In comparison in Germany, lone motherhood is concentrated among the German population and not the Turkish, Yugoslav and Italian communities (Engstler 1998, 77).

Lone mothers' socio-demographic characteristics in Britain may influence the social problem discourse in this country. Briefly, British lone mothers are more often never-married, younger and continue to have more children. German lone mothers are older, have fewer children and have more and higher educational qualifications. They are also more likely to be in paid employment and to work full-time than their counterparts in Britain. While lone mothers have a social class profile similar to coupled mothers in both countries, never-married mothers in Britain are more likely to have a working-class profile.

Family theories develop differently in different parts of the world not just because of socio-demographic characteristics but they are also deeply embedded in intellectual, social and historical contexts (Cheal 1991, 8). Social problem discourses can be traced back to a long-standing academic tradition of social policy in Britain that focuses on the usefulness and the application of acquired knowledge and management of social problems. Therefore, this research is 'reactive' because it either reacts to certain problems of current public concern or tends to evaluate the implementation of specific social policies. In Germany, the academic tradition is more likely to consider instead the role of cultural values and individual attitudes on family change. It places lone motherhood within a wider sociological context of late modernity. The influential sociological discourse underpinning the view that lone motherhood is a result of social change is the concept of individualization (Beck and Beck-Gernsheim 1990 and 2002). This concept has also become the orienting concept of the research that forms the basis of this book.

2 Reynolds' (1998) study found that lone mothers felt that economic constraints pushed them into being in paid employment and argues that full-time work is central to an Afro-Caribbean mothering identity in Britain. This is a result from their historical, cultural and socio-economic experiences of slavery, colonialism and migration. Historically, the fathers could not live with the family nor become their breadwinner. The women had to work to support their children.

Chapter 3

Lone Motherhood – Late Modernity and Individualization

Family changes are perceived as essential elements of late modernity and Giddens (1987) and Beck and Beck-Gernsheim (1994 and 2002) have brought 'the family' back into the centre of sociological concerns. This has coincided with a renaissance in sociology itself (Smart and Neale 1999, 6). Although lone mothers are not a specific subject they are part of wider diversities in family forms and gender relations that are studied closely in order to re-conceptualize society (Beck and Beck-Gernsheim 1994 and 2002; Beck-Gernsheim 1994 and 2002; Hoffmann-Nowotny 1989).

Lone motherhood is a particularly intriguing family form for modernity, because it presents the conflict between emancipation and family tradition. For example, mothers may value stable intimate traditional relationships, particularly when children are involved or may stay together for the sake of the children. On the other hand, they may also value identity development that implies a more individual emancipatory experience away from an unequal power or an otherwise unsatisfactory relationship with a male partner. This two-sidedness is a dynamic process in which both sides need to be negotiated and is interrelated and overlapping. Within this conflict, lone motherhood is viewed as threatening as well as promising (Cheal 1991, 39). State-benefit-dependent lone motherhood is a particularly interesting area, as Giddens (1997) suggests that in areas with low-wage jobs or permanent unemployment there is little to foster continuity in marital relationships. In such circumstances the hold of tradition has perhaps become even more thoroughly disintegrated than elsewhere (Giddens 1997, 147 and 1991, 86).

Giddens (1998) characterizes late modernity as a space, place and a 'series of flows', that rework the older forms of economics, social, cultural, geographical and educational organizations. Late modernity marks conditions of complexity, contradiction and diversity as the global economics of capital restructuring reach down into the local/e to radically *dis*organize prior social forms of collective and political identity and allegiance (Giddens 1998).

According to Giddens (1991) in the post-traditional order of late modernity, the self becomes a project; it has to be explored and constructed as part of a reflective process of connecting personal and social change. We are not what we are but what we make of ourselves. Self-actualization is understood in terms of a balance between opportunity and risk. It is not true that the psychologically liberated person faces risks while the more traditional self does not. In the post-traditional order lifestyle choices are inevitable because: 'modernity confronts the individual with a complex diversity of choices and, because it is non-foundational, at the same time offers little help as to which options should be selected.' (Giddens 1991, 80).[1] According to Giddens, the driving force for change in late modern society is individualization. For Beck and Beck-Gernsheim and Giddens, this term does not stipulate that women *can* choose but that they *have* to choose the way they live:

> Individualization has been the driving force for change in late modern societies. Men and women gain not only the freedom to choose their own values and lifestyles they are also obliged to make their own choices because there are no universal certainties and no fixed models of the good life. (Giddens's foreword in Hakim 2000).

This book discusses to what extent the thesis of individualization can explain the experience of state-dependent lone mothers. The concept of individualization distinguishes itself from previous sociological theories, such as the functionalist theory, in the way that the family is viewed as a fluid and changing concept that is viewed in the context of all the other changes that are occurring under late modernity (Beck and Beck-Gernsheim 1995).[2] The concept acknowledges that the family is location, experience, kinship as well as an ideological construct.[3] It allows for a variety of 'families' or 'family practices' that emphasize that the family is a dynamic, fluid and heterogeneous concept (Morgan 2002). My aim is to discover patterns of diversity and dynamics in lone motherhood and this individualization concept is certainly a useful orienting concept for explaining lone motherhood.

Lone motherhood and the concept of individualization

This chapter is the theoretical foundation for the book's research question: To what extent can the concept of individualization explain the experience of state-dependent lone mothers? It begins with the introduction of the concept of individualization and what it means to relationships, families and lone motherhood. It also discusses the concept more critically, particularly with regard to social class, individualism, gendered inequality and detraditionalization. I am interested in the relevance of tradition and detraditionalization in these mothers' lives and I also want to find out how 'actively' mothers negotiate their lives as well as their motivations for this negotiation. What is the dynamic between lone mothers' difficulties to comply with the traditional nuclear family and their drive for emancipation and self-actualization? Beck and Beck-Gernsheim (2002) acknowledge that individualization may also

1 A lifestyle can be defined as a more or less integrated set of practices which an individual embraces, not only because such practices fulfil utilitarian needs, but because they give material form to a particular narrative of self-identity (Giddens 1991: 81).

2 Reflexive modernization throws all basic social principles into flux in that it undermines modern society; as simple modernization has undermined the traditional society. Reflexive modernity maintains that there are new rules for political and social systems that sociologists should set out to explain (Beck, Bonß & Lau 2001: 2-8).

3 'The family' implies a naturalistic grouping and an ideological construct with its fixed gender roles. It distorts differences of class, race, and religion and presumes heterosexuality and blood or marriage ties as the norm (Morgan 1996).

prompt resistance among people who pursue 'traditional' ways of life in search for routine and stability.

The concept of individualization

The individualization thesis concerns people's everyday lives and it has become a core metaphor through which sociological analysis of family life is now pursued (Smart and Shipman 2004, 491). As a consequence of urbanization and industrialization, biographies are no longer predetermined by tradition, religion or the state. It claims that where classic modernity was characterized by class-based societies that shaped people's lives as 'destiny', in late modernity individuals are left to shape their own destinies.[4] As a result, the strength of social ties and obligations, which previously bound people into groups and networks have become weaker and less permanent (Irwin 2000, 2). This allows for individuals' lives to be dynamic and diverse.

Individualization means the disintegration of previously existing social forms – for example, the increasing fragility of such categories as class and social status, gender roles, family, neighbourhood, etc. In (…) modern societies new demands, controls and constraints are being imposed on individuals. Through the job market, the welfare state and institutions, people are tied into a network of regulations, conditions, and provisos. (Beck and Beck-Gernsheim 1996, 24 and 25).

In modern society individuals have to apply these new modern regulations and conditions to their own biographies through their own activity. The normal biography becomes the 'do-it-yourself biography'. Individualization assumes that more and more choices and negotiations have to be made and are possible with progressing modernization, equal rights and emancipation. 'Life, death, gender, corporeality, identity, religion, marriage, parenthood, social ties – all are becoming decidable down to the small print; once fragmented into options, everything must be decided.' (Beck and Beck-Gernsheim 1996, 29). 'Even not deciding, the mercy of having to submit is vanishing' (Beck and Beck-Gernsheim 1996, 30). For example, many lone mothers make a decision not to make a decision with regards to their pregnancy. Instead of a termination they end up giving birth. Therefore, people are condemned to actively contribute to their biography.

Beck and Beck-Gernsheim (2002) stress the explicit ambivalence of individualization, which does not mean greater equality or the liberation of an individual, and entails at the same time new opportunities and new risks:

> If we think of it not just as a growth in options and freedoms, but more as a way of life under certain institutional constraints and demands or, indeed, as pressure to put a life together under often contradictory and partly incompatible conditions – which poses manifold difficulties that many do not manage to resolve (Beck and Beck-Gernsheim 2002, 126).

---

4 To Giddens (1987: 187), late modern society is characterized by a process called reflexive modernization. It is essentially an acceleration and radicalization of the development of core institutional features of modern society, which are capitalism, industrialism, state administration and military power.

Hence, the do-it-yourself biography can easily turn into a breakdown biography. Today, an individual has to be able to adapt to changes and to be able to organize. It helps if one has initiative, tenacity and flexibility, just like the pioneers have in my proposed type categories. They can also find their own rules and have reflective judgement; essential traits in reflexive modernity (see chapter 7). Reflective judgement does not mean that people today lead a more conscious life based on conscious and rational decisions. Beck and Beck-Gernsheim (1996, 28) accept that everyone acts on routines that are internalized, preconscious or semiconscious. For Beck, 'reflexive' has more to do with reflex than reflection. Reflexes are immediate and cope with a world of quick decision making (Lash in Beck and Beck-Gernsheim 2002, 3).

Individualization, relationships and families

The result of women's emancipation and the educational revolution in the 1960s and 1970s are that women have the obligation to have to create their own biography. Beck and Beck-Gernsheim (1996) list five reasons for the changing gender contracts besides paid work and they call it the liberation from the feudal 'gender fate' in which men were considered to be breadwinners and women as homemakers who conducted unpaid work: 1. Women live longer than men and are not just child bearers and carers but have a life after that. 2. Home work has been rationalized and is isolated. Women are not fulfilled nor rewarded by this and want to go out to work. 3. Women can decide when to have children because of the availability of contraception and abortion. 4. Because of the welfare state and divorce laws, women are liberated from dependency on a man (see chapter 4) and 5. Women can play a part in the labour market due to access to education. All five points coupled with the Women's Movement imply that marriage and the family have lost many of their 'functional' meanings, as they are no longer a constraining economic arrangement based on the traditional male breadwinner/female homemaker role. Of course, these five points are based on assumptions that valorise education and paid work. I will show that not all mothers have access to education and that not all mothers want to go out to work, but some are quite fulfilled looking after their children.

Individualization does not mean giving up old traditions, such as marriage and a family. Instead, their structural constraints and economic dependency have been replaced with individualization and emotional dependency (Beck-Gernsheim 1994, 115 and 134). Marriage has become a 'safe harbour in a heartless world' and has emotional satisfaction and intimacy attributed to it. Love has become the fundamentalist belief to which almost everyone has subscribed. For Beck and Beck-Gernsheim (1995) the fear of being lonely is the most stable foundation of marriage and this is one reason why the departure from cohabitation leads sooner or later into another cohabitation. Another characteristic of the third state of individualization is that marriage is no longer predetermined but also full of negotiations, full of arguments. This is partly because the new form of gender construction presents other difficulties as both partners are under pressure to continuously 'improve' something because of their 'drive to expand' and their 'drive to change' to reach maximum self-fulfilment. This attitude causes conflict and makes living together difficult because rather than improving a marriage, compromising and working on its shortcomings, it is being constantly compared and its shortcomings exposed (Beck-Gernsheim 2002).

> It is a result of individualization that relationships have become paradoxical: they have become hostile but also serve as a refuge, a part of a security system, an emotional base to which the couple has entrusted itself. This then is what the authors mean by the 'normal chaos of love':
>
> The nuclear family, built around gender status, is falling apart on the issues of emancipation and equal rights, which no longer conveniently come to a halt outside our private lives. The result is the quite normal chaos called love. ... Love will become more important than ever and equally impossible. (Beck and Beck-Gernsheim 1995, 2)

A consequence of this paradox of increased personal freedom and choices and unrealistically high romantic expectations is that marriage has become fragile and it is only upheld under certain conditions (Beck and Beck-Gernsheim 1995, 2; Giddens 1992, 98; Hoffmann-Nowotny 1989, 28). As a result, family life becomes a 'doing' as supposed to a 'being' (Silva and Smart 1999, 8). Bauman (2001, 29) speaks of the transformation of kinship from what was once solid and certain into something highly contingent. For Bauman, choice might be integral to modernity but its availability is the undoing of fixed relationships, or their deinstitutionalization. Marriage and family can now be differentiated into divorces, cohabitations and separations. Moreover, through divorces and remarriages, families overlap each other and make whole networks of interrelated extended families, whose structure is difficult to see from the outside. Beck and Beck-Gernsheim (2002, 98) and Beck-Gernsheim (2002, 10) postulate that the traditional family does not disappear but it has lost its monopoly. New forms of living together represent a more post-family community, based on 'an elective affinity' that include good friends. Lone motherhood represents the future of families or what the authors call the contours of the 'post-familial family'; a result of individualization (Beck and Beck-Gernsheim 1995).

One feature of the post-familial family is the shifting focus within families. Parenthood can be split from sex and from marriage and vice versa. Marriage can be transformed from being partnership-centred to being children centred (Nave-Herz 1994, 124). Besides the increased demands on individuals to fulfil emotional needs in partnerships, there are also more demands placed on parenting (Beck-Gernsheim 2002). Families have become more children centred and pedagogical because the 'well-being', development and rights of children have been given increased importance as their economic importance vanished. While love between women and men becomes unstable and predestined for failure, the relationship with a child gives permanence and stability. This may be a reason for lone motherhood. Romantic love for a man, who does not fulfil the expectations, is being replaced with love for a child, who cannot hurt nor leave the woman. Because of the instability of relationships the children become the final alternative to loneliness – a safe haven. Single households and lone parent families are integral to individualization and are a by-product of emancipation and the drive for improvement:

> The fact that work and family are incompatible remained concealed as long as marriage was synonymous with women at home and man at work; it has surfaced with great turbulence now that each couple has to work out its own division of labour. Demanding equality along market lines has the effect of turning the partners into rivals and individuals, competing with one another for the good things in modern life. This is no mere speculation; in Germany and elsewhere the number of single households and single parents is rising. (Beck and Beck-Gernsheim 1995, 144).

The striving for the 'good things in modern life' is also what the authors call the 'status struggle' that comes after the class struggle. Because people have a high level of prosperity and social security as well as democracy, the contradictions between family demands and personal freedom become obvious. There is no longer a daily struggle against misery and oppression and there is also more leisure time. As a result, the individual becomes focused on his or her own growth and self-development and fulfilment.

Critique of individualization

It has been suggested that the concept of individualization is the most influential societal theory of the present (Junge 2002). Nonetheless, the concept of individualization has also been criticized for its sweeping generalizations about the direction of change in western society (Brannen and Nilsen 2005, 413). Many misunderstandings of the concept may be due to the lack of historical and empirical evidence (Burkhart 1998, 107; Wagner 1999, 69). Due to its vague definition the concept evades criticism because any development can be seen as proof for individualization and it is difficult to verify it or prove it wrong. There have also been claims that there was considerably more fluidity and diversity in past relationships than is recognized (Rose 1996). The next three sections deal with three main criticisms of individualization regarding the persistence of social class, individualism, gendered inequality as well as with detraditionalization.

Individualization and social class

The concept of individualization does not ignore structure or the social sphere but states that institutional reference points such as class and social status, gender roles, family and neighbourhood are becoming increasingly fragile (Beck and Beck-Gernsheim 2002, 50). In post-industrial societies each individual has to create their own biography and can no longer rely on stable social and moral milieus.

Family sociologists agree with the increase in opportunities but find that individualization does not sufficiently incorporate structural constraints that determine our lives, such as class, ethnicity and gender (Burkhart 1998; Crow 2002, 291; Crompton 2005; Irwin 2000, 10; Strohmeier 1993, 13). These authors recognize that the mobility between class and status has increased but it has not disappeared. Also there are new developments such as the movement towards class-specific family structures. There is now a polarization of those life forms with and without children. Parenthood is found to reduce individual freedom substantially and this increases with the number of children (Strohmeier 1993, 17). In other words, the number of children has become an important indicator for social inequality and is ever more closely associated with social class position (Hammer 2005). Other empirical evidence finds that the experience of lone motherhood is very different for women from working-class backgrounds compared with other women (Rowlingson and McKay 2005). Thus, if social structure and the existence and number of children can differentiate the extent and direction of individualization, life forms must be more limited than proposed by Beck and Beck-Gernsheim (1996).

This is a misunderstanding as Beck and Beck-Gernsheim (2002, 31) realize that nothing essential has changed and inequalities do not disappear, but instead social crisis appears as individual crisis. They are now redefined in terms of an individualization of social risks, in terms of psychological dispositions. This marks a shift from 'ascribed' to 'acquired' roles. In other words, people must take an individual responsibility for the emergent situation, for which there was once certainties and supports, such as class adherence at their disposal (Beck and Beck-Gernsheim 2002, 48). Beck and Beck-Gernsheim (2002: 201) dub class – along with other concept of first modernity such as the family – a 'zombie category' as the idea of this category lives on even though the reality to which it corresponds is dead. They stress that new demands of control that are being put forward modern society such as the labour market and various institutions. I would like to suggest that Beck and Beck-Gernsheim clear up the conception of class and to illustrate why and how class is outdated by delivering evidence.

Working-class lone mothers are not necessarily able to benefit from 'modern social advantages', the basis for individualization. It can also not be taken for granted that everyone in Western industrialized countries has a secure material existence that allows them to go and search for their self-fulfilment (Burkhart 1998). Here, the concept of individualization, in which 'everything is up for grabs', may be a speculative discussion by intellectuals. It does not bear much relationship to the life of ordinary people in which very little is actually 'up for grabs' (Campbell 1996, 166). Again, I find Beck confusing, as he seems to supports his critics by stating that self-fulfilment is reserved for the better educated and those with a higher income. The 'less well-educated' 'clearly continue to be tied to the value system of the 1950s and its status symbols' (Beck 1998b: 47).

The thesis of individualization was highly instrumental in levering class off the academic agenda. It almost certainly shifted attention away from the material and structural roots of inequality and sanctioned a psychologized view of class distinctions in terms of personal qualities (Brannen and Nilsen 2005, 413; Giles 2005, 835). Hence, the responsibility for issues encountered in day-to-day life is increasingly placed on the individual rather than on society.

Processes of individualization deprive class distinctions of their social identity. Social crises appear as individual crises and individuals vary systematically along these and other lines in the power that they have to negotiate with each other and with representatives of the State (Crow 2002, 291). The purpose of my study is to find out how lone mothers negotiate their own situation within state benefits and single motherhood in Germany and Britain, and how they negotiate their rules within varying social contexts.

Individualization and individualism

Anxieties about individualization also centre on the rise of an ethic of self-interest and on presumptions that people make selfish and easy choices (for example Irwin 2000; Lewis 2001). The thesis of individualization is also disputed for its claim that personal relationships have become more contingent, negotiated and self-directed while empirical research points to the continued importance that individuals place on family ties and obligations (Barnes 2000; Finch 1989). McCarthy and Edwards (2002, 208) make the point that individualization has different meanings in different spaces and that it is always relational, never individualistic. This is supported by empirical family research that shows that people give priority to support and obligation between family members (Ribbens McCarthy et al 2003).

The individual of the individualization thesis seems to exist without parents, without kinship ties, and with concerns only for their own psychic well being (Smart and Shipman 2004, 503). Certain kinds of self-seeking behaviour might be acceptable in public life but they are certainly less so within the home. Sevenhuijsen (2002, 141) suggests an alternative standpoint that believes in inter-dependency; that individuals exist because of, and through their relationship with others. Humans cannot be regarded as separate, individualized subjects but instead selves are embedded in a network of care and responsibility. Her 'ethics of care' approach suggests a culture of 'care as a democratic practice' to achieve a balanced family life (see chapter 11).

The individualization concept may lack international applicability and it took some time for it to be discussed outside of Germany (for example Brannen and Nilsen 2005; Smart and Shipman 2004). It has also been criticized as it presupposes an affluent society and has made middle-class experience normative (Brannen and Nilsen 2005, 422; Gillies 2005, 835). Burkhart (1998, 128) feels that the individualization concept is deeply embedded within a German context and is an ideology popular among the German academic middle-classes. It uses German conditions as the reference parameters and represents a certain culture in which the seeking of self-fulfilment is taken very seriously: 'There is no need to deny that people are "dancing around the golden self", or going astray in the jungle of personal growth offers.' (Beck and Beck-Gernsheim 1996, 42). Individualization may be more attractive in Germany, where the individual is valued as a reaction to atrocities of the mass movement of National Socialism. In Britain, individualization's popularity has perhaps been hindered because there has not been much of an out-of-parliament movement (for example Green Party movement). In British sociology, individuality may not be contested but it continues to be viewed as strongly embedded within class, race and gender.

Individualization and gendered inequality

Although opportunities in life for women have increased, individualization is not equal for women and men (Rerrich 1994, 203). Moreover, mothers have to reconcile more conflicting conditions and expectations in addition to dealing with labour market inequalities. In other words, besides new sets of norms and standards, old gendered sets of norms and standards are still valid in the division of labour (Ferri and Smith 1996, 13; Walker 1996, 53).

Admittedly, Beck and Beck-Gernsheim (2002, 58) are careful to point out that progress towards gender inequality is not linear or revolutionary and that there is a long way to go yet. For women, individualization is incomplete and is 'in an intermediate stage' as they are able to develop self-awareness but still care for others. The concept of individualization can be criticized for assuming first, that women want to escape patriarchal structures while ignoring their own contribution to them (Koppetsch and Maier 1998, 143). Secondly, the concept clearly valorizes paid work over caring. Individualization implies that women's individualization can only be completed if they become more like men, in continuous paid employment and without caring obligations. Nonetheless, Beck and Beck-Gernsheim (2002) point out that as long as men do not increase their caring work, women will continue to be discontent.

Individualization and detraditionalization

Individualization is supposedly a process of detraditionalization. It lends itself to criticism by social theorists who emphasize continuity and find that the concept of social change in personal relationships is overstated. Adam (1996, 143) rejects individualization because it differentiates itself from a fixed 'others' past when in fact tradition remains a central feature of contemporary society. Rose (1996, 301) finds that one cannot draw on structural events such as industrialization to explain how individuals experience themselves and others. Instead of a detraditionalization of the self, there is merely the ever-evolving modification of regulation. In this Foucauldian approach, political systems and power relations penetrate the self. This position points to a largely enduring status quo, particularly in terms of gender and class dynamics.

Smart and Shipman (2004, 494) criticize the concept of individualization for depicting a vision of family and married life that is culturally monochrome. Beck and Beck-Gernsheim (2002, 39) predict that whole cultures will move into certain directions of detraditionalization, sharing the same values and practices, which is too one-dimensional. Smart and Shipman's (2004) study of trans-national families in Britain finds people that hold very different kinds of values to those depicted by the individualization theorists. Families with different cultural traditions, and where traditions have different significance and meaning, live next door to each other in post-industrialized societies. In these families, traditions, religion and culture may have very different significance because of the experience of migration and trans-nationalism. Their accounts also reveal that even one person can be committed to both, change and tradition. Smart and Shipman (2004) plead for attention to complexity, context and culture in empirical research to avoid sweeping generalizations about individualization and family life. In fact, women can live very different lives even when sharing the same religion, culture and gender. Individualization clearly ignores the unevenness of experience and life-trajectory.

Conclusion

The individualization thesis is criticized for being vague, not historically and empirically grounded enough as well as too individualistic. It seems to underplay the structural conditions and gendered inequalities, material circumstances and cultural differences. Nonetheless, it may be able to explain the experience of state-dependent lone mothers to an extent.

In a post-modern fashion it allows for 'families', rather than one type of family. It accepts that lone mothers' lives are not straight forward but heterogeneous and dynamic. It emphasizes the need to make choices and allows for the individual to exercise those choices within constraints such as contradictory societal norms. I like the idea that we can no longer take the stages of our biography for granted but have to piece it together. It encapsulates different ways mothers can piece their biography together and this helps in discovering distinctive patterns of diversity in lone motherhood. This is what is most compelling about the concept as it contrasts social problem discourses that emphasize lone mothers' lack of choices. In other words, within individualization it is conceivable that state-dependent lone mothers may view state benefits not just as an emergency exit out of a partnership, but also as a tool for actively creating their own biography. It highlights the way that humans have some agency and shape their futures.

The extent to which the concept of individualization can explain the experiences of lone mothers will be further explored in my small scale and comparative research. I am interested in how individuals create their biography within their social and cultural context, in Germany and Britain. It emerges from the data that there is a wide range of state-benefit-dependent lone mothers. Some perceive their situation as an opportunity that enables them to actively negotiate their lives in search of self-fulfilment. Here, structural constraints happen to overlap with women's priorities of how they want to create their biography (see chapter 7). Other mothers find social change problematic and contradictory because they aspire to the traditional male breadwinner/female homemaker ideal or perceive to have no choices to either actively create their biography nor to strive for self-fulfilment (see chapter 9).

The research could ascertain a third group in which a transformation of traditional values and norms has taken place, that is not necessarily a demise of tradition. Here, mothers acknowledge and accept some parts of the concept of individualization, such as men's participation in household chores, while other parts of the concept may not fit into their concept of 'good' mothering, such as being in paid employment and being a lone mother (see chapter 8 and 10). It seems that some mothers want a 'different' individualization. The next chapter considers how the ideological and historical development of the German and the British welfare state may have aided or restricted the individualization of lone mothers.

Chapter 4

The Positioning of Lone Mothers in the British and German Welfare States

This chapter analyses how social policies reflect and influence concepts of gender in the German and British welfare states because concepts of gender are deeply rooted in the structure of institutions. Germany and Britain have always varied dramatically in their family policies and in their treatment of lone mothers. The movement towards a single European market and closer political union, and indeed harmonization of social policies and an ever-closer relationship between family policy and employment policy has not changed this (Daly 2005, 392).

The aim of this chapter is to find out about the context in which lone mothers negotiate their lives as mothers and as dependants. The first part of this chapter highlights how gendered characteristics concerning caring can be traced back to the ideological and historical development of the British and German welfare states. This chapter pays particular attention to the different cultural developments in the East and West Germany welfare states as well as the effects of reunification. By doing so, this demonstrates how social policies vary cross-nationally and how their implementation and effect is entwined within societal contexts such as culture (societal ideals, meanings and values) and local labour markets (Pfau-Effinger 1998). The chapter discusses to what extent lone mothers in Britain and in West Germany were treated as dependents rather than as workers as in East Germany. The second part of the chapter compares and contrasts state benefits that were available to lone mothers at the time of the fieldwork. It also analyses the efforts that both welfare states are making to transform lone mothers into workers.

Women in the British welfare state

The post-war British welfare state was similar to the German welfare state as both played an important role in 'reinforcing male supremacy and, under pressure from women's movements, in transforming it to some extent' (Ginsburg 1992, 6). Both were set up with the notions of a male breadwinner and a female homemaker (who would carry out unpaid caring) (Lewis 2002). In Britain, social insurance for sickness and unemployment had been implemented in 1911, but initially it covered only the male worker. Only gradually, in 1925, did it provide allowances for widows. In accordance with the nineteenth century Poor Law, lone mothers were defined as workers who had to support as many of their children as they could, the rest were sent into 'workhouses'. Most unmarried mothers had to resort to workhouses anyway (Kiernan et al 1998, 98).

It was only in the middle of the twentieth century that the emphasis shifted to their role as mothers (Lewis 1997, 51). The 1948 British National Assistance Act transformed the lone mothers' position from worker to carer because state-dependent lone mothers with children aged less than 16 years did not have to make themselves available for work to be entitled to social assistance (Lister 1994). Although social assistance was modest, for the first time a lone mothers' reproductive and caring work was acknowledged. It was assumed that women ought to be provided for by their husbands, and many married women only became included in the social insurance scheme through their husbands (Clarke and Langan 1993a).

While Germany dealt with the labour shortage after the War by only recruiting migrant labour, the British government also actively recruited married women as the reserve army of labour in education, health and welfare services, albeit mainly part-time (Land 1994; Williams 1993). In Britain, despite different ideologies about motherhood, working-class married women and lone mothers always felt compelled to be in paid work to support their families, although some lone mothers were supported by relatives or the absent father (Lewis 1997). Unmarried mothers continued to be perceived as delinquents and tended to live in Homes for Unmarried Mothers, where some resorted to giving their children for adoption (Spensky 1993; Zulauf 1997, 14). Lone mothers' dependence on social assistance started to increase with the change in living patterns and changes in sexual morality at the end of the 1970s. At that time social security and housing benefits reached a level that allowed lone mothers' an autonomous existence, albeit at a low level of income (Kiernan et al 1998).

The Finer Committee on lone parent families agreed in the early 1970s that there was little incentive for a lone mother to be in paid employment unless she could command a high wage. It was also acknowledged that marital and reproductive behaviour could not be controlled in a democratic society and that 'the clock could not be turned back' (Millar 1996, 97). The Committee suggested that it should be left to the mother to decide whether or not to go out to work (Ginsburg 1992). These ideas were not adopted by the then Conservative government, which introduced a Family Income Supplement (FIS), which encouraged the uptake of paid employment (Sullivan 1996). The lack of public childcare made it difficult for all mothers to combine motherhood and a working life; most married women worked part-time. This lack of public childcare was not remedied when the Labour Party was in government between 1974 and 1979 although the Party did implement measures which benefited all women, such as the 1970 Equal Pay Act, the 1975 Sex Discrimination Act and the important abolishment of the 'married women's option' in 1975 which ended the unequal treatment of women in the social security system (Sainsbury 1996).

The Conservative government of 1979 was dominated by a neo-liberal opposition to the post-war Keynesian consensus and to the principles of the welfare state (Clarke and Langan 1993b). The structural diagnosis of poverty and inequality shifted towards an individual provision and consumption of services (Williams 1993). After the weakening of the unions and of local governments, there was little resistance left against these welfare state changes (Kiernan et al 1998). During the time of the Conservative governments (1979-1997), particularly under Thatcher (in power until 1990), entitlements shifted from social insurance based benefits to a) the privatization of pension, sickness and maternity benefits and to b) means-tested benefits. These changes reinforced gender based economic inequalities. They left some women either with no income or with low earnings or in casual work which excluded them from the National Insurance system, let alone from occupational pension benefits (Sainsbury 1996). The influx of women into the labour market has not led to a parallel increase in their entitlements (Bruegel and Perrons 1996). While more married women took up paid employment (albeit mostly part-time) more lone mothers became dependent on Social Assistance (or Income Support). Lone mothers were also given the Lone Parent Premium, which positioned them more as dependents than carers.

The public perception of lone mothers changed during the end of the 1980s when the increasing rate of divorce, extra-marital childbearing, teenage motherhood and lone mothers' increasing state dependency became viewed as a social threat, morally and financially. The image of lone mothers changed from a group struggling to do their best for themselves and their children, to blaming them for seeking welfare dependency (Gauthier 1996; Phoenix 1996) (see chapter two).

While the Conservatives were in power, there was no positive commitment to family policies, no increase in public childcare facilities, and no training schemes or work-related programmes for lone mothers (Evans 1992). Instead, in order to decrease public expenditure and to discourage lone motherhood, the Conservative government implemented the Child Support Act. This has been spectacularly unsuccessful, partly due to the failure of the electronic system supporting it but also due to poor enforcement (Ridge 2004). The Child Support system was an ideal opportunity for the Labour government to address child poverty, which had risen three-fold under the previous Conservative government. However, despite several reforms to the Child Support Agency which attempted to solve its tensions and problems, the system continually experiences poor compliance and considerable resistance to assessments (Ridge 2004). The Labour government, elected in 1997, promotes 'paid work as the best way out of poverty' (Gordon Brown, Chancellor of the Exchequer, 1998). One of the Labour government's pledges is to halve child poverty by 2010 and to eradicate it by 2020. The diverse range of policies and specific benefits that were put in place are discussed in the later part of this chapter.

Women in the German welfare states

Germany was split into two very different welfare states in the period between the end of the Second World War and reunification in 1990, when the West German welfare state system was adopted for the whole of Germany.[1] The 35 lone mothers in East and West Germany who were interviewed for this research, had very different experiences depending on whether they were in the east or the west; these experiences still influence them today. Therefore, the East German and the West German welfare state are discussed separately before a third section analyses the enabling and

1 Before reunification East Germany was the socialist German Democratic Republic (GDR) and West Germany was the capitalist Federal Republic of Germany (FRG).

restricting effects the adoption of the West German welfare state system had on women in the eastern part of Germany after reunification.

Lone mothers in West Germany: carers and dependants who work

The West German and the British welfare states primarily benefit men in paid employment. In West Germany, there was an ideological re-enforcement of this directly after the Second World War when social policy and the law became extraordinarily patriarchal, perhaps to compensate men for fighting in the lost war (Ostner 1993). Following Adorno's argument, Ostner (1993, 98) suggests that the post-war reinstatement of the male as the gatekeeper of the family can be explained as a response to the Nazi's exploitation of the family. For the Nazis, the private sphere of the family was no longer protected from surveillance and propaganda: the private sphere was opened up to the public sphere. After the war, any mention of group day-care was associated with the Nazis, who shared with the communists the goal of transforming children into loyal servants of the state. With the re-privatization of the family and its protection by the constitution, the intention was to re-establish a democratic society as well as to defend against communism. Many women retreated to the private sphere, if they could, after having had to fend for their families during the war. In fact, married women could engage in paid employment only if it did not conflict with their primary duty to their family. Until 1957, the husband was the overriding decision-maker and this was upheld in the constitution (Grundgesetz) (Chamberlayne 1993, 180). Lone mothers were in a 'double bind' (Ostner 1993, 6). On the one hand, female employment was considered to have a detrimental effect on the children and on the other hand, lone mothers were financially unable to retreat into domesticity.

Even during the increased demand for labour in the 'economic wonder years' (Wirtschaftswunderjahre) at the end of the 1950s and early 1960s, the integration of women into the labour market was not an option; instead migrant workers (Gastarbeiter) were 'invited' (Seeleib-Kaiser 2004). During a time of low unemployment, the 1961 Social Assistance Act (Sozialhilfegesetz) replaced fragmented and minimal poor relief and confirmed citizens' rights, including a mothers' entitlement to public assistance (Leisering 1998, 70). This benefit is still subject to the system of subsidiarity and steps in only if the husband or the immediate family fail to provide (Bast and Ostner 1992 cf. Chamberlayne 1993, 175).

This long history of a woman's subordination to her husband and her domestic role chanced a little with the Social Democratic government of the mid 1960s. They saw this model impeding both women's and children's emancipation, and so childcare facilities were promoted mainly to equalize children's life chances, not to facilitate mothers' employment (Chamberlayne 1993, 179). The student uprising of 1968 contributed to more liberal attitudes towards mothers in paid employment and towards lone mothers. With the oil crisis, the economic recession in 1979, and the new Catholic-Liberal government of 1983, there was a return back to the promotion of the housewife model with a veneer of modernization. Part-time working women were more acceptable, allegedly to attract more women voters (Chamberlayne 1993, 180). Childlessness was a greater concern and policies were introduced to reverse the trend by supporting previously unpaid caring work (Bellers 1992, 99). There has been an increase in female employment to 59 per cent in 2004 (Statistisches Bundesamt 2006). From the beginning of the twentieth century until then, it had remained constant at about 35 per cent until 1975 (with the exception of the First and the Second World Wars) (Bellers 1992, 98).

Since the rise is mainly due to part-time employment, a sort of compromise seems to have been reached for married women, which has been adopted in reunited Germany too. There is no strong movement towards full-time education for children, and the majority of women seem to support the socio-cultural consensus that married mothers are in part-time employment and continue to be dependent on male breadwinners. Pfau-Effinger (2005) uses the term 'modernized male breadwinner contract' for this situation, which can be classified as a 'compromise' between women's increasing demands for fulfilment and independence while at the same time continuing unpaid care work whilst remaining dependent on a male breadwinner. This model is in fact supported by national social policies and tax incentives, and is aimed at married rather than lone mothers. In 2003 in West Germany, 14 per cent of mothers with children under the age of 18 were in full-time employment, in contrast to 41 per cent in East Germany. Lone mothers are more likely to work full-time, with 28 per cent in West Germany and 39 per cent in East Germany (Statistisches Bundesamt 2006).

In the beginning of the 21st century, fertility is decreasing, and German women seem to be either in paid employment or to have children. As a result, the government is promoting a better life-work balance by increasing childcare tax allowances, increasing childcare availability and parent time (a paid Childrearing Leave that allows working up to 30 hours a week). The family minister states: 'The key for success is that we make it easier for men and women with children to be in paid employment. Families need income, time for their child during the working week and high quality childcare and education provision.' (Bundesministerium für Familien, Senioren, Frauen und Jugend 2006)

Nonetheless, the increase of caring benefits, parental leave and means tested benefits reinforces lone mothers' status as home makers, carers and part-time workers at the most. The accreditation of 'socially useful' activities that are presented in this chapter confirm the traditional principle and the robustness of West Germany's social market economy. Nonetheless, the acknowledgement of the principle of care does enhance lone mothers' social rights and makes it difficult to dismiss this system despite its gendered aspects.

Lone mothers in East Germany: workers

The East German welfare state positioned women differently before reunification, before the West German welfare state was imposed on the whole of Germany. In post war East Germany the bureaucratic collectivist state system of welfare, that was exported by the Soviet Union, was particularly well developed (Deacon 1993). It came to an end in 1990, after the reunification of Germany. Throughout its existence (1949 – 1990) East German welfare state policies clearly positioned mothers, both married and single, as full-time workers (Annesley 2002; Giddings et al 2005, 121).

In 1988, before reunification, 89 per cent of all lone mothers were in full-time paid employment, in comparison to just 57 per cent in West Germany (Walther 1992).

Several interdependent factors are responsible for the remarkable differences in mothers' employment rates in East and West Germany before reunification. These include labour market factors (the pressures on mothers to work, and the structure of women's employment opportunities), cultural factors (norms about the care of young children), political factors (strategies for achieving gender equality) and policy factors (Schenk 2003). Contraception was free and abortion legal. Childcare was available, flexible, free, open long hours and had very high-uptake rates (Hank et al 2001; Veil 2003). Childcare was mostly from six am to six pm, 80 per cent of all children under three were cared for, and 95 per cent of children between three and six went to Kindergarten. While childcare can be viewed as enabling mothers to be in paid employment, it can also be viewed as an ideal environment for state indoctrination of children, where conformity not creativity was fostered (Ostner 1993, 108). Non-marital children always had the same legal rights as marital children, and divorce procedures were straightforward and cheap. Every mother had the right to a 'baby year' in which she continued to receive her income, every working mother had special rights, and lone mothers received subsidies (Drauschke and Stolzenburg 1994a and 1994b). Throughout the existence of the East German state, lone motherhood was socially much more acceptable; this was underlined by the high number of lone mothers and the high divorce rates.

The East German government thought that by promoting employment for mothers it would also promote gender equality, but this was not the case. First, although men and women had reached equal levels in education, vocational training and labour market experience, women were paid less than men throughout the country's entire history. Women's earnings were about 75 per cent of men's (Behrend 1995). Secondly, lone mothers remained the poorest family type, although they did fare better than their West German counterparts (Dathe 1996, 88; Notz 1994, 303; Sorensen and Trappe 1995). Thirdly, the women tended to do the bulk of the housework and the government failed to promote a father's domestic and childcare contributions (Ellermann and Klatt 1995, 224). For example, only mothers were granted a monthly 'household day' for their domestic affairs and a years maternity leave, a baby year.

In hindsight, social policies reinforced a traditional gender ideology, rather than removing it. Therefore, egalitarian attitudes to gender roles did not increase social freedom for women (Sorensen and Trappe 1995, 404). In the public discourse, working lone mothers were portrayed as 'super-women' who could manage everything: work, household and childcare (Klett-Davies 1997). However, the socialist ideal of a family was the nuclear family with two to three children, increasing the population, with parents in full employment and active in society (Keiser 1997, 52).

In practice, women's participation in the labour force ultimately weakened the traditional role of the father as the head of the household. In fact, many lone mothers that I have spoken to in East Germany manage differently by living without a male breadwinner and using state benefits. The interviewed lone mothers in West Germany prefer a male breadwinner/female homemaker model.

Gendered policies in unified Germany

Reunification in 1990 has quickly changed East Germany's bureaucratic state collective system into a capitalist welfare system (Deacon 1993, 185; Leibfried 1993, 136). Lone mothers in the East were almost immediately confronted with the West German social market economy and they rapidly submitted: 'the East German government and population appeared willing to be completely taken over by the West Germans' (Maleck-Lewy 1995, 65).

Following reunification, the two parts of the country converged toward the gendered arrangement in which men are employed full-time and their female partners hold down part-time jobs, although there is some evidence of continuing differences between East and West (Rosenfeld et al 2004, 103). The restructuring of the labour market in East Germany following reunification has seen a massive increase in unemployment and a contraction in the typical male sectors. Suddenly, men were competing with women in formerly female work spheres and women were pushed to the margins of the labour market.[2] The number of comprehensive childcare facilities also decreased (Hank et al 2001).

While the cost of living (rent, utilities, childcare) and the number of consumer products (car, telephone) increased quickly after reunification, wages have increased disproportionately more slowly and are still below West German standards. Unemployment was high and women have been called the 'losers of reunification' as their situation has deteriorated most - although of course both men and women originally welcomed the new-won freedom in East Germany (Schröter 1996; Liebecke 1994, 221). Over time, this situation has become more apparent. For example, the risk of unemployment is reduced for those employed in the public sector, those who have qualifications and those without young children (Rosenfeld et al 2004). Most remarkably, East Germany experienced a massive fertility decline: the birth-rate has halved since reunification (Dienel 2005; Hank et al 2001); now, Germany is the country with the fourth lowest birth-rate worldwide (Pinl 2003, 8).

The withdrawal of East German women into the private sphere has been defined as a step into a 'new modernity'. Before reunification, paid work in East Germany was obligatory and was less valued as a means of self-fulfilment than it was in West Germany, where the struggle for a woman's right to work has been fought in terms of individual freedom and self-fulfilment (Braun et al 1994). Also, before reunification the young generally had no post-adolescent, single adult phase but started adulthood earlier than in West Germany (in paid work, childbearing and marriage, for example) (Engstler 1998, 99). Reunification gave lone mothers the opportunity to escape the double burden of motherhood and paid work and enabled them to rear their child themselves with support from modest state benefits such as Childrearing Benefit and

2 Previously mixed sectors have tended to become male dominated and former male dominated sectors have become even more single sex (Schenk and Schlegel 1993: 375). Segregation was accelerated by West German protective legislation to remove women from certain jobs (Chamberlayne 1993: 186).

Income Support (Keiser 1997, 223). My data analysis tends to support this finding to some extent.

Empirical research into the issues of women and paid employment in East Germany in the mid 1990s tends to disagree with the concept of 'new-modernity' and instead argues for a concept of 're-traditionalization' (Großmann and Huth 1996, 182; Huth et al 1996; Kaufmann 1995; Keiser 1997; Leisering and Leibfried 1999, 234; Quack and Maier 1994). Here, the effects of reunification are viewed as a backlash against emancipation towards a re-traditionalization of gender values. Women in East Germany may have had no other choice but to work before reunification, but this gave women financial independence and social integration, which translated into emancipation. After reunification, East German women became unwillingly re-traditionalized due to capitalist market forces, more precisely labour market restructuring and privatization and gender segregation.

Studies find that lone mothers in East Germany are particularly motivated to be in paid employment and that they are reluctant to restrict themselves to the private sphere, that is into full-time motherhood, or to adopt a West German 'modernized male breadwinner' orientation. Financial independence is considered to be very important, and state benefits are disapproved of. Paid work is also seen as a means of integration into society, financially as well as socially. Women's decreasing labour force participation is explained by the adoption of a West German market economy which systematically disadvantages lone mothers in the labour market. The number of mothers in paid work in East Germany decreased particularly for those with pre-school aged children and those in full-time work (Engstler and Menning 2003). This, together with the economic recession, deteriorating childcare facilities, continuing job segregation and an increasing 'poverty trap' is a contributing factor to the fall in lone mothers' employment levels in East Germany (Brand and Hammer 2002; Nestman and Stiehler 1998; Rosenfeld et al 2004; Schneider et al 2001) (see chapter 2).

Keiser (1997, 223) considers that reunification introduced an enormous 'backlash' against women. For example, liberal abortion rules are being reduced to traditional West German conservative standards. These consequences also disappoint West German feminists, although it can be argued that West German women have benefited from reunification in terms of better pension rights, the right of a Kindergarten place for every three-year-old child, and the Kindschaftsrecht, without actively fighting for it (Meyer 1996, 62).[3] Furthermore, pension credits for childrearing were reduced although this meant an increase in West German mothers' entitlement.

Women in East and West Germany grew up under different sets of gender values. These different gender values continue to influence women's lives. West German feminists still view the labour market much more critically than their more pragmatic East German counterparts. Some West German feminists also want to enable mothers to enjoy motherhood at home and prevent mothers from capitulating to the public sphere dominated by men and the masculine project of capitalism. East German feminism is largely concerned with policies for working mothers and other subsidies, and it could not fully comprehend the West German concerns about

3 The Kindschaftsrecht from 1998 gives illegitimate children the same rights as legitimate children and makes shared custody possible (Bundesmisterium der Justiz 1998: 7).

the combining of home and work (Milz 1996, 339). West German women, and particularly women with lower educational qualifications, felt that mothers should look after their children full-time and leave the labour market completely until the child goes to school aged six (Henze and Klar 1996, 165). East German women have never visibly viewed children as impeding their career, unlike in West Germany or Britain perhaps. While East German women believe in the coexistence of mothering and paid work ('Gleichzeitigkeit von Beruf und Familie'), West German mothers' life courses are organized in stages which are kept separate from each other ('Mehr-Phasen-Modell') (Henze and Klar 1996, 167).

These different feminist beliefs towards support for women's care-giving versus engagement in the labour market go beyond West and East German approaches and can be categorized into so-called 'care' (or difference) feminists' who call for new conceptions of citizenship that recognize women's care giving and argue for policies that acknowledge and remunerate care (for example Lewis 2002). In contrast, 'employment' (or sameness) feminists stress the importance of gender parity in paid work. They argue for policies that strengthen women's labour market attachment (Rosenfeld et al 2004).

There is evidence that women in the eastern part of unified Germany are determined to maintain their active role in the labour market, despite the introduction of the west German welfare system. In 2003, 43 per cent of women with at least one child under three were in employment in East Germany, in contrast to 30 per cent in West Germany (Engstler and Menning 2003) However, the reunified German welfare state positions lone mothers with very young children as carers and later as state-dependents who could be paid workers. Nonetheless, lone mothers have gained democracy and are no longer compelled to be in paid employment without state support. Even at the beginning of the 21st century, German society is split between working mothers in East Germany, who continue to depend on public child care, and women in West Germany, who tend to waver between private care and a demand for more state support (Veil 2003, 12). Pfau-Effinger and Geissler (2002, 81) suggest that women's paid work orientation is part of a strong cultural legacy from the Communist period, which includes the disdain for the traditional housewife role as demeaning to a modern woman. This may also act as a demarcation, as part of the East German identity, in which East Germany turns out to be more progressive than the West.

The face-to-face interviews with lone mothers show that state dependency has various meanings and that their lives are complex and dynamic. From the mothers' perspectives, state-dependent full-time lone motherhood can mean either a step into new modernity or a move into re-traditionalization. The mothers perceive state-dependent lone motherhood as a welcome choice over paid work that gives them the opportunity to look after their children after they had not had that chance before reunification. This view would fit into the new modernity discourse. Other mothers fit into the re-traditionalization discourse as they feel constrained and would prefer to be in paid work.

Gendered characteristics of the German and British welfare state

The British welfare state has been called a liberal welfare state regime which subscribes to traditional and liberal work-ethic norms 'in which means-tested assistance, modest universal transfers, or modest social-insurance plans predominate.' (Esping Andersen 1990, 26). Here, social rights tend to cause socio-structural polarization among groups of the employed (Pfau-Effinger 2005, 323). Social insurance contributing employees may view themselves as paying for the benefits provided to lone mothers who should be able to rely on their partner or fend for themselves. This is different in Germany, where the granting of social rights was hardly ever a seriously contested issue and social insurance contributions are not perceived as a tax (Wilson 1993, 141). Germany's welfare state is considered 'status conserving' because it links workers' contributions with their entitlement to benefits.[4] Many employees in Germany seem to have nothing against state-dependent lone mothers, perhaps because their own needs are met by the social insurance system.

Only at the beginning of the 21st century did the German government began to support the one-earner family as well as the 'one-and-a-half earner model' (Pinl 2003). The latter also seems the most popular cultural model of the family in West Germany. Instead of promoting informal care in the family based on financial transfers, German social policy is extending public childcare provision to a substantial degree. Hence, care policies are no longer adequately described by Esping-Andersen's description of a 'conservative' welfare regime (Pfau-Effinger 2005, 324).

The second difference in welfare ideology is the German focus on related individuals and on institutions based on the Catholic principle of subsidiarity. According to this principle, the smallest unit of welfare is the individual and their family who have the primary responsibility for social welfare and are fairly autonomous (Hoff 2001). In Germany there has been a shift from the subsidiarity principle to one that emphasizes public responsibility to guarantee the maintenance of lone mothers' children. Where the absent male breadwinner/biological father does not fulfil his obligations, the state pays 'advanced maintenance payment' (Unterhaltsvorschuß) without waiving the fathers' obligation. However, German local authorities (as with Britain's Child Support Agency (CSA) have been fairly unsuccessful in reclaiming the benefits from the father (Bundesministerium für Familien, Senioren, Frauen und Jugend 1998). Family members, such as parents, grandparents, biological fathers and ex-spouses are legally obliged to support the state-dependent lone mother. Only if their income does not exceed certain limits is social assistance paid in full. As the German welfare state is constructed on interdependence, the role of the family seems to be particularly strong (Seeleib-Kaiser 2004). This is unlike Britain, which is moulded by the liberal tradition and where social rights are based on obligations, not interdependence (Hoff 2001). Britain lacks the system of subsidiarity and citizens tend to rely more on the state. Therefore the state, and not the autonomous church, has responsibility for the underlying philosophy of the welfare state (Seeleib-Kaiser

---

4 By 'Germany' I mean a) Germany before the existence of East Germany (GDR), b) West Germany between 1949 and 1990 and c) East and West Germany after reunification 1990 if not stated otherwise.

2004). This often-overlooked feature is an important difference between the Britain and the German welfare states and may explain some of the differences between the situations of lone mothers.

The third difference between the German and the British welfare state is that social policy changes are not as easy to introduce in Germany as in Britain. The Christian Democratic Party (CDU) has dominated the political landscape in West Germany since the Second World War, and was in government without interruption between 1983 and 1998. The CDU was dedicated to conservative as well as religious values. Although the Social Democratic Party (SPD) has been in coalition government with the Green Party from 1998 until 2005, the changes that it imposed were not as dramatic as in Britain, where social policies vary much more depending on the political party in government.

There are several reasons for these differences: Both of the main parties in Germany search for the middle ground in order to get elected, and social policy tends to be discussed on the basis of expert analysis rather than right or left ideological standpoints (Clasen and Freeman 1994, 5). Due to the German principle of subsidiarity, the many layers of support mean that social policy and its organizations are complex but also fragmented, which contributes to the difficulties in implementing changes in social policy. Also, Germany is a federal and semi-sovereign state and power is divided between municipalities (Kommunen), 16 individual states (Länder) and the national government (Bund). Most importantly, social policy in Germany is unlikely to change because the constitution characterizes Germany as a Sozialstaat (social state) which legally obliges it to honour certain social justice commitments.

In contrast to Britain, Germany also seems slower with regard to social policy innovation because of the number and variety of players involved. Powerful church welfare organizations, the Constitutional Court, political parties, a government by coalition and a decentralized federal system can all impede innovation of social policies and limit cuts in welfare (Mählmann 1998, 56).

A fourth distinguishing feature is that the Germany social insurance system is heavily based on a 'generational contract'. Those who make social insurance contributions today for the retired, sick, disabled and unemployed will become recipients of others' contributions when it is 'their turn' in the future. The system works as long as every generation keeps to this contract. This may be one of the most crucial reasons for the more positive feelings to lone mothers and their caring work in Germany, because their children are viewed as future contributors of social insurance who will thrive best with their mother. This may also be a reason for positioning and reimbursing mothers as carers and not as workers. Lone mothers are more positively viewed than, for example, childless couples and women who 'break' the generation contract. Fifthly, in Germany, lone parents fall into the domain of the Family Minister, which might be more beneficial for their image than in Britain, where lone mothers are dealt with by the Department of Work and Pensions.

Despite a resilience to change, an argument has been made for a 'dual transformation' of the German welfare state at the beginning of the 21st century. Seeleib-Kaiser (2004) highlights the decreasing emphasis on guaranteeing the achieved living standard of workers through wage-earner centred social policies on one hand and an expansion of family-oriented policies on the other hand. Through the

'Hartz IV' reform in 2005, the state has seemingly moved away from the wage-earner approach. Unemployed workers are increasingly dependent on means-tested benefits. Other measures include a partial privatization of the pension system and subsidized reemployment and self-employment (Bruttel and Sol 2006). Also, welfare-to-work programmes for unemployed individuals who receive social assistance benefits have been intensified and increased emphasis is placed on work to combat poverty, just like in Britain (Annesley 2002). In other words, the active labour market policies are becoming similar to those implemented in Britain (Bruttel and Sol 2006). Hence, because of unemployment, demographic change, and political developments, Germany no longer follows all principles of a 'social market economy'.

On the other hand, and as a result of the decline in fertility, family-oriented benefits and services have been expanded. Child Benefit has increased and childcare facilities are being enlarged thus facilitating mothers to go back to paid employment, irrespective of their particular family arrangements. However, the political climate is not going to force mothers with small children into employment (Bleses 2003). Even the Christian Democrats have modernized their approach towards the family and supposedly refrain from imposing a specific family model. Hence, Germany can no longer be categorized as a truly conservative welfare state.

Britain and Germany are members of the European Union which exerts considerable pressure for unified social policies and for a more corporist gender equality model that can be traced back to an 'equal opportunities at work' discourse in the 1980s (Duncan 2002, 305). For example, the introduction of the individual legal right for children between three and six to publicly financed childcare was largely influenced by the European law (Pfau-Effinger and Geissler 2002, 79). The two welfare states show a greater similarity with regard to their welfare/work model. There is some evidence for this in the meeting between Prime Minister Blair and German Chancellor Schroeder during which they discussed Giddens's (1998) idea of the 'Third Way' in 1999 (Lewis 2002, 337).

In the same year, the welfare state theorist Esping-Anderson (1999) argued that women's employment rate had to be increased first, because of the decreasing number of male breadwinner/ female homemaker households and secondly, because the tax base of the male breadwinner/ female homemaker model is unlikely to be able to sustain their welfare state. Measures to achieve the 'reconciliation of work and family' are now the dominant theme in the EU Policy on the family – work relationship. The flagship policies for this are tax credits, growing childcare provision and parental leave arrangements (Daly 2005, 392).

It seems that the move to a citizen-worker model is the replacement of one type of 'model family' (the male breadwinner/female homemaker) with another singular model (the working family). Daly (2005, 393) criticizes governments for not responding to the need for diversity in policy response and for ignoring the complexities of the issues inherent in the gendered division of care work. Women are still performing the bulk of unpaid care work, which was their obligation under the male breadwinner/ female homemaker model and which remains poorly valued. Lewis (2002, 341) also finds that welfare state policies are in danger of increasingly assuming women's self-provisioning when the majority of women work on a part-time basis only.

Specific benefits available to lone mothers in Britain and Germany

The British and the German welfare states reinforce gender inequalities because of the way they are structured. The work-oriented social insurance system continues to be more beneficial than means-tested and caring benefits (Blossfeld and Rohwer 1995; Seeleib-Kaiser 2004). We could therefore speak of a 'dual system of welfare' in which women's claims are based on need and men's as earners (Hantrais 1994, 136).

Nevertheless, the British welfare state may be less polarising than the German welfare state. British social insurance benefits translate into modest flat-rate benefits, not dissimilar to social assistance benefits. In Germany they continue to be earnings-related and status-conserving. Therefore it could be proposed that for state-dependent lone mothers it is more advantageous to live in Britain than in Germany. Daly (1996, 104) agrees because Britain is a better 'gender equaliser' although the German welfare state more effectively alleviates poverty, 'For, judged in terms of overall poverty levels and the income standard attainable by lone mothers, Germany is the better place to live, for women as well as men.' (Daly 1996, 104)

Sphere of care

In Britain, working mothers primarily rely on informal childcare arrangements, such as relatives, partners and friends (Pfau-Effinger 2005). This reliance on informal and unpaid care may partly determine married mothers' part-time employment. Recently, there has been increased effort to ensure more public childcare in Britain to facilitate the entry of mothers into paid employment. In 2005, 57 per cent of working families used formal childcare services, while 67 per cent used informal care (Bryson et al 2006). For lone mothers too, low paid employment has become more financially viable, as tax credits can pay up to 70 per cent of the cost of registered childcare (Evans et al 2003, 8).

Since 1998 the British government has been spending £300 million annually to boost childcare under the National Childcare Strategy. This includes a childcare tax credit for low income families. Since 2004, all three- and four-year-olds are entitled to free part-time early education (Bryson et al 2006; Ford and Millar 1998, 15). Nevertheless, implementation of free education places may vary between local authorities and take-up rates depend on local labour markets and gender cultures. However, the increasing state involvement in childcare as well as welfare-to-work programmes for lone mothers, such as the 'New Deal for Lone Parents' indicates that Britain is about to follow a more liberal-communitarian model, just like Germany.

In Germany, since 1996 every child over the age of three has had a statutory right to a place in a Kindergarten (Rechtsanspruch auf einen Kindergartenplatz). In 1998, every child over three had a place although there were large regional variations, with around 80 per cent provision in West Germany and an over supply in East Germany. Few nurseries offer full-time places to the over threes, with poignant differences between East and West (19% in West Germany and 98% in East Germany in 1998). In 1998 only three per cent of children in West Germany attend public child care, in contrast to 36 per cent of children who are provided for in East Germany (Engstler and Menning 2003, 120).

Hence, we can speak of two care cultures, one for East and one for West Germany. Mothers with children under the age of three can be viewed as being discouraged from paid work, particularly in West Germany. In West Germany Kindergartens close at midday. Thus, either working part-time or not working at all seems to be promoted, as is continuous state dependency. In East Germany, the full-time working mother ethic continues. Hence, the principle of financial dependence of mother-carers upon the state or male breadwinners is not fundamentally changed, at least not in West Germany.

The positioning of lone mother's caring work in Germany

The German pro-natal Childrearing Benefit (Erziehungsgeld) is aimed at lone and coupled mothers in households with small and medium incomes (Bundesministerium für Familien, Senioren, Frauen und Jugend 1998, 93). It consists of a two-year benefit of up to Euro 300 (about £207) a month which is paid to the main carer for up to two years. In effect, the parent with the lowest opportunity costs, usually the mother, becomes the home child carer or a part-time worker at most. Nevertheless, this policy particularly aids state-dependent lone parents and keeps them above the poverty line. This is because other state benefits such as the German equivalent of Income Support, Housing Benefit and Child Benefit are not counted as income when calculating eligibility (Erler 2004). Since its introduction in 1986 its recipients are almost always the mothers (Engstler and Menning 2003, 115). I would argue that these policies position lone mothers as caring mothers for the first two years of the baby's life because they can maintain a socially acceptable standard of living on the benefits offered and may even be better off than in low paid full-time paid employment. My research shows that some lone mothers actually view this benefit as a 'salary for caring'.

The two-year Childrearing Benefit (Erziehungsgeld) was introduced in 1986 and the three-year Childrearing Leave (Erziehungsurlaub) was introduced in 1992, which in 2001 became Parent Time (Elternzeit). These policies undoubtedly recognize work in the home while allowing a top-up income. While until 2000 parents were allowed to work up to 19 hours a week, they can now work up to up to 30 hours a week and choose to take the one-year Parent time option with higher benefits (Engstler and Menning 2003, 114). To encourage fathers to take up parent leave, two-months 'daddy leave' has been added. However, Childrearing Benefit is seen to have effectively lowered young mothers' paid employment participation rates (Erler 2004). Long leaves and deskilling may be responsible for lone mothers' lower earnings and lower pensions. Lone mothers more so than any other mothers are in jobs with short-term contracts and in shift or seasonal work (Erler 2004).

Despite the development of these policies, labour market employment continues to be highly valued in Germany as well as in Britain. First, the most comprehensive maternity benefits are structured around labour market status, with the intention of compensation for loss of earnings. Secondly, mothers in paid employment do not lose out as much on their pension contributions as caring non-employed mothers (Gardner 1998, 6).

In Germany, lone mothers with young children under two years are clearly treated as carers, while lone mothers with older children are 'punished' for staying out of paid employment for too long. Lone mothers are in 'no man's land' when the child is between two and three years old, as they are positioned neither as carers nor as workers. The expiration of the two-year Childrearing Benefit (Erziehungsgeld) represents an estimated 30 per cent fall in monthly public transfers and suggests their positioning as workers. However, they continue to be positioned as carers because for another year lone mothers are still entitled to Childrearing Leave/ Parent Time, and have not yet earned the statutory right to childcare (Rechtsanspruch auf einen Kindergartenplatz). In theory, once the child turns three, state-dependent lone mothers may be treated as workers. In reality, state-dependent lone mothers in Germany are only required to register for paid employment, if 'it does not jeopardize the proper/orderly rearing of the child.' (Bundesministerium für Familie, Senioren, Frauen und Jugend 1998, 106). As most childcare places are part-time and term-time only, especially in West Germany, the mother is limited to applying for part-time jobs. The next 'marker' is when the child reaches age seven. Then, a state-dependent lone mother loses even more of her regular state benefits to encourage her to shift from being a carer to being a paid worker. Therefore, there is a time limit on Lister's concept of 'defamilialization' in which lone mothers are able to maintain a socially acceptable standard of living, 'independently of family relationship, either through paid work or social security provision' (Lister 1994, 37). However, schools in Germany also continue to offer only half-days at least in wide areas of West Germany (Pinl 2003).

Nevertheless, lone mothers may not be obliged to enter paid employment everywhere. Formal local authority enforcement policies vary here too, and are dependent on the gender culture and local unemployment rates. The issue of implementation has often been overlooked in social policy research. Annesley (2002) mentions that the workfare component in Germany's social assistance law is in part pragmatic and in part ideological. For example, in 2000 a law was passed that requires employment offices to co-operate with the authorities that administer social assistance. However, Bruttel and Sol (2006) find welfare-to-work programmes at an early stage in terms of rules in terms of their compulsory elements.

Also, lone mothers do not yet feature prominently in debates about increased work incentives for social assistance recipients. Since lone mothers are not (yet) specifically targeted in work programmes, this may show that the welfare state continues to substitute the male breadwinner in part. Hence, the traditional features of the German social welfare system are retained, while lone mothers remain in poverty since the social assistance levels are not high enough to lift recipients out of poverty (Annesly 2002).

The positioning of lone mothers' caring work in Britain

The British welfare state gives out mixed messages because it positions lone mothers as carers and workers but primarily as dependents. In the late 1990s, when the fieldwork took place, policies have not been linear but have been 'Janus-faced in often condemning lone motherhood and yet giving lone mothers the means of subsistence.' (Kiernan et al 1998, 277). As carers, state-dependent lone mothers entitled to additional benefits are as yet under no obligation to register for paid work and they have no benefits withdrawn. Nonetheless, social assistance and caring benefits tend to be more modest than in Germany. As a consequence of this and of low employment, more lone mothers' in Britain experience poverty than lone mothers in Germany (71% and 49% respectively). Never-married lone mothers in the UK are almost twice as likely to be at risk of poverty compared to their counterparts in Germany (46% and 25% respectively (Ruspini 1998, 39).

The Conservative government's agenda, during its time in power between 1979 and 1997, was very pronounced in discouraging lone motherhood altogether by reducing access to benefits rather than promoting paid employment for lone mothers with young children. Instead, the government reinstated the biological father as the source of support with the 1991 Act. They not only wanted to reduce public spending but also to reinforce the fathers' responsibilities to maintain their family. Bradshaw et al (1999, 2) argue that the CSA is an example of bad policymaking. It was badly designed and suffers from low compliance.

The in-work benefit 'Family Credit' only encourages low paid, part-time jobs, because of its disincentive to increase earnings above a certain threshold. As the research data shows, lone mothers on Income Support are caught in a 'poverty trap'. They cannot afford to enter paid employment, particularly full-time employment, because higher earnings will be offset by a deduction in benefits in cash and kind, in conjunction with a parallel increase in costs, such as childcare, travel and work clothes, National Insurance contributions and Income Tax. While paid employment does alleviate poverty to a certain extent, this is not the case for low paid employment, and this policy has clearly failed to place lone mothers as workers. Another reason for its limited influence has been insufficient understanding of this benefit by the supposed recipients and their biased perceptions. The Labour government, in power since 1997, has been improving in-work benefits, but these changes have not had any effect at the time the interviews took place.

The Labour government clearly wants lone mothers' transformation from state-dependents to paid workers and not to carers. It has acted to push lone mothers into the labour market, in the face of strongly shared values among some women that prioritize care work. Policies to 'make work pay' include the introduction of the minimum wage in 1999 and generous wage subsidies in the form of tax credits, such as the 2003 introduction of the Child Tax Credit and the Working Tax Credit. These have increased the financial gains from part-time and low paid work, as well as the New Deal for Lone Parents (Lewis 2002).

The New Deal for Lone Parents

In October 1998 the 'New Deal for Lone Parents' (NDLP) was introduced nationally. The programme's main objectives are to encourage lone parents on Income Support to improve their prospects and living standards by taking up paid work and to generally improve their employment opportunities (Ford and Millar 1998, 15). The Department for Work and Pensions has a target to have 70 per cent of lone parents in employment by 2010. In 2003, the figure was at 54 per cent, up from around 40 per cent in 1995. 317,000 lone parents have participated in total until September 2002 and poverty rates have fallen from 62 per cent in 1996 to 54 per cent in 2002 (Evans et al 2003).

The programme is voluntary but through the introduction of a compulsory Personal Advisor Meeting in 2001, the participation in the programme has increased from 5-10 per cent to 20 per cent. The Personal Advisors could not only work out whether lone mothers were 'better off' in paid work and assist lone parents in finding paid work, but also build confidence and break isolation. The NDLP has been subject to extensive evaluation. Evans et al (2003) calculated that by 2002, the programme reached nine percent of lone parents claiming Income Support. Those least likely to participate have two or more children, have a child under the age of three, or have health problems or a disability.

Those most likely to participate are most motivated, those with the shortest claim history, and those who do not mind working for a minimum wage (Evans et al 2003). It could be argued that these lone parents might have entered employment even without the programme. The main barrier to work was found to be childcare, although in some cases interrupted education, health problems and caring responsibilities for relatives or children with illness were also problematic (Knight and Thomas 2006). Almost a third of participants who find work through NDLP move back to Income Support within one year. Those lone parents who are looking for higher-level jobs that may require some specialist training tend to be poorly served in the scheme (Bruttel and Sol 2006). Also, lone parents in general are almost twice as likely to leave their job compared to single childless women, particularly those with young children, more than one child and in a low paid part-time job (Evans et al 2004). This is despite in-work and childcare subsidies (Department for Work and Pensions 2005).

Since this programme concentrates on the labour-supply side, it is more likely to be successful in a well-functioning economy, but would not be sustainable during a recession. This can be backed up by a study that also found that favourable economic conditions and tight labour markets appear to have played a larger role than welfare policies in increasing the economic activity of lone parents in Norway (Kjeldstad and Ronsen 2005, 85). To reach the government's employment target of 70 per cent, it will need to involve far higher participation rates from the non-employed lone parent population with very young children and those with more disadvantages and barriers to work (Berthoud 2003).

The programme also obscures massive inequalities in terms of work rewards and conditions as well as class and gender inequalities at work (Stewart 2000, 4).

The activities of employers providing low paid or insecure jobs are not questioned (Duncan and Pfau-Effinger 2000, 3). The rationale for positioning unskilled mothers as workers may be political and cultural but it is not economic as they are likely to continue to receive benefits. Moreover, 'society' seems limited to the employed. Caring work is not considered essential nor a productive contribution to society.

Conclusion

This chapter has shown that although lone mothers 'fall out' of the male breadwinner model, they are paradoxically repositioned within this model, with the state substituting to a limited extent the breadwinner under certain conditions. Nevertheless, the care policies of Germany in particular, reflect and support the principle that informal care plays an important role also in the modernized cultural concept of the family.

There are some common trends in what the German and the British social-democratic governments have done with respect to the promotion of labour market activation and 'making work pay'. In both Britain and Germany, policies on the family are a growing area of intervention, but one which has narrowed in scope. In Britain especially, it seems to have become more of an arm of employment policy. However, to this day, the German and British welfare state provisions prove remarkably resilient to change in some aspects. Lone mothers in Britain as in Germany are ultimately neither catered for as full-time workers nor as paid carers, but as dependants, since caring is not comparable with the security that full-time employment provides.

Germany, although now one country, continues to exhibit two national trends regarding lone motherhood labour force characteristics and participation rates. The importance of East and West Germany's different cultural and historical development with regard to lone mothers' attitudes and behaviour has been analysed. It seems that the British welfare state is no longer prepared to perform the male breadwinner role for lone mothers, and has placed state-dependent lone mothers as mothers who should be workers. Social policies have been implemented to reinforce this. The New Deal for lone parents and the 2008 Parent Time show that both the German and the British labour governments are devoted to labour-market activation. This is effectively a move towards the creation of a citizen worker model (Lewis 2001). Both, the German and the British model have compulsory elements. In Britain, state-dependent lone mothers do not have to register for paid work – only for an interview with a 'Personal Advisor', unlike in Germany, and their benefits are not reduced as the child gets older.

Social policies cannot solely explain why women, including lone mothers, act the way they do. For example, social policies in Germany discourage lone mothers' labour market participation by providing few and only part-time childcare facilities. However, lone mothers participate in the labour force despite remaining poor and facing a double burden. Of course, there is no reason to believe that social policy should explain how mothers live their lives because lone mothers do not act in a rational economic manner to maximize benefits.

The research data shows that we need to look at social expectations, moral obligations, discourses and possibilities - as well as local labour markets, class, qualifications and ethnicity when explaining lone mothers' lives. A variety of factors influence lone mothers to enter paid employment. This research looks not only at state benefits but also at their personal characteristics, their 'stage' of lone parenthood, their attitudes, their social and neighbourhood networks and their personal cost-benefit assessments of employment. Here, the concept of individualization is useful as it recognizes that lone mothers' are diverse and that their lives are dynamic.

Nonetheless, welfare state ideologies and specific social policies are important parameters within which lone mothers negotiate their lives. It is argued that the welfare state can make women feel either oppressed or empowered or both. However, would these women not feel empowered if they had a genuine choice to undertake care work, if their care work was recognized and valued? The choice to care depends on valuing care. Lewis (2002) argues that a form of basic income is necessary for there to be the security to choose different forms of humanly and socially necessary activity, such as care. To benefit all members of society, instead of women and mothers adapting to a masculine model of employment, perhaps men need to become competent in flexible paid work as well as in care and family work.

Chapter 5

Mothering and Paid Employment – Views and Experiences

The purpose of the research is to find out how mothers define themselves regarding paid or unpaid employment and motherhood. Specifically, the research sought to establish what it means to be a good mother and/or a good worker, and how these two roles may relate. The research involved in-depth analysis of the views and comments towards motherhood and work following face-to-face interviews. A theoretical sampling strategy was used rather than a representative one (Miles and Huberman1994). I interviewed 70 lone mothers, split evenly between London and Berlin (see chapter 1 and appendix).

The chapter starts by analysing why lone mothers with an employment orientation are not in paid employment. It will show how reasons between the interviewed lone mothers in London and Berlin vary. The second part of the chapter explores the concept of mothering and mothers' identities as mothers within the concept of late modernity.

Reasons for staying out of paid employment

Table 5.1 shows in more detail the unprompted reasons for staying out of employment that emerged from the data. Already we can ascertain that there are lone mothers who use state benefits to further their education, for personal and occupational reorientation or for an artistic career by concentrating on music or art. This adds to the three mothers' orientations Duncan and Edwards (1999) describe (primarily mother, primarily worker and mother/worker). The responses in Table 5.1 were unprompted and the following sections analyse each issue in turn.

Table 5.1 Reasons for staying out of paid employment in per cent

	London	*Berlin*
Other reasons	14	11
Cannot earn enough money	54	0
Childcare issues	20	23
Want to pursue education	43	37
Cannot find job	6	14
Cannot find flexible work	37	20
Want to be with children	46	49

*It is possible to give more than one reason.

Many mothers prioritized being with their children or pursue education over being in paid employment. The mothers who were interviewed in Berlin perceived different barriers to paid employment than London mothers. Berlin mothers had problems with the availability and flexibility of childcare and felt discriminated against by employers. London lone mothers had difficulties commanding a sufficient income to replace benefits and the cost of childcare.

Other reasons

This category included mothers who either could not enter employment because of ill health or because they had other interests. The London group contained mothers who were ill or had children who were ill (for example asthma or spina bifida). In Berlin, there were mothers who were ill, or heavily pregnant or had children who were ill.

Issues of ill-health and disability are a recurrent theme for lone parents. This is a clear work barrier, either because of the mothers' caring responsibilities or because of their own ill health (Millar and Ridge 2001, 183). It would be useful to know more about needs and circumstances of families in poor health, but so far there has been little research on this (Casebourne and Britton 2004). These mothers are not individualised but constraint in their choices.

For one London mother, state benefits were an enabler to achieve her creative goals, 'My goal is to become a professional songwriter. It is not really about getting a job, paying the gas bill or getting a job to buy my daughter some new shoes.' Here too, the state benefit system is viewed as an acceptable breadwinner for a while (Mädje and Neusüß 1994a and 1994b). In accordance to the concept of individualization, these mothers use state benefits to increase their life choices. They can live their lives differently, rear their child and pursue an artistic career that may not be financially viable. Here, 'self-fulfilment' has a higher priority than financial independence and the state takes the role as a 'patron of the arts'.

Cannot earn enough money

Half of the mothers in London, but none in Berlin, mentioned the inability to earn enough money as a barrier to employment, mainly because they thought that they could not command an income to compensate for the loss of state benefits and the cost of childcare. In other words, they were caught in the poverty trap.

There are many reasons for this, most of which include the type and length of the mothers' work experience, the age of their children and their educational and vocational qualifications. These women may not have been aware of the in-work benefits and tax credits available to them. Also, programmes such as the New Deal for lone parents as well as the Childcare tax credits were only introduced after the interviews took place.

Much British academic research confirms the relationship between the level of qualifications and a mother's probability of returning to work after the birth of a child. This may go some way in explaining why Berlin lone mothers are not afraid of the poverty trap. The lone mothers I have interviewed in Berlin were much more likely to have educational qualifications than the lone mothers in London. Of the London lone mothers interviewed, 37 per cent of mothers had no educational qualifications in contrast to 14 per cent of Berlin lone mothers. Without qualifications it is likely to be difficult to command a decent wage. For mothers with no qualifications, the prospect of becoming a lone mother may not be a negative one, as ife on benefit may not result in a substantial drop in income (Rowlingson and McKay 1998, 197).

The type and length of work experience prior to the women's first pregnancy is another predictor of their chances to enter 'sufficiently' paid employment (Noble et al 1998, 41). Contrary to the popular portrayal of unmarried mothers, who are typically seen to be young, unemployed with no work experience, all but four of the 70 mothers interviewed have a paid-employment record, working mainly full-time before having had children. The Berlin lone mothers' paid employment record was longer, partly perhaps because they had their children later and they had fewer children.

In both Berlin and London, the women's jobs varied before they became pregnant. Typically, their employment was a reflection of academic and vocational training that had been achieved. Roles included receptionists, care assistants, catering assistants, sales assistants, housekeepers, clerical assistants and waitresses. They were mostly in low-skilled, flexible and traditionally female occupations. Amongst the London lone mothers interviewed, there were also a couple of nurses. In East Berlin, women also worked as farm workers, warehouse workers and nursery nurses. In West Berlin, the picture was similar, but there was also an academic researcher, an accountant, a dental assistant and a few factory workers.

Cash in hand work

During the interviews, mothers in both the London and the Berlin respondents had no hesitation in discussing work in the informal economy but more women in London than in Berlin received an income from 'cash in hand' work (10/35 and 4/35). Figure 5.1 shows the relevance of income from the informal economy to top up state benefits over other additional benefits and financial support by relatives. Only two mothers, both living in London, received regular financial support from relatives. Casual work tended to be irregular, flexible and low skilled and did not appear to be offset against benefits. Women mentioned jobs such as a cleaner, waitress, babysitter, receptionist, tele-sales person and sales consultant. Obviously, mentioning independent income is a very sensitive issue. Nonetheless, crosschecks led me to believe that the accounts were genuine.

It is supposed that the relative low take-up by Berlin mothers of informal employment may be influenced by the fact that they had younger children. For one in three of these mothers, state benefits were topped up by a £200 Childrearing Benefit, which the mother receives until the child is two years old (see chapter 4). Therefore, they may not have been a 'need' to top up their income particularly since rents and living costs are lower in Berlin.

All of the lone mothers in this research were dependent on state benefits. Their income level varied with the number of children and the amount deducted in debt repayments by the Department of Social Security. In London, every second mother

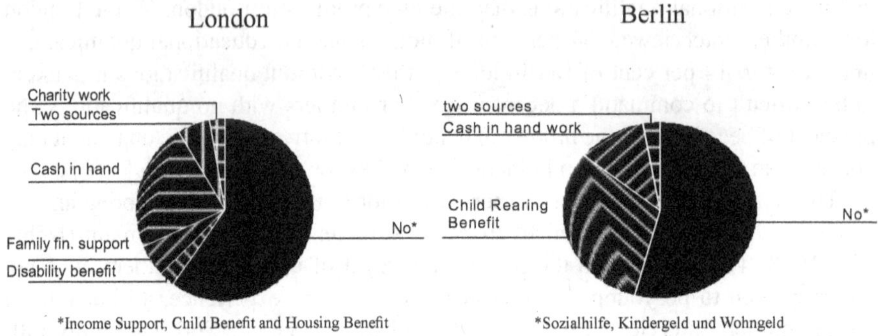

Figure 5.1 Lone mothers' income sources

had debts with either the Department of Social Security (which provided a loan for moving costs), or with private catalogue companies, where items are paid for in instalments.

Cash in hand income ranged from £10 to £50 a week. In other words, rather than maximising consumption, lone mothers worked cash in hand to minimize the risk of an economic disaster. In Berlin, all mothers received the German equivalent of Income Support, Sozialhilfe. Berlin mothers had less money available to them each week than London mothers but their income range varies more. The three Berlin mothers with school-aged children were worst off of both groups because their state benefits were cut by a quarter and they had to pay for mandatory health insurance. Those mothers with one child under two were best off because they received Childrearing Benefit on top of their usual state benefits. Even after excluding rent, London lone mothers on benefits still had a higher disposable income than Berlin lone mothers – on average £94 and £84 respectively. However, the cost of living in London is 20 per cent higher than in Berlin (*The Economist* 2002). As other research has already suggested, lone mothers seem better off in Germany, at least materially (Daly 1996, 194). German mothers worried about other barriers such as flexible childcare instead.

Cost-benefit analysis

In London, many women were under the impression that they could not earn more in paid work than on state benefits. Many were unaware or unsure about the in-work-benefits and tax credits available to them. In Berlin, Lydia gave this cost-benefit analysis, comparing a three-year Childrearing Leave from paid employment with the two-year Childrearing Benefit of £200 a month,

> For me, to be honest, I said straight from the beginning, two years I stay at home because then the money is right and because then I still have time for the child and stuff, that's not bad. And after the two years we no longer get the money but I think that then they have a good age that they should be with other children, otherwise they deteriorate. Always with the mother at home is not so good.

German social policy encourages lone mothers with young children to be 'good mothers'. Childrearing Benefit in Germany – now called Parent Time – assumes that people make cost-benefit type decisions to maximize personal gain both for the parent and child. This research has found that lone mothers are rational utility maximizers in part since they indeed weigh up the costs and benefits with respect to their own interests.

Duncan and Edwards (1999, 279) coined the term 'gendered moral rationalities' to explain mothers' socially negotiated understandings about the proper relationship between good mothering and paid work. Duncan and Pfau-Effinger (2000, 7) recognized that mothers make economic calculations but this factor needed to be set in context with another model of rationality that is socially negotiated and non-economic. It is an understanding about what is morally right and socially acceptable. These negotiations depend on particular cultural and neighbourhood settings, local labour markets and welfare state regimes.

Edwards and Duncan (1996, 119 and 128) emphasized the importance of geographies because mothers who are members of particular social groups, living in particular areas, collectively negotiate moral rationalities. While I agree with Duncan and Edwards (1997, 70) that gendered moral rationalities are collectively negotiated in social groups, I feel that the concept undervalues the individual's agency and overvalues the importance of geography. Mothers' social groups are not necessarily confined to a specific neighbourhood, as this research shows. Nonetheless, the local availability of formal childcare, transport facilities and jobs remains significant, as well as the attitude of the local authorities in Germany in pressurising lone mothers with older children to enter employment.

The concept of gendered moral rationalities also under-emphasizes that collectively negotiated norms can be confusing, unclear and paradoxical. The result is that lone mothers as individuals have difficult choices to make. This fits in with the concept of individualization that proclaims that it is left to the individual to design their 'do-it-yourself biography' (see chapter 3).

The decision to work is not an obvious one and can depend on many factors, not just on institutional conditions, neighbourhoods, local labour markets and social policies, but also on factors that cannot be 'counted', such as the psychological reasons, past experiences and the individually perceived needs of the child.

Childcare issues

Academic research in Britain has accepted that in London the cost of childcare is a major constraint for women's employment (Bryson et al 2006; Evans et al 2004; Finlayson and Marsh 1998, 194; Ford 1998, 224; Noble et al 1998, 46; Sinha 1998, 73). A recent study found that even after the 1999 introduction of the childcare element of the Working Tax Credit many lone parents still felt that childcare was too expensive (Bell at al 2005, 5). Noble et al (1998, 3) confirm that the number of children dampens the exit rate from Income Support. As a result of high childcare costs, of those mothers interviewed for this research who had pre-school children in Britain, only three had formal childcare in place, which was highly subsidized. The other mothers relied on informally exchanging babysitting or support from relatives and friends, as is typical for Britain (see chapter 4).

In contrast, German research has found less flexible childcare arrangements (Hank et al 2001; Pinl 2003; Rosenfeld et al 2004; Veil 2003). In West Germany, young children usually stay at home with their mother. Some mothers have some form of public childcare in place, mostly part-time (5/16). Most mothers rely on informal occasional childcare support from their social network, mostly by their own mother. Exchanging babysitting is also a popular practice. This is similar to London, although there children enter school one to two years earlier.

In East Berlin, being out of paid employment does not mean that the children stay at home with their mothers. As most of the comprehensive childcare provision of the former socialist East Germany still exists, one third of the mothers stay at home with their children (7/19) while the majority has secured a full-time Kindergarten place. Here, the availability and low cost of public childcare may in turn influence lone mothers' drive for education in East Berlin. It may also stem from the culture that was carried over from before reunification, when the combination of paid employment or education and children was not only socially accepted but also financially supported (see chapter 4).

After close examination of the data in Berlin and London, the research reveals that mothers may feel under pressure to be seen to aspire to paid employment. I have found that some mothers used their constraints to justify or legitimize full-time mothering. With some, it was the perception that matters rather than the experience of barriers, such as lack and inflexibility of childcare. Five women in West Berlin made employment decisions based on the opening times of *one* Kindergarten only. One example is Susanne who was torn between wanting to go to work and wanting to be with her children, 'I would have probably had problems with my daughter because Kindergartens are not open until six o'clock. Somehow I want to be there for my two children.'

Cannot find job

The low rate of lone mothers in paid work in economically deprived neighbourhoods in inner city areas in Britain is connected with their limited job-search areas as well as associated problems (Speak 2000, 33). Lone mothers' commuting time is limited by domestic responsibilities and transport costs and difficulties. A further obstacle is the restructuring of labour markets. Duncan and Edwards (1997, 68) refer to the concentration of new 'high-tech' and production service jobs outside older industrial areas and cities in the 1980s. In this study however, the conditions of local labour markets were a less significant barrier than the labour market discrimination that the interviewees in Berlin mentioned.

Labour market discrimination

Only few ethnic minority women reported racial discrimination but many lone mothers in Berlin felt discriminated against because of their status as mothers. Employers consider them less flexible and less reliable. This may be a result of the female homemaker culture in West Germany, but it is also an effect of a law that states that a lone mother has the right to take up to a maximum of 20 days off a year to look after each of her sick children; 50 days is the maximum (Paragraph 45 des Fünften Sozialgesetzbuchs). Seven East Berlin mothers and six West Berlin mothers felt discriminated against for this reason. One West Berlin example is Manuela:

> I am panicky about not being able to get work because of the child and things. Because you have to tick [on the application form], lone parent or whether you have a child or whatever. And that is where it starts, lone parent and child? When the child becomes ill is the mother missing and then you have to add 20 days [as an employer] because the child has the right to 20 days. And when the child is ill, then the mother is absent too.

Labour market discrimination is not only about perception held by the mothers. In five cases Berlin mothers reported that they have been told that they would not get the job because they had children. West Berlin's Burcu applied for an apprenticeship in a typically female occupation, a dental assistant, after her second child. She stated: 'that dentist was a woman. She won't take mothers with children.' In contrast, only two London mothers felt discriminated against by employers because they were lone mothers.

There are several explanations for the differences found in my interviewees' experiences of labour market discrimination in Germany and Britain. Germany's labour market is only now in the process of being 'flexibilized', a process slowed down by the unions and by the principles of the German social market economy (see chapter 4). In Germany, the employer may not want to employ lone mothers because they feel a) mothers should be with their children, b) they are too expensive because they have too many rights and c) they are not flexible enough. In Berlin, lone mothers blamed employers' attitudes towards them for their high rate of unemployment, while in London, lone mothers mainly blamed the state of the labour market and their own lack of skills and work experience. The lone mothers I have interviewed in London may have also been more 'streetwise' and hidden the fact that they are lone mothers.

Lone mothers' expectations

Lone mothers in Berlin and in London may also be in receipt of state benefits because they are not prepared to just take any job that comes along but have expectations about hours, income and 'enjoyment'. One example is Angela who has a school aged son:

> If I am gonna be taken off the dole it's gotta be for a job that I actually enjoy. Otherwise I am not going to stick with it and then it is difficult for me to get back onto the dole and get all my benefits.

When asked what they are looking for in a job, lone mothers in both Berlin and London, mentioned enjoyment and flexibility before other motivations such as money, social opportunities and career prospects. A job must be interesting to compete with the alternative of being a full-time mother. Nonetheless, some mothers I have interviewed held unrealistic career prospects: they may have not yet been confronted with the realities of the labour market because entering the labour market was not imminent.

Psychological factors
The interview data shows that some mothers could not imagine entering paid employment as they have lost confidence and aspirations. Two Berlin women and at least three London women could not imagine other scenarios and were resigned to their situation. In East Berlin, Connie realized that she would not be able to find interesting work, which pays more than benefits, but state benefits also made her phlegmatic:

> Mhmm, I want to say that it has been internalized. Let's say, when you have never been properly in work, apart from the two years in the apprenticeship, then it is phlegmatic more or less, I would say. I am more or less used to staying at home all the time. Other people get used to work, like I got used to staying at home more or less.

Research by Finlayson et al (2000) also found a very clear association between severe hardship and low morale. A lack of self-esteem adds to women's general lack of work contacts and makes it difficult to secure employment. Psychological barriers can be hidden behind external reasons, such as problems with inflexible childcare. In East Berlin, Beate, a trained milkmaid, admitted late in the interview that her lack of confidence impeded her chances of paid work:

> I am pretty shy and I not daring at all. And then I, I just can not do it, to apply for a job. To go somewhere, to chat with people. I do not know ... and convince them to take me. I just can not do it.

Not only long-term state dependency but also mothers' recent experiences were responsible for lack of self-esteem. Some lone mothers have gone through traumatic separations and needed time to recover. In London, Cordelia explained her problem with paid work:

> Cause like when I kicked his dad out my self-esteem was so low, I couldn't have gone out to work cause I was just, I'd get to an interview, they'd ask me a question and I'd start crying, cause I was so low after kicking her dad out. And it took me like two years to recover.

As part of the psychological factors that made lone mothers want to stay at home with their children is the discovery of what I would like to call 'serial mothering', that is mothers who have three to five children by as many fathers. This research found at least one mother in East Berlin, West Berlin and in London. All three liked the continuous experience of being pregnant or of having young children that are needy, perhaps because of the result of depression or fear of loneliness. For West Berlin Burcu, it was an escape from difficult situations:

> I think that having children or becoming pregnant is a type of escape from my situation. It is a nice experience. I like being pregnant and I like bearing children especially when it gets difficult or, as the other children get older and become more demanding. That

> wasn't good. When I am pregnant then I am occupied, busy. And I have, I do not know, something for myself somehow. I do not know how you can explain it. Somehow it is a substitute. Other people eat, become mad and I like to be pregnant.

Other research confirms that pregnancy can increase a woman's self worth. For example, their body experience enhances women's' feeling of being 'special' at this time and of having an additional value culturally (Baily 1999, 341). It is therefore entirely possible that a serial mother uses pregnancies not only to bring permanence to relationships but also to improve her self-worth. For these women, having a baby is also about controlling their environment by making it intimate, and placing themselves firmly in charge. Babies may offer the stability and security some lone mothers lack perhaps because of their circumstances and negative childhood experiences. These tentative explanations show the need to both analyse lone mothers' psychological issues and also to provide social support in the area of mental health.

Cannot find flexible work

This section portrays mothers who wanted to combine mothering and paid employment. Flexible work can be defined as a wide variety of working patterns, such as part-time, flexi-time, temporary and seasonal contracts to name a few. Hakim (1997, 5) coins women who want to work part-time 'adaptive women' but in my research, these mothers are not very adaptive because they really wanted employee-friendly flexible work that is secure, part-time and fits into childcare and school hours. In other words, they wanted employee-friendly flexible work rather than employer-friendly flexible work (Perrons 1998).

Flexible work may be an example of how deeply internalized women's family obligations are. It is also an example of the highly practical way women go about meeting conflicting demands but may also be result of a cost-benefit analysis of in-work benefits and tax credits that favours part-time work. An example in London is Polly who viewed her life as not just about being money but also about mothering a happy child:

> It is very important to me that I can bring my child to school and that I can pick him up. And that he is OK and that he is happy. It is not just about money. It is also about the child and his well being.

More London mothers than Berlin mothers were looking for work but found it difficult to find flexible work. It is unique to the London lone mothers that they were also concerned about the cost of childcare and the rules of tax credits, while Berlin lone mothers voiced concern about childcare availability and hours. Some of the barriers are experienced; some of them are anticipated, such as labour market discrimination, Kindergarten opening hours and the inability to earn a sufficient income. Both, 'actual' and 'perceived' barriers influence and further the decision-making processes and serve as justification of the decisions made. Millar and Ridge (2001, 148) also report about work barriers that might arise from misconceptions, for example about the real cost of childcare. Duncan (2006) explains how constraints are connected with social moralities. Lone mothers' decisions refer to social identities that present different mixes of preference and constraints. Both are socially and culturally created through the development of biographical experience, relationships, and through normative views in social networks. In this way, preference and constraint become social moralities. This is even more encouragement to look beyond work barriers and into their orientations towards mothering and education.

Education orientation

Many of the mothers who currently did not seek paid employment were interested in pursuing some form of education or are already studying. It emerges from the data that education is a facilitator for a multitude of motives and other research finds that it facilitates mothering, is viewed as an alternative to unemployment and as improving labour market chances at best (Evans et al 2004; Winterborn 1990, 11). By entering education, state dependence can be regarded positively as an enabler rather than a personal failure (Mädje and Neusüß 1994a and 1994b). However, there is hardly any information available about mothers' desires for education (Millar and Ridge 2001, 184).

It emerges from the data that education was used for personal development too, as one way of rethinking and restructuring mothers' lives without losing out on benefits, or to avoid unemployment. For Connie in London, education was more flexible and less stressful than full-time paid employment:

> I want to go on to university and do a degree. I want to devote a lot of time to studying because when I'm studying, I think it's easier than working and I can spend more time at home. So if I am studying it takes a lot of the pressure off. It's a different sort of pressure.

There were more East Berlin than West Berlin mothers who were about to start education and all six mothers who were already pursuing higher educational or vocational qualifications live in East Berlin. This may be related to the fact that they came from a slightly more middle-class background than the West Berlin mothers I have interviewed. East Berlin mothers grew up in a socialist culture, which supported mothering while studying and, also, their previous occupations may have been no longer relevant in a restructured economy. These mothers could also now study their chosen field of interest and had a chance to improve their educational qualifications regardless of their political orientation or pressure to be in full-time work. Mareike in East Berlin said:

> I say now that it is more comfortable to get Income Support and to do 'A' levels in *peace* and then to do something else. I do not think I would do it, where I go out of the house and come back at six and get the same money. That sounds tough but it is like that. I do not want to lie. I prefer to do it, like I do it now, to do 'A' levels and then work somewhere part-time perhaps.

Education not only improves chances in the labour market but also enables professional orientation as well as reorientation. Colleges and universities were perceived to be more interesting, less time-consuming and therefore more accommodating towards mothering. Moreover, while waiting for a course to start or while being in a vocational retraining course, Berlin benefit offices do not pressurize mothers on state benefits to seek paid employment. Course fees and childcare costs served as a deterrent to education for London lone mothers who often wanted to wait until their child was of school age when there are no more childcare costs. In London, Sarah stated:

> I'd like to go into social work or teaching. But it's just getting the qualifications. I can not afford to go to college, because again, having to pay for childcare. I can not afford to do the Open University, when I do it at home because I just can not afford to pay for the course [of £360 a year].

There are many commonalties between the London and Berlin lone mothers with regards to their attitude towards education. Nonetheless, education was primarily viewed as a facilitator for mothering. Mothers in London and Berlin 'chose' education or 'resigned' to it, but only London mothers experienced barriers because of benefit rules, childcare costs and school fees. It may also be possible that my presence and position as a researcher in an educational institution may have kick-started the thinking about education as an attractive alternative to their current situation.

Want to be with children – Professional mothering

Views on paid employment are inseparable from the concept of motherhood, or mothering. While some mothers resigned to full-time motherhood because of lack of employment opportunities, in both London and Berlin, about half of mothers stayed out of paid employment because they preferred to be with their children.

The term 'professional' mother encompasses meaning and purpose and is used for women who declare that they *want* to be a full-time mother and who perceive their self-identity as a full-time mother. These women feel that only through full-time mothering can they give their children love and a sense of security, as well as moral guidance in shaping their children's emerging characteristics. German research has also found mothers who increase their self-worth by their ability to create a harmonious and intimate family setting (Koppetsch and Maier 1998, 149).

There may be a dissonance between the image of professional mothering and its practice, but I refrain from evaluating it as this was not part of the study. Some mothers work towards their children's cognitive development and report that they take them to many activities and outings where they socialize with others. Others may value the emotional development: the fact that the mother is there for the child only. Professional mothering may be valued in terms of the amount of time spent with the child or the quality of time spent with the child. In London, Laura defined mothering as a teaching job: 'I take being a mum as being a job and I do all the things that I would do if I was a teacher.' Again in London, Moira's account of the emotional development is also characteristic for a professional mother in that it is elaborate, informed and analytical about mothering:

> I want her to be emotionally secure as she can be. This is why I keep breastfeeding her for longer, why I want her to know her dad. I know they go through separation anxiety from six to nine months. The more I am with her without being overbearing or clingy then the more confident she is going to be.

While I initially assumed that professional mothering was influenced by the desire to compensate for being the only parent, only one woman explained mothering like this. Attitudes to professional mothering vary over time according to mother's needs and how they perceive their children's needs. Research recognizes that the age of the youngest child is one of lone parents' foremost concerns regarding work re-entry in Britain (Evans et al 2004; Ford 1996). In Germany, Mothers may also decide to become a professional mother after they have made their cost-benefit analysis. In Berlin, the Childrearing Benefit rewards caring work. In contrast, London mothers may professionalize mothering as a response to limited earning opportunities. In London, Julie made a financial and emotional cost-benefit analysis:

> I do not have family here. All my friends work. I'd basically be working just to pay childcare more or less and you pay poll tax that you get benefits for and it wouldn't have been worth it. There is no point. It would basically be feeding him, cleaning him and put him to bed. And that would be all and there would be no play with him or any sort of communication you have with a child. It would be like having a pet dog. You know, make sure it is walked in the morning. Rather than a human being it's only really the practical side. And I think I will be much more stressed out.

A few mothers used professional motherhood to rectify something they perceive as being a mistake. Some regretted that they have not been there for their first-born, who were now teenagers. Alternatively, they wanted to repeat the experience of having a young child. It is also possible that those external constraints that increase when the first child grows older may make mothering a less demanding and more easily obtainable option. The London mother Lisa said she has missed out on much of her now 16-year-old son's childhood and did not want to repeat this with her two-year-old daughter:

> I missed so much of him being a baby, because he used to stay with his grandparents sometimes at weekends and I'd be working in the pet shop. I missed so much. I wanted to not miss it this time. Before I even considered that I would fall pregnant or anything like that, I thought, oh God, I've missed so much of his growing up and he's so big now. Look at him, he's a man, all of a sudden, he's gone from that to that. I missed half of it. I can never, ever get that back again. Never. And I'd sit and look at his picture and cry. But I've got it back again.

Interestingly, the professional mothers tended to be the older women. Other research confirms that lone mothers over 35 are less work-oriented than their younger counterparts although their children tended to be older (Noble et al 1998, 49). Perhaps older lone mothers feel more 'at ease' in stating that they would like to stay at home with the children than younger lone mothers, who feel pressurized to enter paid work. Also, they may have already found a career and feel more confident about returning to it later, or they might feel they are not missing out by not working. Some of these interviewed women have delayed childbearing and view looking after their own children as a 'career break'. They found that working life is not that fulfilling and that money is not everything. Full-time mothering may have been their way out of an early 'midlife crisis'. Children may be used to 'escape' work they no longer find fulfilling and they were no longer be prepared to wait for 'Mr Right' to come along. What these older work-experienced professional lone mothers had in common is that they did not feel ashamed about their state-benefit dependency: they viewed it as a fair exchange to taxes paid in the past and in the future. Particularly in Germany, lone mothers validated professional mothering and state support because they were raising the next generation of taxpayers and kept to their part of the 'generational contract' (see chapter 4).

Professional mothering is influenced by a multitude of reasons and some may serve as a rationale for others. It may be difficult to keep constraints apart from choices but I consider professional mothering as dominated by choices rather than constraints. I would argue that the women I have spoken with did not just maintain traditional views passed on from generation to generation but were highly individualized in parts. In other words, these mothers negotiated their commitment to mothering rather than following a moral rule viewing mothering as a constraint (for example Finch 1989). Obviously, mothers on state benefits are not all self-fulfilled professional mothers, and the notion of choice has to be questioned. A case of self-justification that serves as a coping strategy to themselves as well as a justification to the public has to be taken into consideration although it is difficult to detect. The next section analyses how choices are located in gender, and how meaning and identities are also constructed within a material and cultural context (Miller 2005, 55).

Motherhood and late modernity

Within Western cultures, there are changing and complex contexts in which motherhood is experienced. This will be explored by looking at the pervasive ideologies that shape expectations of motherhood. Obviously, motherhood and the notion of good mothering is a site of contestation, not only in political culture but also in modern feminist theory (for example DiQuinzio 1999).

The development of the motherhood concept

Historically, the social construction of mothering takes the altruistic and normative values for granted and assume that it is in mother's nature to nurture. This has been introduced with the normative concept of motherly love (Mutterliebe) (Müller 1989, 55). Coupled with the development of the nuclear family during the Industrial Revolution in the 19th century, the norm of mothering has become one of devotion to the child in return for emotional enrichment, as altruism. The nature – nurture debate has since been criticized, but values and norms about good mothering tend to persist (Schütze 1991, 6). In fact, the irrational devotion to the child or the myth of motherhood has been rationalized as the necessary behaviour for the child's well being.

Within modernization, mothering and children's development has been medicalized and psychologized while mothers have experience 'limited individualization'. A 'bad conscience' became instilled in mothers as the effects of 'maternal deprivation' became emphasized and were supported by child psychology and psychoanalysis (Brannen 1999, 146). Here, motherhood is socially constituted in terms of a response to children's needs. In other words, motherhood becomes a social category that is formed on the basis of the 'childhood' category (Lawler 1999, 65). For example, the role of lone mothers with very young children is perceived as a full-time carer. This is based on the psychological assumption that the first years are the most important in a child's life (Mählmann 1998, 66). These gendered values are surprisingly persistent and are valid across all social classes, particularly in Germany (see chapter 4). These gendered values come together with the very powerful experience for women who become mothers (Miller 2005; Szypkowski 1997).

Professional mothering

There is a danger that my definition of professional mothering is misinterpreted as promoting an essential motherhood. The psychoanalysist Chodorow naturalizes women's mothering as natural or instinctual mainly because a woman has parented a women too. As a result, men are 'emotionally secondary' in women's lives in that 'men do not become as emotionally important to women as women do to men.' (Chodorow 1978, 197). Mothers may then become and stay lone mothers because of an emotional unequal relationship with the father of the child. With the birth of a child the relationship with the father of the child becomes secondary in mothers' lives but remains primary to their partner. There is a danger that this 'social' feminism also has the tendency of essentialising women as carers (Ruddick 1980, 367).

The account of the professional mother highlights the fact that the mother is a critical agent who creates cultural meanings and moral values for herself and for others (Everingham 1994, 8). This is evidence for late modernity, in which individuals are reflexive agents. In a study of childrearing, Ribbens (1994, 213) comes to the conclusion that parenting is based on fundamental differences in views about the nature of social life. For example, in my study there are mothers that cared for their school-aged child despite the stigma attached to it. Moreover, some lone mothers adapted to stigma by ceasing to participate as citizens in any form of public space, getting on instead 'with seeking their own satisfaction strategically', using those parts of the formal institutional structure that are advantageous and finding ways around the rules and regulations that limit them.

Mothers' negotiation of mothering

Mothers negotiate and interpret meanings as they socially position themselves, participate and construct their gender and caring roles. The motivation to 'invest' in a subject position such as motherhood often depends on the rewards associated with each of these, including both intangible benefits, such as emotional satisfaction, and tangible benefits, such as access to power (Moore 1994, 61). Women shape mothering in ways that suit their own needs and interest (Silva 1996, 34). This is not to ignore the fact that full-time mothering means being there for the child 24 hours a day and restricting ones own needs and desires substantially. It is one of my main arguments that motherhood is actively negotiated and constructed out of self-interest and interest for others. This extends the findings of the milestone study by Finch (1989), who finds that moral obligations and commitments between kin are not reducible to a static sense of duty but instead to empathy and affinity.

The case of professional mothers in their late-thirties who enjoy their break from paid work to care for their children is evidence for the self-interest and active negotiation argument. These women are also proof that full-time mothering is not only based on a financial cost-benefit analysis as many of them have had their benefits cut. If a mother aspires to professional mothering then the emotional benefits may far outweigh costs such as relative deprivation. There are a multitude of factors influencing the decision to stay at home with their children, some more obvious than others and some are more 'socially acceptable' than others.

In late modernity, motherhood has other benefits too, as it can become a catalyst for escaping a former identity and for actively negotiating a new one. Other research confirms that the transition to motherhood offered many a new sense of cohesion and direction, and motherhood was welcomed as an opportunity to change their self-identity (Baily 1999, 351). Here, motherhood operates as a narrative pivot in the construction of a reflexive biography, and is an opportunity for renewed narrative movement. The self-interest thesis is supported by Bauman (1996), who has argued that in the post-modern era people are incessant seekers of experiences to escape binding identities. He evokes the image of the 'tourist' as appropriate to life-strategies for identity building. Women, perhaps more so than men, describe motherhood as 'entering a new world' and there may be a grain of truth in Schön's (1989, 29) essentialist views of mothering as a liberalising experience, as it may be the last resort in which one can live an existential connectedness with holistic life processes. Obviously though, even an identity change is still gendered and remains structured by inequalities (Jamieson 1999, 477).

Pregnancy is often the catalyst that leads women to resign themselves to a more traditional gendered identity. While motherhood adds to women's' valuable experiences and adds another dimension to their life, it also takes away opportunities in a male structured public sphere. Hence, this perspective on becoming a mother could be evaluated as reinforcing traditional gendered inequalities as well as being explained in terms of individualization in late modernity. The reality of the situation may look like an extension of tradition albeit in a modified form.

Many years ago, Rich (1977) and Oakley (1974 and 1992) discussed the social construction of mothering and its relationship to the oppression of women, stating that the emancipatory potential of liberalism cannot be extended to women. This approach – that has its foundation in critical theory – devalues mothering. This chapter has shown that it is not possible to say whether professional lone mothering is either inherently emancipatory or inherently repressive. Motherhood may be the affirmation these women seek. Of course, not all mothers who see advantages in full-time mothering feel that they had a choice in making this decision.

This brings us to the notion of 'choice' in becoming a professional mother. Hakim (1997, 3) coins the term 'preference theory', arguing that some women choose to be ‘full-time homemakers’. For these women, paid work and a career are of secondary interest to them because they maintain traditional views of women’s roles as homemakers. The problems with this theory are threefold: while Hakim leaves ‘choice’ unquestioned this chapter has shown that first, there are genuine barriers to and in paid employment, and secondly, that social moralities are constituted by both preferences and constraints (Duncan 2006).

Thirdly, this idea presumes a dichotomy between traditional and ‘emancipatory’ determinants, between ‘being there for others’ and ‘self-realization’. Obviously, professional mothering attitudes have to be viewed as deeply internalized family obligations or as ideologies within material and cultural contexts (Phizacklea and Wolkowitz 1995, 79). Other research testifies to women’s extensive and automatic assumption of obligation and responsibility as mothers (Ribbens 1998, 33). This research tries not to overlook the ideological over-determination of mothers’ accounts of their experiences.

There may not be a dichotomy between full-time mothering as the traditional component and mothers who are in paid-work as the emancipatory component. Instead of a demise of tradition we can presume a co-existence of both, tradition and its demise. Mothers may view good motherhood and paid employment as dichotomous, but their personal choice and situation does not prevent them from agreeing with a general model of equality for women and men, and from accepting that other lone mothers may prefer to be in paid employment.

Justification of full-time mothering

This chapter grapples with the idea that lone mothers needed to justify their state-dependency and that they felt the need to discern barriers to paid employment because they felt under pressure to be in paid employment when it did not fit into their concept of good mothering or their current phase in life. Lone mothers negotiated their status of professional mothering by arguing that they are raising the next generation of future taxpayers, and they viewed state support as a wage for full-time mothering. Others viewed it as a fair exchange between temporarily receiving benefits and taxes paid in the past and in the future. The interviewed Berlin mothers particularly felt that they have more moral rights to claim benefits - more so than asylum seekers and drug addicts for example - while many of the interviewed London mothers felt that they had no choice because of the poverty trap.

This research identifies two types of justifications for not being in paid employment: ‘socially accepted’ reasons and ‘socially objectionable’ reasons. I would suggest that perceived potential employer prejudices, caring for a young child and the poverty trap are socially acceptable justifications for being out of employment. They may cover up socially objectionable reasons, which sometimes tend to surface eventually during the interview. Socially objectionable reasons include the desire to be a full-time mother of a school-aged child, lack of confidence, the habitual receipt of state benefits and finding the double burden too stressful.

Conclusion

The women in this study viewed the world through the lens of motherhood. They perceived themselves as mothers and struggled to be providers within that context. In Berlin as well as in London, education is chosen partly to improve income potential and to find more self-fulfilling work in the future. Barriers to paid employment varied. London mothers were concerned with not being able to earn enough money and Berlin identified discrimination by employers. The reasons for not being in paid employment and for drawing state support are manifold and multi-faceted. Categories are useful for establishing patterns and trends, but they necessarily gloss over many of the specificities.

Moral decisions about 'the proper thing to do' are also characterized by their ambiguity, and emerge over time and in specific social and cultural contexts (Finch 1989). While mothers may agree about the right thing to do in principle, they may feel it is inappropriate in a specific circumstance (Smart and Neale 1999, 116). For example, many mothers in this study were in principle in favour of lone mothers being in paid employment, but based on their individual circumstances they felt that looking after the children is what they wanted to do. Mothers' individual circumstances include financial support, age and number of children, class, ethnicity, educational qualification, work experience, childhood experiences and self-esteem. There is no one single factor responsible for professional mothering; such generalizations cannot be made. There are professional mothers who have delayed child bearing, who have school-aged children and little financial support, and there are mothers with young children with greater financial support.

This research has presented some women who took a very reflexive approach to their biography and who were aiming for self-development in education or an artistic career. This would fit in with the concept of individualization that is part of late modernity that specifies that traditional roles can no longer be taken for granted, but that they need to be negotiated in the drive for self-realization. For self-realized professional lone mothers in this study the state becomes an acceptable breadwinner. Professional mothers take emotional responsibility for children whilst handing over responsibility for other areas of life to men, or to the state in this case. Here, professional motherhood offers women an alternative refuge from the working world, where it is imperative to keep personal issues separate from the demands of the job. A child provides one with a chance of finding a firm footing and a home. Committing oneself to a child holds the promise of being loved by someone and for an authentic relationship. It can also be a projection screen for unrealized and utopian dreams (Beck and Beck-Gernsheim 1995, 106).

There are some mothers who were full-time mothers because of barriers to paid employment. Mothers may experience 'freedom from' the limitations of a partnership of marriage but they do not experience 'freedom to' secure their livelihood through paid work. In the absence of a wider range of choices the post-rationalization of advantages of professional mothering may serve as a coping strategy. However, these mothers can simultaneously be 'modern' and 'independent' through the revaluation of mothering and paid work. Nonetheless, they arguably remain 'traditional' not only because they remain financially dependent. Perhaps we should not be talking about a replacement of tradition but acknowledge that the two exist simultaneously. This is also applicable in women's dual orientation of mothering and paid employment that has itself become a norm as this book has shown.

Mothering is constructed within a nurture-nature debate and mothers are still expected to 'devote' themselves to the children as well as 'sacrifice' their individualization, at least in parts. In other words, mothers' individualization is limited because of the social construction of childhood that demands mothers' presence with the children. Professional mothering then may just be a 'repackaging' of traditional female roles and not a transformation, however, the data shows that norms are not passively followed but rather lives actively negotiated.

This chapter was concerned with the different reasons for being state benefit dependency and concludes that while women are made responsible for bringing up their children 'properly', they are only given limited resources.

Chapter 6

Creating and Interpreting Meaning – The Use of Type Categories

The main theme of this research is to find out how lone mothers negotiate their lives with respect to full-time mothering, state benefits, poverty, paid work and stigmatization. This study identifies three type categories of lone mothers.

'Real' types offer an overview of the data and relate cases and their characteristics to each other while they show the mothers' diversity as well as their homogeneity. The validity of typologies constructed in this research is derived from their inductive approach as types are constructed from the data and not vice versa. They are also helpful for highlighting the trends and dynamics of lone motherhood in Berlin and in London. This chapter explains the use, the problems and the development of type categories in general and it outlines the type categories 'pioneer', 'struggler', and 'coper' in more depth.

In-depth qualitative research is ideally suited to this exploratory approach as the aim is to gain a wide understanding of lone mothers' entire situation (see chapter one). An inductive approach is also appropriate for exploring new ideas and theories. It can detect different factors that may influence the variables and it can show the interrelations and interaction between these. A variable is any attribute that changes values across things being studied (Hoyle et al 2002). For example, through these interviews and open-ended questions I was able to find out that various perceptions of further education exist. While some lone mothers saw further education primarily as a means for personal development, others perceived it as means to improve labour market chances and to bridge unemployment. Additionally, further education is linked to mothers' perception of full-time mothering as it can facilitate the process of mothering.

The use of categories

Categories help researchers make sense of the data. I was inspired by the study of the sociography of an unemployed community in the village of Marienthal in Austria in 1930. Here, the researchers Jahoda, Lazarsfeld and Zeisel (1971) categorized citizens into the following four divisions according to their basic attitude to their perceived economic pressure: 'unbroken', 'resigned', 'in despair' and 'apathetic'.

In Britain, Duncan and Edwards (1999) used crude type categories to distinguish between 'worker', 'mother' and 'worker/mother integral' orientation. They explain lone mothers' orientations in terms of the notion of gendered moral rationalities as discussed in chapter five. Hakim's (2000) categories describe women's work-family orientation based on individual preferences. Preference theory highlights some of the dilemmas associated with typologies. The developed three types are: the 'work-centred', the 'family centred' and the 'adaptive' woman. Besides playing down external constraints and neglecting different capacities for overcoming constraints, Hakim's categories also underestimate the fact that individual preferences vary over the lifecycle, particularly with the age and number of children, social policies and structural backgrounds. Furthermore, the type categories do not distinguish between short-term and long-term work perspectives, which may well be different from each other and not only dependent on preference but on circumstances.

My research takes a more holistic view and persists with the use of 'real' types. Real types offer an overview of the data and relate cases and their characteristics. Moreover, finding commonalities among the diversity of lone mothers not only heightens our understanding of them but can also offer guidance for social policy. The three type categories are developed by contrasting cases along an agency/structure continuum. Agency consists of personal and social identities and is not just dependent on the individual's capability or power to 'do' things but also on their perception and identity to 'do' things, as a creative capacity (Schilling, 1997, 742).

My research examines lone mothers' reflexive shaping of self-identity, and finds that it cannot be reduced to material circumstances. Some 'poor' lone mothers are able to enrich and negotiate their lives satisfactorily despite scarce financial resources. Therefore, the main objective in the development of type categories is to take a holistic view and a multidimensional approach on single mothering, and not merely to examine their coping strategies under economic pressure: an approach that assumes a lack of agency. The 'Sense of Coherence concept' (SOC), discussed in the following section, is a useful analytical tool for understanding the mothers' coping strategies, and how these strategies influence their perception of their own confidence and complex identities.

The Sense of Coherence concept

Antonovsky (1987) works within the sociology of health, and explains the origins of health in terms of success in coping with stressors. He developed the SOC concept to explain this, which is defined as:

> a global orientation that expresses the extent to which one has a pervasive, enduring though dynamic feeling of confidence that (1) the stimuli deriving from one's internal and external environments in the course of living are structured, predictable and explicable; (2) the resources are available to one to meet the demands posed by these stimuli; and (3) these demands are challenges, worthy of investment and engagement. (Antonovsky 1987, 19).

Thus, successful coping is dependent on being able to make sense of the stressor (comprehensibility), to strike a successful balance between demands and capabilities (manageability) and to be flexible in selecting coping behaviours (meaningfulness). The comprehensibility concept involves the degree to which information seems to be ordered, consistent, structured and clear, rather than chaotic, random, inexplicable and accidental. The manageability component evaluates the manageability of the demands posed by these problems. In other words, it evaluates the perceived locus of control or a confidence that 'things will work out' (Antonovsky 1987). A tendency to see life as meaningful provides the motivational drive to engage in confrontation with the problems. Meaningfulness is the emotional component of the three concepts. It incorporates the social valuation or stigmatization of the person's activity by either society or by significant others.

I have tried to operationalize this approach by breaking it down into a series of assessments used in the interviews, for example in lone mothers' negotiating process with state benefits and lone mothering. A strong SOC provides a 'strong' basis for the successful resolution of problems has a positive impact on well being and acts as a stress-buffer (Antonovsky and Sourani 1990).

The SOC is made up of three intertwined components: manageability, comprehensibility and meaningfulness. Hence, these components are examined with regard to particular variables that came out of the data could be grouped into: mothers' perceived experiences and their evaluation of: mothering, state benefits, relative deprivation, paid work, education, social support networks and lone mothers' general outlook on their own future. I have found that most of these variables can be given three distinct 'values'. The values are a good indicator to distinguish types. Three types could be generated through the data and their differences - and not by preconceived ideas about a typology.

Operationally, lone mothers' accounts have been organized according to these particular 'variables'. Their characteristics were then examined according to the three components that make up the SOC concept: manageability, comprehensibility and meaningfulness. The evaluation of these 'variables' according to this principle led to the formation of three groups of lone mothers: those with high, medium and low SOC's. Lone mothers with a low SOC feel that most aspects of their lives are unmanageable, incomprehensible and meaningless. The concept itself proved an invaluable tool that could be used as the basis for the creation of the three type categories.

According to my judgement based on a thorough analysis of the interviews, three distinctive patterns arose out of the data that made sense of the differences between the mothers' complex identities: pioneer, coper and struggler. Pioneers have the highest SOC while strugglers have the lowest SOC. In other words, pioneers convey the sense that most aspects of their life situation are particularly manageable, comprehensible and meaningful. For example, a pioneer is able to manage her situation between demands and capabilities and finds it meaningful to be a full-time mother and can make sense of her situation. In contrast, strugglers feel that most aspects of their lives are unmanageable, incomprehensible and meaningless. The copers may score high on one component and low on another but are likely to have many mediocre SOC ratings in the relevant variables. The individual case studies that follow in chapters seven, eight, nine and ten show in more detail how the three levels of the SOC concept were identified.

Types of lone mothers

The pioneer feels in control of her life not only because she intentionally created her present lifestyles but also because she embraces change positively and tends to be optimistic. She resembles Sennett' (1998) 'surfer' types who accept that decisions must and can be made under conditions of uncertainty: this feeds an optimistic outlook to life. The strugglers perceives that she has no control of her life because she sees it as externally determined. This bears some similarity to Sennett's (1998) 'drifter' types, who experience the contingency and fragmentation of life as a loss and a threat.

The motto for the pioneer woman could be 'I've got what I want' as they do not wish their situation to be different. The coper's motto could be 'I make the best out of my situation' and the struggler woman's motto would be 'It's really difficult'. While the pioneer is an optimist, the coper has a more pragmatist approach and the struggler is something of a pessimist. She perceives that her life is based on constraints while the coper feels she has choices as well as constraints. The pioneer emphasizes the choices she makes and external factors do not usually feature in the decision making process. The struggler makes constraints mainly responsible for her situations, and externalizes those responsible for them.

The pioneer type category

As the type categorization emerged from the data, the main distinguishing factor of the 'pioneer' type was that this woman viewed motherhood as a positive event, as an achievement, which she chose whether intentionally or not. A couple of mothers in this type took active steps to become pregnant because they perceived their fertility as decreasing. Here, lone motherhood was viewed as the only option of motherhood. Lynn in Hackney was afraid of becoming infertile, and because her desire to be a mother was stronger than her desire for a partner, she chose artificial insemination. The pioneer type may lead an alternative lifestyle but, as found in other research, she may not be part of a particular sub-culture (Duncan and Edwards 1999). The pioneer seems to embrace changes positively and this marks her out from the coper and struggler type. She does not seem to simply follow conventional roles and expectations that usher women into mothering as if it were their nature. Instead, she develops their own ideas. In her perception, motherhood becomes a chosen profession instead of conventional paid employment. She experiences motherhood as giving an identity, as fulfilling and satisfactory and she wants to 'enjoy' motherhood, even if this means living on state benefits (Mädje and Neusüß's 1994a).

Motherhood may serve as a career break after a long period of paid employment, or it can act as a catalyst whereby the birth of a child can be a key milestone in making a biographical change, even a transformation (Baily, 1999). Linda from Wembley used to be a tour guide on tourist buses. State dependency enabled her to become a full-time mother as well as to rethink her professional orientation. State benefit dependency may be the anticipated result of choices made by some women and may be used strategically as a 'means' to facilitate a lifestyle choice such as full-time mothering, being an artist, education or hobbies (see chapter five). One pioneer in East Berlin had time to paint and meet her friends when her child was in Kindergarten. One year after the interview she told me that she intended to travel around the world while her child stayed with a close friend. Another pioneer in East Berlin used to be a nurse and state benefits helped her to fulfil her ambition to re-evaluate her life through personal development, while mothering was equally important to her.

Here, state dependency is not perceived as a sign of dependency but as a means to an end or a guarantee of personal independence and autonomy, a kind of citizens' right, as a wage for professional mothering or as a fair exchange for paying taxes in the past. In contrast to the coper, the woman in this pioneer type views her socio-economic interests and employment as secondary after her personal interests. For her living with a small income is a temporary worthwhile sacrifice and is sometimes even viewed as an asset. Some pioneers are optimistic about the temporary nature of their deprivation and take a viewpoint of delayed financial gratification. This type of woman does not have negative views of unemployment and lone motherhood.

A pioneer type lone mother may be momentarily disengaged from the public sphere, but may live in her own private sphere as well as in an alternative sphere, an 'alternative Lebenswelt' (Habermas 1985). The pioneer's family and friends are not always supportive. Of course, it is sometimes difficult to assess whether a pioneer woman is simply post-rationalising, or self-justifying a situation that she has not 'really' chosen. However, a pioneer type is defined as a woman who takes responsibility for her situation, who is clearly a 'reflexive agent' and who perceives her situation as meaningful, manageable and comprehensible. She may have plans for the future but views the present as more important. In contrast to women in the other categories, the pioneer may not necessarily 'escape patriarchy' in the sense that she has given up on men. She may be non-conformist and have ideals of gendered equality but nonetheless, I found that some have an underlying desire to be provided for and to be looked after, financially as well as emotionally. The pioneer is different from the coper because she rarely conforms to a socially accepted norm as she utilizes state benefits to fulfil her lifestyle choice.

The coper type category

The coper is a pragmatist and manages a problem satisfactorily even if her ultimate goal is out of reach. She has not 'chosen' her situation as an ultimate lifestyle choice although she works within it as constructively as she possibly can by trying 'to make the best of it'. She regards internal and external factors as responsible for her situation and accepts her situation on state benefits as temporary although she has no specific end in sight. State benefits facilitate 'coping' and accumulated savings or casual work may ease the financial deprivation. State benefits are accepted as a legitimate form to secure a living as a temporary arrangement only. Some may be registered as students while receiving benefits. I suspect that some mothers fail to declare that their partners are living in their households in order to avoid benefit cuts but only one woman in Berlin admitted this to me. This type use their benefits constructively and 'make the best out of a situation'.

While economic resources are not a high priority for pioneer types, the coper may choose to ease her financial deprivation by doing casual work. Furthermore, the coper has more conformist traits and may choose education to improve labour market opportunities rather than for personal development. It is difficult to focus on the coper's employment orientation because it has many layers. On the one hand the coper shows a paid employment orientation but at the same time her expectations, needs and skills may not be compatible with the labour market. She may not be prepared to work full-time and is unable to demand a sufficient wage working part-time. She may appear to 'resign' herself to full-time motherhood or education. Nonetheless, it also shows that even in resigning herself to full-time mothering there is an element of choice because the coper is not prepared to lower her job expectations. State benefits facilitate full-time mothering as well as further part-time or full-time education. The coper may have to go through a separation from a partner but this does not jeopardize her existence permanently. Children give meaning and help to get over crisis situations and the coper type can rely on social support by friends and family. This is in contrast to the struggler type who feels left alone with her problems.

The struggler type category

The struggler type is characterized by her low sense of coherence (SOC). A mother in this type has low self-esteem. Everything seems too much for her; she might despair, be apathetic, or highly dissatisfied. She has difficulties in caring for her children, problems with institutions, with budgeting and debts, and she feels financially deprived. She feels that there is nothing she can do to change her situation, and instead depends on institutions such as the government, from which she expects the help to come. The struggler does not take any responsibility for her situation and blames either the 'system', others or some other external force. Her high expectations are disappointed, and any contact with Social Services, the local state benefit offices and Job Centres is perceived as negative and discriminatory rather than supportive. As a lone mother on Income Support, she feels stigmatized and excluded from a society to which she would like to belong but never has, not even before she became a mother.

The disruption to her life brought about by having a child is not greeted as a welcome opportunity to 'collect experiences'. The struggler feels lonely, has little or no social network, but has relatively high expectations of her friends and family, and she is disappointed that they are not offering sufficient support. She believes that having children and especially the unsatisfactory childcare system are the cause of her unemployment and state dependency. The struggler type might have had experiences of domestic violence as well as negative childhood experiences, such as her relationship with parents, institutions and schools. Pioneers tend to have a more positive experience but I have refrained from including this in the table as not everyone talked about their childhood and copers can have a negative or positive experience. In the struggler category, some of the women may be ill and suffer from depression.

Borderline cases between coper and struggler

A borderline case of a mother between the coper and the struggler type category tries to cope with some problems and has little confidence. She views her situation as a result of undesirable events and her situation may be unstable and prone to crisis and she may have to deal with depression and low self-worth. She may not have a clear aim but still aspires to paid employment, a male breadwinner, childcare and/or education. She makes external factors responsible for her situation, such as the labour market structure and the poverty trap. These external factors become coupled with internal factors and the knowledge of her own limits is experienced as stressful, thus lowering her self-worth even more. For example, she may be frustrated that she cannot find sufficiently paid employment and that she has to rely on state benefits but may do little to seek an appropriate job at all or cannot imagine taking a job which has to be topped up with supplementary benefits. Nonetheless, financial deprivation and debts may be an issue but are not an overwhelming problem.

Borderline cases between coper and pioneer

Not every mother can be clearly defined as either a coper or a pioneer and some have both traits and are on the borderline of either type. This borderline type is able to actively respond to changes and tries to be conscious of change as a means of steering it. Although this borderline type may have an ultimate goal she is able to modify it or postpone it. She makes the most out of her situation and state benefits are a facilitator for autonomy and independence. She may even be better off now than when she had a partner or was in paid work. This mixed type may not be as driven as the pioneer and does not necessarily use income support as a means to an end. In other words, she makes the best out of her current situation, enjoys it and accepts responsibility while relative deprivation is viewed as the cost of being able to rear children at home. Here, personal interests are as important as economic interests. For example, paid work is important for economic and personal reasons and it has to be challenging, fulfilling and meaningful. In the absence of this, state dependency is used for personal development, for therapy, for learning. Some mothers may rationalize professional mothering as a result of not being able to enter paid employment. Some may also have psychological problems, illness and family responsibilities.

Type category characteristics

The case studies presented in the following chapters are descriptive and are meant to contribute to our knowledge of lone mothers who receive benefits in Germany and Britain. They are also an attempt to present and analyse the data fairly and to give a holistic view of the individual and her situation. By describing and analysing lone mothers' interviews, we learn that the boundaries between phenomenon and context are not clearly evident and how values of variables are interrelated (Yin 2003).

Table 6.1 presents a useful summary of the three type categories and their distinct characteristics. The table discerns between variables (for example full-time motherhood evaluation) and their values, or characteristics, that I found relevant when analysing the interviews. Although the table may have a causal flavour it presents a useful summary and it identifies patterns that emerged from the data rather than being deterministic. It also clearly shows how the values of variables are related. The set ranges of experiences of each lone mother may not fulfil all but most characteristics for her particular type category. The subsequent chapters present detailed case studies to make each type category livelier as well as giving them more substance. The case studies are constructed biographically to show the dynamics in lone mothers lives as well as to show their influence in mothers' negotiation of their current situation.

The case studies vary distinctively between each type category. The variables describe lone mothers' negotiating process with full-time mothering, paid work, state benefits and education and their evaluation of relative deprivation and support networks. I have included all characteristics that are specific to each type category and have not distinguished between their explanatory and their descriptive values. Although they are obviously related, the research cannot prove that they are interdependent. I do not even distinguish between lone mothers' orientation and their situation because in my view, even their 'definition of the situation' is a construct of their orientation, an evaluation.

Table 6.1 shows the seven variables used in the type categorization. Their values determine whether a lone mother is a pioneer, coper or struggler. All seven variables are evaluations based on the lone mother's account of this particular variable. Mothers' particular accounts were analysed and evaluated to construct three different values for each variable. Each of these values corresponded to one category, to the pioneer, coper or struggler. A mother is a 'single' type if she fits into at least six out of the seven values that relate to one category. A mother is a 'double' borderline coper/pioneer if she meets three to four criteria of either the pioneer or the coper category. A borderline coper/struggler also has only three to four values in the struggler or coper category each. In the interviews with 70 mothers there was no evidence of a 'triple' borderline coper/pioneer/struggler case.

Table 6.1 Type categories and characteristics

Type category characteristics	*Pioneer*	*Coper*	*Struggler*
1. Evaluation of full-time mothering	Highly satisfied. Is chosen. career break, catalyst	Satisfied. Because it is temporary due to lack of suitable paid work or childcare or currently on maternity leave	Unsatisfied.
2. State benefits evaluation	Satisfied. Is used to fulfil ambitions/wage for mothering	Ambivalent, It's temporary because of lack of paid work income or earning partner	It's vital. Couldn't do without
3. Relative deprivation evaluation	Sufficient income. Money is low priority, anti-consumerist attitude	Sufficient income through careful budgeting or income is increased through casual work, gifts, Child-rearing Benefit or grants in Germany	Insufficient income. This is accelerated by the inability to budget and/or debts
4. Paid employment evaluation	Not in work by choice.	Not in work mostly due to constraints. Lack of suitable work and part-time or flexible hours, childcare, poverty trap or discrimination	Not in work. Current situation is difficult enough
5. Further Education evaluation	If in education, then for personal development or re-training	If in education, then to improve labour market chances, to bridge unemployment and to facilitate full-time mothering	Not in education. Current situation is difficult enough
6. Support network evaluation	Not important/ no reliance on it	Satisfactory/ can rely on it	Unsatisfactory. Perceived isolation
7. Outlook on Future	Optimist	Pragmatist	Live from one day to the next day

Variables

Evaluation of full-time mothering

What is it like to be a full-time mother? A mother is a pioneer type if her primary goal is the upbringing of her children, often by providing the childcare herself without contemplating any other options. She perceives full-time mothering as meaningful, comprehensible and manageable, and it can act as a career break and a catalyst, a life-changer. For her, it becomes almost a vocation. In comparison, the coper considers full-time mothering as a temporary situation. She likes being a full-time mother but she is also aware of a lack of employment that is flexible, part-time and lucrative. She also perceives childcare facilities as too inflexible, unavailable or too expensive. However, the coper does not lower her job expectations. Struggler and struggler/coper borderline cases are dissatisfied about full-time mothering and would like to be in paid work instead.

State benefits evaluation

This variable describes how lone mothers evaluate receiving state benefits, how they perceive it or even justify or defend it. For pioneers, state benefits are either a means to an end or a guarantee of personal independence and autonomy, a kind of citizens' right, a wage for full-time mothering or a fair exchange for paying taxes in the past. The pioneer perceives her situation as so meaningful and comprehensible that she does not feel stigmatized. She may just shrug it off because pioneers rarely conform to a socially accepted norm.

The coper is more ambivalent about receiving state benefits and emphasizes that it is a temporary situation because of the lack of paid employment, income or earning partner. She may well be embarrassed about it and may hide her situation and not tell anyone about it. The strugglers evaluates state benefits as essential, which she just could not do without. She is beyond hiding the fact that she is in receipt of benefit and feels stigmatized because she already feel excluded from a society to which she would like to belong but never has.

Relative deprivation evaluation

How do single mother get by on state benefits? The strugglers suffers most from being poor. She cannot manage on their state benefits because she has never learnt how to budget and to manage finances. She has run up debts that she finds difficult to pay back. For the pioneer, living with a small income is a temporary worthwhile sacrifice and is sometimes even viewed as an asset. Others are optimistic about the temporary nature of their deprivation and take a viewpoint of delayed financial gratification. A women in this pioneer type perceives her socio-economic interests and employment as secondary after her personal interests. The coper manages on the income by careful budgeting and sacrifices but in many cases state benefits are topped up with casual work. In Germany, lone mothers with children under two years old cope financially because they receive Childrearing Benefit of about £200 a month.

Paid employment evaluation

Why are lone mothers on state benefits not in paid employment? Lone mothers are not in work either because they do not want to or they have not searched for work because of the perception of barriers such as the poverty trap, insufficient or inflexible childcare or perceived and/or experienced employers' discrimination of lone mothers with children (see chapter five). In Germany, every lone parent qualifies for 20 days a year paid sick leave that can be taken for each child that becomes ill. The coper as well as the struggler feel that they are discriminated against because of their children. Both know that they would not be able to command a wage to live on (poverty trap) and feel that childcare is either unavailable or too inflexible. The struggler finds it hard to cope with her daily life so paid work or education is not really an option. In this category, copers and pioneers can overlap as both copers and pioneers can choose to be a full-time mother. The coper seems more resigned to it while the pioneer embraces the opportunity.

Further education evaluation

Education was another variable that came up by surprise. It was not integral to the interview schedule but it came up in many interviews as mothers contemplated paid employment for the future. A woman who views education as a tool for personal development or as a means for self-fulfilment – or to retrain in a new chosen field – is a pioneer. When a woman perceives education as a way to improve labour market chances or to bridge unemployment she is categorized as a coper.

Support network perception

Here, the mother evaluates her social network- how friends, family and even institutions give her financial and/or social support. The struggler feels lonely, has little or no social network but relatively high expectations of her friends and family and is disappointed about the social and/or financial support offered. Also, her contact with Social Services, the local state benefit offices and Job Centres is perceived as negative, as discriminatory rather than supportive. The coper type can rely on social support by friends and family and this is in contrast to the struggler type who feels left alone with her problems. The pioneer perceives her network as satisfactory but irrelevant or not important. She is fairly self-sufficient and may not even have a social network, nor does she seem to greatly rely on her friends, family and authorities.

Outlook on Future

This variable relates to the final part of the interview in which lone mothers discuss their near future or any plans they may have. The SOC concept can be applied very well here. The struggler's outlook is pessimistic and she sees the future as unmanageable, incomprehensible and meaningless. Her coping strategy is to take one day at a time. Likewise, the pioneer does not necessarily have plans for the future but this is because her life is currently so manageable, comprehensible and meaningful. She wants to enjoy the present and not plan too much into the future. Nonetheless, she appears to be an optimist while the coper could be described as a pragmatist who often has plans for the future laid out.

Chapter 7

Pioneers

Anne

I met Anne in the summer at Katzenhain state benefit office in East Berlin and interviewed her later in a park nearby. She was at 44 years of age the oldest mother. While her six-year-old son rode around on his bicycle we talked on a bench. This interview was - at two and a half hours – not only one of the longest interviews but also one of the most intriguing because of her perception of state dependency, relative deprivation and mothering. She fitted all nine characteristics of a pioneer.

Anne was born into a middle-class family in East Berlin and had an idyllic childhood. Her father was a theatre actor and her mother a housewife, which was unusual because most mothers used to be in paid work in the GDR. She trained to become a theatre hairdresser and make-up artist and worked in film and TV across countries. Nonetheless, as a single person she was not allowed to work outside socialist countries for fear that she may abscond to a capitalist country.

Anne was already a successful freelancer when she met her partner, an acting student, 18 years ago. She supported him financially and their relationship had to fit in with her demanding work hours and travel schedule. She always wanted to have a child, and saved up for it because it was never her intention to combine work and mothering. Therefore, after fifteen years in employment she was ready to give up work. Only then did she feel she had reached the level of maturity necessary to cope with a child:

> Previously, there were so many things I wanted to do and you cannot combine both. Then I decided that I was mature enough and that I had finished partying and done what I wanted to do as a young person. Therefore, I had enough time. That is the way it was and I enjoyed it. If I had to choose again I would do it exactly like this.

When she was 38 years old, Anne had Thomas with her partner of 12 years, who was unable to support them. He was unemployed and did not live with them. She and her son lived in an un-modernized bed-sit in central East Berlin but spent the majority of their time at her grandparents' house in the suburbs.

Anne only reapplied for state benefits when her savings were all gone. According to state benefit regulations she should have been searching for paid work once Thomas was three years old. Instead, she negotiated an additional three years Childrearing Leave with the authorities. Although unemployment benefits would have paid more, she did not want to be available for paid employment. Anne felt that her state benefits were a fair exchange for her tax contributions in the past. She also had no problems shaking off allegations from friends and former colleagues who thought that she was lazy to be living off benefits. She did not mind this stigma as she knew that her son would later pay the taxes that formed the basis of their pensions. She also knew of parents that had regretted that they not spending enough time with their children while they were young. Anne managed well on a low income partly because she knew it was only temporary and partly because she perceived her anti-consumerist attitude as a virtue. She saw state benefits as a privilege that enabled her to stay at home with Thomas:

> I do not need anything, because I have everything. I have everything but nothing new. I do not need clothes. I do not need anything new. I have no television set. I can live with what I've got. Somehow it works, because I told myself, it is much nicer and more important that we experience something rather than consume something. I can cope well on state benefits. I have no problems whatsoever and I am not embarrassed at all. The opposite is the case. That I can receive Income Support now and be able to stay at home, that makes me proud and happy; that I have the opportunity to care for my child and the state pays for this.

However, Anne had dedicated her life to her child by making sure that she was always available to him and letting him decide how and where they spent their time. For example, she rarely met her friends because she did not want to exclude Thomas and leave him to play by himself. Her social network is not as important as was her relationship with her son. She did also go to bed with him until he was asleep after which she got up to do the domestic chores. Furthermore, she was so child centred that she could not be a partner as well as a parent. The father saw his son about twice a week, but only if he could fit into their routines.

> Somehow they (men) get left behind. Because of this responsibility, that you have on your own with a child. It goes chop, chop, chop, one thing after another. You have your commitments. He has to go to school and so on. You cannot consider anymore whether it suits the man or whether he has time or whether I can spend my free time with him. Because of this great responsibility, he has to see that he does not get left out, when he wants to see us.

Although Anne experimented with part-time work at a theatre, she gave it up because she was convinced that the children of working mothers experienced separation anxiety. This was also the reason why she breastfed Thomas for five years, until he gave it up himself:

> The children of working mothers will have an unfulfilled life because they constantly yearn after comfort and security [Geborgenheit], because they have never experienced it during their childhood. And that results in communication difficulties, in paranoia, and partnership problems. I think that nature designed it that way, that the children cut the umbilical cord to the mother and not the other way around. In our society I feel it's the other way round and the children cannot leave. They cannot get rid of the feeling that they are constantly left by someone.

I define Anne as a pioneer because she negotiated her set of values without much support from her friends and family and without being part of a particular sub-culture. Her views may be essentialist and naturalistic but they are her own. She intentionally broke up her biography into stages and viewed her professional life phase (Lebensphase) as separate from her mothering phase.

Anne did not conform to the male breadwinner/female homemaker model in principle. Since she had been the main provider in the past, she had expected to be provided for at least temporarily. However, her younger partner did not change from a 'kept man' into a responsible and committed provider. Although she recognized that he was a victim of economic restructuring after reunification, her disappointment with her partner has coloured her view of men in general. Interestingly, while she expected her partner to fit in with her, she has let her son dominate their relationship, and she fitted in with him. It is possible that by living apart from her partner and raising Thomas in an anti-authoritarian way she has avoided conflict. In fact, she admitted that she had a great need for peace and harmony.

Anne was a pioneer on all levels. Anne enjoyed motherhood and had no immediate plans to return to paid employment. She may have been unaware of her employment opportunities but she was optimistic about them. When I interviewed her a year later for the second time, she still had no immediate plans to return to work but was involved in volunteer work at the alternative private Steiner school that her son attended, and for which he had won a scholarship.[1] Her social network was not as important to her as was her relationship with her son. Anne and her son lived on a very low income, but she did not feel poor because state benefits enabled her to realize full-time mothering. Talking with two friends of hers, and interviewing her again a year later, confirmed that her narrative was consistent.

Victoria

Victoria was white, 40 years old and lived in a working-class and aspiring East London borough. She was raised by middle-class parents on the outskirts of London and had positive childhood memories. As her father was a self-employed composer and her mother was a singer who was often on tour, she was brought up by her father and by au-pairs. She had little contact with her younger sister who was a designer.

After her O levels Victoria did a nursery nursing course but failed the exam twice. She worked as a receptionist for about four years until she became ill with a fallopian tube infection. She subsequently lost one tube. Since then she had not been back in paid work and had received sickness benefit for 15 years because of ongoing infections. She has had low grade pain almost all the time and she had to take care not to get too tired because that would make it flare up again. She has had several further operations, more cysts, and recently has lost her last ovary.

1 The Waldorf education was founded by Rudolf Steiner. It balances artistic, academic and practical work in a holistic approach in a developmentally-oriented curriculum. Imagination, cognitive growth and creativity are cultivated as well as a sense of responsibility for the earth and its inhabitants.

Victoria moved in with her partner when she was 17. After thirteen years she left this relationship because she wanted children and he did not. After narrowly escaping a hysterectomy, she decided to have a child by artificial insemination. She felt her time to have children was running out:

> I went down to the operating theatre, not knowing what I was going to come back with. And that was quite hard. I desperately wanted children and that was it. I wasn't having any children. I went down to the theatre and they had managed to save my womb which was great. I had at that time been toying with artificial insemination, simply because I did not know what else to do. I couldn't see another relationship on the horizon. I was 30 and I had no children and I was still not well. What do I do now? That was hard. I wanted a child that much and I couldn't see how else to do it. There was quite a lot of publicity about that [artificial insemination] at that point. I heard about it and read about it. So I had the operation. Whilst I was in hospital I actually talked to my mom a bit about doing artificial insemination. I thought I better start laying the seeds now and see what happens. And she was amazing. I was doing it through the clinic at that point and she offered to pay for treatment and she said 'At least it would be ours.' Which I thought was just like wow. Because she knew how much I wanted children. She also wanted grandchildren I think.

After the operation she went through the process of artificial insemination with frozen sperm at a London clinic. After five months of trying, two of her girlfriends' partners offered to donate fresh sperm for her to inseminate herself with at home. She became pregnant immediately but had no idea who the father was. She was reasonably open about her action and did not perceive it as any more selfish than two parents who have children:

> I never came across anyone thinking that what I'd done was wrong. Sometimes I was a bit confused who to tell, but in the end, what I've done, I told loads of people and I feel quite strongly the more I tell about it the more acceptable it may make it for somebody else who thinks they want to go through it; and also the more it becomes acceptable in society. It isn't this thing that raving lunatic lesbians do. It is something someone who wants children does.

She had since been in one long-term relationship, but was unable to conceive a second child with him despite using fertility drugs. As she was unable to commit to paid work, she enrolled into counselling training courses. She became a volunteer for a women's health support group and she was involved in the tenants association on the estate that she lived in. For two years she had also been involved in running the community nursery. In the future she was considering setting up an infertility network or working in counselling. She perceived herself as a full-time mother and dearly wants to raise her son by herself:

> I tried to put 'mother' on forms. I think housewife sounds so twee. I tend to class myself as a mother. I think a lot of times it is underrated as an occupation. On the one hand I fully appreciate that some people want to go back to work when they've children but, for me, I feel strongly that we are bringing up the next generation. And I think its very valid. It is not something that should be underrated and slagged off. And the time and effort we put into our children is what makes them into responsible adults as time goes on. ... I could have not left my child with other people. For me, I could see no point in it, I particularly

> went through to have my child. Particularly when I realized what a miracle it was that I had him. ... All I ever wanted was to be a mother. And I resent people making it seem as if it is a second class occupation. I wasn't someone who wanted a huge career path. I always knew. It was always part of who I was.

She lived on Child Benefit, One Parent Benefit and Invalidity Benefit which was a little more than Income Support. There were also debts on her credit card which she tried to ignore as money issues were a low priority for her. However, being a single mother meant freedom to her and she cherished the time she could spend with her son:

> I manage ok but I think a lot of people do not. The benefit system is existence rather than living a lot of the time. It is like anything in life. You either have time or you have money. And if you live on benefits you have time but not a lot of money. If you are working, you have money but not a lot of time and then probably not a lot of money either (...) We can do what we want. I like not to be consistently thinking of somebody else but me and Alex.

Victoria had been living on the same estate for 20 years and lived in a three-bedroom flat. She liked the estate because she knew the people and could rely on their support. For example, she and her son had meals with her best friend and her three children who lived in the same block. She was also thinking of getting an adult male 'buddy' for her son as he mostly associated with women. The idea was that they would come maybe once a week to take the child out to the park and to go swimming.

> More than anybody I had a choice and I made a choice. I very very much made a conscious choice about having my child. I very much think that I took the upper hand on that. ... I could have been a victim. I could have sat there and gone: Oh I can not have any children because of this and this but I took the upper hand.

Victoria was a pioneer because she actively embraced becoming a single and full-time mother through artificial insemination. Like Anne, Victoria negotiated her set of values; but unlike Ann, she cherished and relied on support from her friends and family and here she fits into the coper category. Her friends even persuaded their former partners to donate sperm. Her mother also supported Victoria's decision to try artificial insemination. She did not mind receiving state benefits because there were many single mothers in her neighbourhood and it enabled her to be a full-time mother. Victoria did not have conformist attitudes and she had not known other women who had chosen to become single mothers in this way.

Victoria felt comfortable with being on state benefits, perhaps partly because of her recent operation from which she was still recovering. She could have been considered a coper in the 'paid employment evaluation' section as her sickness did partly stop her from being in paid employment. However, she was a pioneer, as her illness had enabled her to be a full-time mother and a volunteer as well as studying for a counselling qualification. Victoria was self-fulfilled and had an optimistic outlook on the future. Money was a low priority and she said to herself: 'All I ever wanted was to be a mother.'

Marie

Marie was 28 and her daughter was nine months old. She lived in a house which she shared with eight other people from New Zealand, South Africa and Ireland, who tended to stay for a year or so.

Marie grew up in England and in Ireland. Her father was a lorry driver and a builder and her mother worked in a factory in Ireland. She had two younger sisters and one younger brother. After her A levels she worked as a secretary and changed jobs frequently because she would get bored. When she fell pregnant she stopped her university access course because she needed the money and was already working hard. She never contemplated abortion and she knew her parents would support her decision as they had only moved in together and got married when she was five years old.

The baby's father was a motorbike courier and bike racer. The casual relationship was over by the time she found out that she was pregnant. She started letting him visit them after her daughter was born. Since then he has been visiting regularly and they are on civil terms with each other although she did not really like him. The father was registered and informally paid £30 a week.

Her housemates were friendly, but were not keen on a baby living in the house and she tried to be considerate by not letting the baby cry. She did not want to live in a bed-sit and liked the fact that she had a big house all to herself during the day while everyone was at work. She hardly socialized with her housemates. In the evenings, she rarely went downstairs, because she did not want her daughter to fall out of the bed they share. Marie had no support; she did not seem to mind that she did not see as much of her old friends, and she only knew one other single mother.

She could manage to live off Income Support and Child Benefit, partly because of her budgeting skills and also because she had some savings, and weekly maintenance pay. She did not think that she would be better off working because of childcare and housing costs. Nor did she enjoy her job anymore. Most importantly, being a full-time mother was a break and a privilege to her:

> Actually I am happy to be a mother. ... I am seeing this in a way as taking time out because I am not going back to work until she is about 18 months old. I am trying to think what else I can do so that I do not have to go back to the old way of life basically - secretary at a temp agency. In a way I think I am privileged because I know someone who works who prefers not to but they have to for whatever reason, mortgages or financial or whatever. I can afford to spend the time with Jessica. I do not have a husband to look after or a house to look after.

Marie also thought that not working was the best thing she could do to be a good mother:

> I want her to be as secure emotionally as she can be. This is why I keep breastfeeding her for longer, why I want her to know her dad. ... I know they go through separation anxiety from six to nine months. I figure, the more I am with her without being overbearing or clingy then the more confident she is going to be.

She cherished being a single mother because it made her feel autonomous. She did not have to worry about a boyfriend getting jealous, and she alone chose what to do. Having a child had made her much stronger and much more outgoing as 'there is that real motivation to stand up for yourself when it affects somebody else.'

Marie was a pioneer because she was optimistic and contemplated several options in the future. Ireland was perceived as less stressful, but it also had fewer career opportunities. Alternatively, she could go to college to study biology and science to perhaps retrain as a science teacher or she could work from home as a freelance copy-writer and proof-reader. Marie embraced changes positively and was fulfilled and satisfied. Full-time motherhood also served as a 'career break' and as a key milestone in making a biographical change, a transformation. She did not mind living on state benefits and she did not hide this from anyone. State benefits guaranteed her personal independence, autonomy and time to spend with her child. She also did not seem to mind that she did not have any social support. Marie was happy that she could be a mother without having to conform to a male breadwinner/ female homemaker model. Her life was meaningful, manageable and comprehensible and she felt optimistic about the future.

She was a coper in the relative deprivation category as she only had sufficient income through savings, maintenance and careful budgeting rather than having an anti-consumerist attitude. True, her child was only nine-months-old and she was still happy with her current situation and had yet to try to re-enter the workforce.

Janet

Janet, 40, and her one-year-old son lived north of Central London in a Housing Association flat in a terraced house. Her father was a Croatian farmer who worked in factories, and her mother was a British dinner lady. They were both retired. She grew up with her parents in the East of England. Janet trained first as a nurse and later as a midwife. Nineteen years earlier she moved to London where she was working as a nurse, and she also got a degree in Environmental and Urban Studies. Before her maternity leave, she was a consultant for a medical recruitment agency. In her private life, she mostly had casual relationships:

> I never met anybody that I chose to have a baby with anyway. ... I wasn't desperately looking for a partner. I just think I am one of these people that I am quite happy on my own, quite independent. I have never been dependent on somebody. It's nothing that I have ever missed.

Janet became pregnant shortly after she had the coil removed. She had known her partner for three weeks, a minicab driver who received state benefits. It was a casual relationship and she did not have a lot in common with him:

> I wasn't really that bothered whether I'd get pregnant or not. I do not think I made a decision. I wasn't yearning to have a child. But I had kind of done everything else. You know I was at an age where I'd done a degree and I wasn't particularly fulfilled by it. And I had been to university. You know there wasn't really that much else to do and I know

> that was a kind of hit and miss attitude but it could possible have been why I did not worry about it.

Janet became quite critical of her partner and expected more commitment and their relationship only lasted another six weeks. There was no contact between her and her former partner and she preferred to have no father figure for her son rather than someone who was irresponsible and unreliable. She saw no point in pursuing the father for maintenance as he received state benefit and was suspected of having fathered other children too.

Janet felt slightly stigmatized by the media but she had not experienced any personal criticisms. Her family were quite conservative and were worried about her well-being. She did not see her friends very often because they tended to be in paid work. However, they tried to support her when they could. Her son also went to a nursery twice a week.

She knew that being poor was just a temporary situation and was optimistic about the future. She knew that she had 'got a lot to go for yet' and loved being at home with her child and that enabled her to cope financially too:

> I love it. And I really enjoy being at home. (…) My life has changed. We cut corners on a lot of things. Not going out is one thing that saves a lot of money. Clothes, things that are not really necessary. A lot of stuff comes from charity shops whereas before I would have bought it in regular shops.

It helped that her baby was good-natured and not difficult as he slept through the night and ate well. She felt fulfilled:

> I have always had a decent life style, and social contacts, and money. But as you get older, you do start to think, it could be a bit more. And for me, having had him, that kind of filled a gap. I just think it is worth it.

Janet planned to stay at home until her son started school. She probably would not have another child and she did not want to miss out because they 'grow up so quickly'. Eventually, she was thinking of qualifying as a teacher, perhaps through an Open University course that allowed her to study in the evenings at home. She justified being on state benefits with the fact that she had paid taxes for many years:

> It would basically be feeding him, cleaning him and putting him to bed. And that would be all and there would be no play with him or any sort of communication you have with a child. It would be like having a pet dog. You know, make sure it is walked in the morning…rather than a human being. it's only really the practical side. And I think I would be much more stressed out.

Janet thought that she had an advantage over married mothers who ended up taking the main share of the housework and childcare anyway and she also felt different from other single mothers:

> There may be a slight difference in that I have worked before and, like I said, I've got lots. Well, I've got a car, basic furniture, whereas some younger mothers might be struggling.

> ... Financially I might be better off. But also I am on my own. I've actually got things, I've made a career and been to university and I travelled. If I had had a child when I was younger perhaps I would have been losing out. And now I am quite happy and satisfied to know that I've done that and that I am not missing out.

Janet was a pioneer in all but one category because her social network was relevant to her. Other than that, she perceived her situation as meaningful, comprehensible and manageable. In fact, had she known that having children was not the ordeal she always thought it was, she would have had children earlier. For Janet, her child marked an important change in her life and she was not at all concerned about receiving state benefits. State benefits made it possible to spend time with her child and she chose not to be in paid employment and coped with it because she had a anti-consumerist attitude. She had a positive outlook to the future and was thinking of retraining to become a teacher.

Short Biographies of Pioneers

Sabine came from a middle-class family in East Germany. After she finished school with GCSE levels she became a children's nurse. Sabine became pregnant shortly after having met her then partner. They broke up because it was a long-distance relationship and her partner suffered from depression. Her parents and friends were very supportive and she was really happy being a mother. Financially, she got by on state benefits and topped it up with casual work. She did not want to be in paid employment. Instead, state benefits enabled her to fulfill her ambitions; she was part of a children's theatre group and had enrolled to do her A levels at a college for her own personal development. She was optimistic about her future. She said: 'A lone mother must go her own way, despite the child. You can not sacrifice your life for a child all the time. If you would you become unsatisfied and, the child will notice and become unhappy too.'

Peggy left school after her O levels in East Germany and after her apprenticeship she became a waitress. Her father was a police man and her mother a trained worker in electronics. She fled to West Germany before reunification and became a door-to-door salesperson and fell in love with the head of the group, who turned out to be a gambler. She became pregnant from him at 31 and separated from the father during her pregnancy.

She loved being a full-time mother. State benefits gave her a chance to have a break from waitressing and also the time to paint and concentrate on photography. It was her choice not to be in employment because: 'The first three years in the life of a child are really important and that the mother is there is important too.' She did not feel poor but she topped up her income with casual work. Her friends were deemed reliable and important and she had an optimistic outlook to the future. 'I love my child. I love my life. I love my freedom. I want to do things that interest me.'

Chapter 8

Copers

Steffi

I met Steffi in the waiting corridor of the Hundedorf state benefit department where we arranged the interview for later. I visited Steffi in her light and airy top floor flat in a recently built block in a small council estate. We talked over coffee in her conventionally furnished lounge while her three-year-old daughter played and sometimes demanded attention.

Steffi was 26 years old and had been born into a working-class family. Shortly after she was born, her mother left her father taking her and her three siblings. When Steffi was eight years old her mother remarried a postman who Steffi thought of as her 'dad'. He was proud that he was the male breadwinner and that her mother was a housewife who looked after the children.

Steffi left school with her Realschulabschluss (German equivalent of the GCSE) and trained for two years to become a dental assistant. She continued working for a further five years until her Childrearing Leave. Her pregnancy was unplanned but welcomed by both her and her partner of two years, a physiotherapy student. After one-year childrearing leave, Steffi returned to work, sending her daughter to a childminder. Although her employer was keen for her to return to work in his small dental practice, he fired her six months later because he was concerned that her child's potential for illness would make her attendance unreliable:

> He (the dentist) told me when I returned: you know that I can make you redundant because you are no longer protected. And the reason for the redundancy would be a game of roulette for him, whether I would always be there because of the child. I said, not only can she become ill but I can become ill too. But that would be too risky for him and he wouldn't want to work with only two assistants. Because of that he would like to give me my notice. That's how he told me. Everyone told me I should take him to court but I said no, all doctors stick together. And when you take him to court you will never get a job again.

Initially, she was very optimistic about finding another job as a dentist's assistant but she has had 20 unsuccessful job interviews for a part-time job in the last one-and-a-half years. She felt discriminated against because she had a child, and also felt disadvantaged because of insufficient computer and x-ray skills. She enrolled on a computer course but was not prepared to compromize on the hours she worked. This was influenced by her experience of 'bad' mothering when she had previously worked full-time:

> My partner's sister was my childminder and I paid her to care from eight in the morning until seven or seven thirty. (…) That worked quite well but also in a negative way and I was disappointed and hurt because she started saying 'mama' to the childminder. That is my main reason for not wanting to work full-time anymore. (…) I want to work part-time to have some space for myself somehow, to do things for myself. Somehow I want a distraction too, and not only to be a mother but to have responsibility for other things. And I like my job. It makes me more balanced.

The father did not pay any child maintenance but she was only marginally worse off living on state benefits. She felt that she could live on state-benefits: 'you can live on it alright.' Although she felt ambivalent about state dependency and hid this fact from her friends and neighbours for fear of being stigmatized, she justified it as a fair exchange for her paying taxes in the past and because she had tried to get paid work. She also valued state benefits as an enabler:

> Nowadays it is made easy to give up a family. I do like it that there is such a thing (state benefits). Otherwise you wouldn't know what to do at all. Then you really would have to live on the street with your child. Somehow you are really supported as a lone mother.

Steffi did not want to send her three-year-old daughter into a Kindergarten while she was still unemployed and her daily routine showed that she viewed her situation as comprehensible and manageable:

> We get up at eight in the morning. Then we laze around for a bit. Sometimes we are still tired. Then we go through the flat and tidy up (…). Then we go shopping and eat a snack. Then she should sleep. Then we both have a nap and go to the playground or somewhere else. At the weekends we do something special - theatre, zoo or something. (…) In the evenings I relax, relax from the day. Sometimes my friends come and I watch TV, read a bit or do the domestic work.

She and her partner separated recently but she hoped that they would eventually get back together again. He saw their daughter once or twice a week. They had drifted apart because of his long studying and working hours, but she said that this had not changed her situation much as she had been mostly alone with her daughter anyway. Although she could rely on her family for support. She had also built a wider social network since the separation:

> I am more independent. I go out more. Really, I must say that I cope well with the situation. In a way, nothing much has changed because I did not work and was alone with her most of the time anyway. He worked until nine o'clock and wanted to succeed. It was his aim to have his own practice one day.

Steffi was an interesting case because of her experience of employer discrimination and her integral working/mothering outlook. She was a coper because she perceived some but not all aspects of her situation as meaningful, manageable and comprehensible. She managed to live on state benefits but was ambivalent about state dependency. Steffi only managed not to feel stigmatized because she hid the fact that she was dependent on benefits. She felt positive about the temporary nature of her situation and was pragmatic about it by making the best out of her mothering situation.

She also had a 'conformist' attitude regarding the 'male breadwinner/ female homemaker' family. This positive attitude may have been built on the experience of her mother remarrying when she was eight. Moreover, her mother was not in paid employment and this was endorsed by her stepfather. She may have been following this tradition temporarily, although her unsuccessful job search suggests otherwise. She experienced employment discrimination. It is a fact that dentists' assistants are typically female, young, independent and flexible, although she hardly mentioned her lack of certain vocational qualifications in her explanation.

Vanessa

Vanessa was 28 years old and lived on the working-class outskirts of East London. She had two sons who were nine years and four years old. In her own childhood she had felt neglected by her mother. Her mother was also dependent on Vanessa partly because of a mental illness that made her in Vanessa's words 'jealous and twisted'. There was not enough food, and the flat was cold in winter. Her parents had got divorced when she was five years old. Her mother occasionally worked as a cleaner while her absent father was a plumber who later remarried. Vanessa went into foster care when she was 14 years old, and later into lodgings. She had no educational qualifications. She had a sister who was unhappily married with two children. Until her first son was born she had worked as a waitress in bars and pubs, and also in factories.

She had been in a relationship for one year when she fell pregnant. She was surprised about this; as she had been told she was unlikely to get pregnant because of cysts in her fallopian tube. At 19, she had felt that she was too young to become a mother. However, worried about her medical condition and the fact that this could be her last chancel, she went through with the pregnancy. When her son was 18 months she split up from her partner, a tattooist, because he was not committed to the relationship and often absent.

> As soon as he was born, it was like I had this little baby. I did not want anybody else. I had this little boy, he was all mine and I certainly did not want to share him. And he [her partner] wasn't very supportive, he wasn't there often. I think I got bored as well. I just had enough. I think it got stale as well and we just split up.

Two years later she entered a new relationship with a cabdriver. Although she did not want to have another baby she became pregnant soon after. Her partner was violent and he beat her up when she discovered him in flagrante:

> I found him in bed with the lodger. And she had a baby from him but he did not stay with her. But he really beat me up when I found them. He really beat me. Then he got together with my friend six weeks later. Married her this year and then the marriage only lasted six weeks. I wouldn't go to hospital. I refused. I wanted to die I was so humiliated and just absolutely heart broken. I couldn't believe it. But the doctor was saying I should go.

Her subsequent partner was also violent, and she and her sons had to move a number of times because of this. After his release from prison, he started to become particularly possessive and violent: 'He is dangerous. When he was at home the first time he tried to chop my head off with a machete and if I had not moved I think I'd be dead.' She left him shortly after but had to leave her house and contents behind in order to stay in a refuge. Subsequently, she had to move to another refuge after he found her and harassed them. After this, she had an injunction taken out against him, and managed to obtain a council house for herself and her children.

Financially, she managed to cope on state benefits as she did the occasional cleaning job and was 'really good with money.' The fathers of her children gave no financial support, but she had been given a wreck of a car by the second father. The father of her first son saw his son about once a week, while the father of the second had little contact with his child.

> When I was with their dads I was financially better off. But now that I am on my own I haven't got any of the -, I'll be honest with you - any of the hassle. I do feel better off in other ways. I mean they do not want for much really. They are quite lucky because I do not smoke. I do not drink. I do not go out a lot. (...) If you play around with your money right, then you can cope. It is hard but you can do it. (...) I am quite good at that.

She was not in paid employment as she did not want to miss out on her children growing up, particularly because of her own childhood experiences. She was quite strict with her children and really wanted them to succeed. She was also aware that with her lack of skills she would not get a job that would pay more than what she was on now. Once her sons were in full-time education she was planning to do a full-time college course in law, and she was also going to take a computer course in the near future. Vanessa ideally wanted to become a refuge worker or a solicitor involved in domestic violence because she would enjoy working with other women who have been through what she had been through.' I want to aim for a career. I do not want to live off Income Support. I do not want to be just stuck in a factory.'

She had a support system in place. There were two women at the refuge centre who she visited almost daily. She recently joined the single parent group, Gingerbread, where she met and talked to other single mothers. The evenings made her feel quite lonely: 'Come eight o'clock we are all stuck in our little houses, all on our own.' To her, there were advantages to being a single mother:

> I feel like I do not have to share them. They are more mine. She (her sister) is moaning because she has to do him dinner and clear up. I think, thank god I haven't got all that. Then other times I really wish there would be somebody but that doesn't last long. I think it is better me being on my own than being in a volatile relationship where you hear me arguing and they can feel the unhappiness and the nastiness.

I classify Vanessa as a coper because she managed to 'get by' by careful budgeting and irregular cleaning jobs. She was not resentful and thought that everything happened for a reason, even her negative childhood experiences. She might have been a struggler when she was with her last boyfriend, but she 'wouldn't put up with somebody's behaviour like I have done it in the past, definitely not.' She was satisfied with her support network as well as with full-time mothering. She was not in paid employment because she she would not have been able to command a 'decent wage' with her lack of skills. But she also did not want to miss out on her children growing up, particularly because of her own childhood experiences. She overcame her ambivalence towards state benefits by telling herself that the situation was only temporary. She was quite pragmatic and had precise plans to enter education which would have increased her employment chances as well as contribute to her personal development.

Beate

Beate, 28, white, lived in Katzenhain with her five-year-old son in a one bedroom flat. She slept in the living room on a sofa bed and her son had his own room. She grew up in a small village in East Germany with three brothers. Her parents were farm workers at the large state-owned farm where she had trained and worked as a milk maid after obtaining her basic educational qualifications. To escape village life she followed her boyfriend to Berlin when she was 23 years old. In Berlin, she had worked as a maid in a hotel for five days but was fired because she answered her boss back. Shortly after, she became pregnant:

> I became pregnant by accident. I wanted to look for work and then I wanted to go on holiday and stuff. And then I was late and then it was all over. But when he was there, I was happy. I did not think of marriage because I knew, that one day the relationship would be over. I just stayed with him to be able to move to Berlin.

She continued to live with her partner until her son was four years old. Her partner had no qualifications, was not in paid work, and was an alcoholic who did not share the childcare. When she could no longer tolerate his violence, she moved into a mother-child home. The father now visited them on birthdays and about once every three months.

She felt quite lonely in Berlin and knew no other lone mothers. Her parents never visited her but she visited them when the nursery is closed. Financially, she managed, especially since her parents tended to give her a little when she visited them four times a year. She did not want to go back to the village because only the large farm there provided jobs.

In Berlin, her job centre had offered her jobs as a hotel maid but she has had to turn them down because the nursery did not open early enough to account for the long commute and the early start time. She once worked as a sales assistant at a newsagents but she found the counting aspects of the job too difficult. She really enjoyed working as a care assistant in a residential home but her career advisor did not allow her to train any further, because as a single mother, she would not be able to work shifts. Beate was just about to start a placement as a garden centre worker. This might lead to a retraining programme in green spaces maintenance. 'It's better than sitting at home. Then I will finally meet people.' She is grateful that the job centre organized this placement for her: 'I am very shy and hesitant. I just can not, I can not apply for a job, go somewhere, talk to someone who I do not know and sell myself until they take me. I can not do that.' She is not satisfied with being at home as currently:

> I send my child to nursery at eight and I pick him up at four. So I could go to work if there was a job that I wanted to do. I would like to go to work. My child isn't so much work. All I do is make him tea and he goes to bed at seven thirty. And we play a board game or so. That isn't any work, really. ... During the day I do not know what to do with myself.

She did not feel discriminated against because she felt that 'when you only have one child, then you are not that looked down upon.' She felt that without reunification she would have stayed in her village, with a partner, a job, a child and her own money. At the same time, she was quite proud of the fact that she managed to leave her village and her partner and to have found a flat by herself. In the future, she hoped to find a partner, but she also stated: 'I would be able to manage by myself.'

Beate felt very lonely and isolated because she had no friends and no family living nearby. She was dissatisfied with her situation as a mother. Although her son was in full-time nursery care, she found it difficult to apply for jobs because she was very shy. She was quite lethargic and said: 'During the day I do not know what to do with myself.' She had lost full-time jobs in the past and could not find new ones because she either found aspects of them too difficult or the commute too long. Furthermore, she had got used to living on a small income through careful budgeting and had almost paid off all her catalogue debts. She was ambivalent about receiving state benefits but she knew it was only a temporary situation. She was grateful to her job centre for organising a placement in a garden centre and was considering training in green space maintenance. This pragmatic outlook on the future made her a coper.

Polly

Polly was 30 and had a white middle-class English mother and an Afro Caribbean father. She rented a council flat near central London in a tower block and had a five-year-old son. After her A levels she went to college to study social work, but took two years off to travel and to work as a clerk. She was back in college in London when she became pregnant by her boyfriend, who had already once left her for someone else. She thought she would not get pregnant and was shocked about the news.

> I did not want to have a baby. I take responsibility for making this decision but the decision actually wasn't based on actually wanting to have the baby. I wanted him [her partner]. Also, I did not want to have the baby, he did. He had a child with somebody else in the years in between, but she just kicked him out. In my naivety I thought, yeah, maybe having lost one child, then another is going to help you. Very very young, very naive and because I still loved the bloke. Anyway, I sort of agreed that I would, for him really, I wanted to go through with it.

Already during her pregnancy, Polly had decided to leave him and to take full responsibility for the child, as the father proved noncommittal and irresponsible. Nevertheless, she never imagined that she would be on her own and she felt angry to be robbed of her student life and her youth. After her son was born she was in a long-term relationship, which she finished because she felt that she had to be a mother to that man as well as to her son. These experiences coloured her fairly negative view of men in general: 'The men in society that have got a problem about what responsibility is and what is expected of them as human beings. It is men who deteriorated value wise.'

Polly went back to college to work and to study when her son was eight-months old. As she had to pay for the nursery, transport and rent, she had less money to live on than she did while on benefits. Work and study also left her exhausted. She only managed to finish her degree in social science because she quit her job. Financially she coped relatively well, doing cash-in-hand jobs such as waitressing, decorating and renovating. She felt uncomfortable about not declaring the income, but she justified it by referring to the 'lousy system' that gave little support. She used to have a lodger for the spare room who sometimes did some babysitting too. Polly more or less chose not to be in paid employment because she found it stressful and unrewarding:

> I am choosing to live on a low income rather than struggle, day to day, trying to get my child organized, to school, get myself to work, get back, get the food. clean the place, you know, I am choosing to have less money, less choice, and a less stressful life by not pushing myself. I couldn't have lasted, you know. I tried to do the work thing and it nearly killed me. Not physically so much but the rewards at the end of it, there were not any.

When she left her social work course last year she felt quite depressed and without focus. But she also did voluntary work for an Aids charity and she had just been accepted for a foundation arts course. What she liked about the college course was its autonomy, creativity and control over work hours:

> It is very important to me that I can take my child to school and that I can pick him up. And that he is ok and that he is happy. It is not just about money. It is also about the child and his wellbeing.

She was quite happy with her social network, but none of her family lived in London and her friends tended to be very career-oriented professionals. She could rely on her son's godmother for regular babysitting, and she exchanged babysitting with another single mother one evening a week. Her son's father had no contact with them but paid about 90p a week in child support which was deducted from his Income Support. Polly did not want to become a single mother in the first place. She did have a good relationship with her son, but she also felt also insecure and lacking in confidence as a first-time mother. She felt stigmatized too:

> There is an assumption there that most women have actually decided to become pregnant without necessarily wanting the support of the man. That's the assumption. It's about ideology. It is about the family, about maintaining social control, all that stuff about family and patriarchy. They piss you off. It is very demoralizing. You are struggling and you are being penalized for carrying out your responsibilities. Single parents should be bloody supported.

I categorized Polly as a coper because she was trying to make the best out of a situation that she felt pushed into. She was also worrying about the future and about making the right decisions, but she had trained herself to be pragmatic and tried to enjoy being a mother. She would not have gone through the pregnancy if she'd known she would have become a single mother, and she felt cheated out of her adolescence. She felt ambivalent about state dependency, but it enabled her to pursue higher education, which not only increased her employment chances but also furthered her personal development. Education also accommodated good mothering because it was flexible in contrast to the job she used to have. The financial rewards were just not good enough and the stress too high in paid employment. She was satisfied with her social network and financially, she coped well through a combination of good budgeting, casual work, and the income from a lodger. At the same time, she perceived her life-chances as limited, the portrayal of lone mothers as demoralizing and her housing as unsatisfactory. However, she viewed the mothering and education aspects as meaningful.

Short biographies of other coper cases

Dagmar, 32, white, was from Katzenhain and was one of ten siblings in a three bedroom flat. She did not want to work full-time because she wanted to raise her second son differently and enjoy spending more time with him. Dagmar felt compelled to send her first son to a children's home because she could no longer cope with his difficult behaviour which she put down to her having worked full-time while he was little. She was looking for part-time jobs but thus far had not found a day-time only waitressing job nor flexible childcare.

Dagmar did not want to live with her partner because she was disappointed that he was unemployed, and also because both their benefits would have been reduced. She just about managed to live on state benefits through careful budgeting but she felt that her older son was discriminated against as she could not afford to buy him brand name clothes. She felt ambivalent about receiving state benefits and she hid this from friends, although she could count on support from her family and her partner. She would find further education or retraining too stressful and doubted whether they would improve her labour market chances.

Susanne, 26, white, lived in Hundedorf and had two daughters. She was raised by a lone mother when not in children's homes. She left school with basic qualifications and dropped out of her work programme because she became pregnant at 17. Although she soon split up with her unemployed Turkish partner, she was keen to have her daughter because she wanted to 'reverse' her own negative childhood experiences. At first glance she presented herself as someone who was work oriented and ambivalent about receiving state support. Later in the interview her mother-orientation surfaced as she had never searched for paid employment because she wanted 'to be there for her children' because her own mother was never there for her. She negotiated her situation to her satisfaction by working cash-in-hand and she had quite a few friends with whom she also exchanged babysitting. Ideally, she wanted to conform and not be made to feel 'asocial'. She did not mention further education.

In the future, she plans to work part-time as soon as the children are in childcare or school and, ideally, meet Mr Right, who would work and accept both children.

Marion, 28, white, was born into a working-class family and lived in Hundedorf. She left school with basic qualifications and used to work as a factory worker. During her pregnancy she kicked her partner out of her flat because he gave her no support and was an alcoholic. While she was satisfied with being a full-time mother temporarily, she wanted to enter part-time paid employment or a retraining programme to increase her chances for employment and because her Childrearing Benefit ran out soon. Nonetheless, she already perceived barriers such as childcare, employer discrimination and lack of qualifications. She did feel like a 'beggar' despite the fact that she was still in receipt of Childrearing Benefit. She wanted to escape her feeling of isolation although her parents were very supportive. Ideally, she would like another child with a responsible, committed and reliable male breadwinner partner.

Yvonne, 21, white, was from Katzenhain, was brought up by her mother and step father and continued to have a close relationship with her supportive mother. She had a mother orientation and was pregnant with her second child. Although she had always wanted children she became pregnant by chance in both cases. In the first case she thought she was infertile and in the second case she forgot to take the Pill. She was a lone mother for official purposes only as her partner lived with her although he had his own flat too. She did not want to get married. She planned to move, and planned to concentrate on education for professional reasons once the second child was one year old. She did not feel financially deprived, mainly because of Childrearing Benefit and her partner's support, but she felt bored and isolated, while her partner continued to live a bachelor life. She felt ambivalent about state benefits and she overheard people saying that she was too lazy to work. However, she knew it was only a temporary situation.

Jane, 18, white, lived in South London and was cared for alternatively by her mother, who was a drug addict, relatives, and children's homes while her mother was in prison. She became pregnant accidentally but decided to have the child because she wanted a 'companion', someone to love and someone to love her. Jane viewed her situation as a full-time mother as meaningful perhaps because her daughter was only four months old, perhaps because 'I never really thought about my career'. She had no educational qualifications and little work experience. Jane may become a borderline coper/struggler case soon because she had great difficulties managing her finances as she never learned to budget and state benefits were essential to her. So far she had no debts and at the time of the interview a friend of hers used to buy her groceries so that she did not go without food. She did not feel ambivalent about state benefits because it was nothing unusual as she lived in 'single mothers' land'. All her friends and family also lived in the area. She did not really think of going to work because of the poverty trap: 'what is the point of going to work for dole money when you can just sit at home and get your dole money at the end of the week.' In the future she would like to go to college to gain three 'O' levels but right now she plans only from one week to the next. Also, for now she wanted to be with her daughter: 'She is my little companion.'

Denise, 34, Afro-Caribbean, lived in South London and had two boys aged 18 and three years. Her father was a postman and her mother a care assistant. She has been a single mom on and off but had lived alone for a year now although she may marry her partner eventually. She left school at 16 without any qualifications before her first pregnancy began to show. Since then, she has done two O and A levels and worked in a sweet shop and in an after-school-club. She enrolled in a computer course to improve her employability and also applied for jobs during school hours. The second pregnancy came as a shock to her. 'Then I thought it happened and I just have to get on with life. He brought so much joy into my life even though he wasn't planned.'

She thought that she was different from other lone mothers because she had a good family support system. They never talk about Income Support: 'It is never really discussed. It just never comes up. You just live your life and that's it.' She managed to get by and to buy her children nice clothes because she bought on credit through catalogues. She could ask her partner for money and did the occasional cleaning jobs.

Chapter 9

Strugglers

Mary

I personally approached Mary in front of the post office in Northington. I visited her later on that day in her one bedroom flat on a large council estate nearby. Her simply furnished flat was gloomy because the curtains were drawn and the bare light bulb was not strong. Mary was white, 21 years old, and had a three-year-old boy and an eight-months-old daughter, who played in the same room where our interview took place.

Mary was born in London to working-class parents, who were on Income Support for most of their lives. Her father has been in prison and she had her first experience of care away from home when she was still a baby:

> There are certain things my social worker has told me, like from three-months old I had bruises all over my head, my face ... My dad used to beat me all the time. I was put in care for a little while when I was a baby. Then my parents got me back and from the age of 13, 14, my dad sexually abused me. I was locked in my bedroom. With a bucket as a toilet. (…) When my dad was in prison, I set my mom's flat on fire. I kept the whole house on fire.

She ran away from home and although she requested foster care she also ran away from foster families because she found the places too strict. Instead, she lived on the streets. She was no longer in contact with her parents, partly because her mother did not believe that her father sexually abused her, and partly because they were angry that she collaborated with the Social Services, who sent her brother into care too. At school Mary felt bullied because of her cleft pallet and her learning difficulties. She left school at 15 with no qualifications. Although she was once arrested for hitting someone, she had no criminal record. At 18, she lost her place on a hairdressing course because she could not afford to pay for public transport.

She became pregnant because her Afro-Caribbean partner would not use condoms and she forgot to take the Pill, which made her feel sick. Her partner left her for her 15-year-old sister, who also became pregnant by him: 'I was basically on my own. I was homeless, I was pregnant.' She was against abortion and always wanted children, albeit at a later stage. She was anxious to state that she had not become pregnant to jump the housing queue. During pregnancy she was moved into a council flat in Deptford and then into supervised housing, but she did not stay there for long either:

> I was evicted from there because I was seeing someone and he was threatening me in the building and it was on camera. And they evicted me because of that, because I think we were not allowed men in the Mother and Baby unit. When they evicted me I ended up in another Mother and Baby unit there. From there I got a flat in another area. I moved into there and I had trouble there when he found out where I was living and was threatening me and everything. From there I moved back down here into a hostel near here. When I was pregnant again I got my flat here. I am not happy here.

Mary had hoped to consolidate her situation with another Afro-Caribbean partner, with whom she had had a second child. Although her daughter was unplanned, she had wanted a playmate for her son and they did not use any contraception. She was devastated when she learned that her partner had fathered another child at the same time and that he had given that child the same name as her daughter. Her partner left both mothers and, although he came to visit about once a month he had no relationship with his daughter and did not pay maintenance because he was unemployed. Her son's father denied fatherhood, was no longer traceable and apparently had four children by four different women. These experiences influenced her very negative view of men:

> Because there are a lot of men out there who go out there and sleep around. And once the baby is there they disappear. And that happened to me twice now. (…) That is what men are like. A lot of black men do it.

Financially, Mary experienced serious deprivation because she could not manage on her benefits because she had to pay back a Social Services furniture loan. She also felt incapable of budgeting: 'Sometimes I have to borrow money. I can not budget. I have never been taught how to budget money. Never. So when my money was in my hand, it is gone the same day.' She did all the washing by hand because she could not afford a washing machine and, although her daughter was advized to eat red meat to become healthier she could not afford it. She felt under enormous pressure and was afraid of losing her children:

> I've got to make sure everything is alright. My kids will be taken off me and put into care because I haven't got enough money to support my kids. And it is not right. It is not fair. (…) I've got a social worker. I can not cope. It's hard. ... Sometimes my daughter is not well, like she has diarrhea whatever. I haven't got the money to buy her nappies. He gives me money, couple of times a week or once a week. ... Last year I was homeless and my son went into foster care (for four months while she registered herself as homeless to get a flat).

Mary regretted that she had left school at such an early age and she while her son was at nursery. However, she had no clear perception of further education and had either childcare, journalism or hairdressing in mind. Meanwhile, after one year she was still waiting for her friend to accompany her to the Job Centre. 'I am waiting for my friend, so that she can come with me to go to London Bridge.' Mary remained also ambivalent about education and preferred to stay at home with her daughter because she was afraid that her daughter might experience abuse in childcare since she herself had been abused when she was a child:

> Because why should we go out and work and leave her with a child minder I do not know. When all I know, I can come home and there is a bruise on her face (…) I think lone parents should look after their children because I have been abused.

Nonetheless, she recognized that Jordan was very happy at nursery. He learned and had friends and regular meals there: 'He is no longer so disturbed and he doesn't hit and swear at me.' However, during our interview I observed that she slapped him and he slapped her back. She apologized for his behaviour: 'He has seen the violence in my life. He has seen the threats in my life. He has seen me move from one place to another.'

She was in a vicious circle: she suffered from depression, and she became even more depressed over the fact that her children saw her in 'that state'. She felt socially excluded because she did not like to go out for fear of stalkers and harassment, and she could not rely on support from her family. 'I hate being on my own. I hate being a lone parent. I never asked to be a lone parent.' She regretted having children and had had an injection that stopped her from becoming pregnant again.

> What I have been through. (…) I feel like I am a victim. I have been abused from when I was young. When I have been with men they treated me horrible. I am just a victim of everything. I get the blame for everything.

Mary had been treated for depression but she stopped taking anti-depressants because they made her sick. Throughout her life she had been in contact with institutions and she had a social worker. She was meant to have counselling and I felt she was using the interview as a counselling session. She broke down several times during the interview. She perceived her situation as unmanageable, meaningless and incomprehensible. She had low self-esteem, was lonely and felt poor and isolated.

Mary's case is another example of the importance of housing in lone mothers' lives. In the pioneer and the coper type categories housing seemed to have facilitated the independence of lone mothers and given them a sense of continuity. In contrast, Mary could not cope with living alone nor with the rules of supervised housing. In the space of three years she had moved five times. She had ambivalent and paradoxical views on work and full-time mothering which showed how inappropriate the mother/worker dichotomy is. She perceived herself as both a full-time mother and as unemployed. On the one hand, she thought full-time motherhood was best for the children until they entered secondary school. On the other hand, she thought that she would be better off financially in paid employment. However, she did not realize that she was caught in a poverty trap. She even felt too paralyzed to enquire about education and paid employment and found coping with her current situation difficult enough. She coped on a day-to-day basis. Her depression meant that it was unlikely that social policies such as the New Deal for Lone Parents would be of value for her.

Mary regretted having had her children and is not fulfilled with being a mother. State benefits were absolutely essential to her but she did not manage to live on them as she could not budget. Mary did not take responsibility for her situation and considered that external factors were solely responsible for it. She felt stigmatized and isolated, was disappointed in her family and friends, and wanted the blame shifted to men and non-resident fathers. In fact, Mary diverted all responsibility for her situation to men, her friends and family, government and society in general. Perhaps this is not so surprising if we look at her negative childhood experiences which may well be responsible for her inability to cope with the rules of society.

Michele

Like Mary, I approached Michele, 30, white, in front of the post office in Northington where she received her Income Support in cash. I later met her in her flat in a large housing estate in Northington where she lived with her two sons, who were five and two years old.

Michele was born into a working-class family with fifteen siblings and grew up at home in Northington and in children's homes. Her parents were originally from Ireland. Her father was described as an 'odd-job' man, and her mother stayed at home with the children. Her relationship with her mother was not good and when she was ten years old she was sent to a boarding school for 'difficult children' which she left with no qualifications.

She had her first child at the age of 18. She liked the idea that 'it was something for me to keep hold of, that nobody could sort of like take it away or anything. It would always be mine.' Her parents were not bothered about her pregnancy. She split up from her partner shortly after because of his jealousy and his domineering personality: 'Cause he was sort of like, like dominating me, it was like, the dinners got to be on the table by a certain time in the evening. Well, I can not be told to do that. I'm not a robot, you know.' Shortly after the split, she met her next partner. But she left him too after he started hitting her while she was pregnant.

> Coming in from the pub drunk, when I've got a child with me already and I'm waiting for him to come in to tell him that I've just found out I'm pregnant, and he comes in and starts hitting me. So there was no point in me telling him that I was pregnant. I just left and came back to London.

Before long she had her second child and she became pregnant again by another partner: 'I had a lot of problems, cause I had a serious drink problem for a few years. And when I met Danny, Danny was trying to take me off the drink but it was impossible to take me off the drink.' Social Services became involved, and her first two children went into foster care. She went into hospital to 'dry out' while pregnant with her third child.

> I knew I needed help. And I was losing everything that I ever wanted and that was my kids. So I went into hospital the first time, came out, back on the drink. The second time, the kids went back into foster care, still pregnant with Danny. Still on the drink, even when I had my little Danny. I was still drinking a lot. (...) I was seeing things, I was hearing voices, and my personality was changing. Without a drink, I'd get really violent. I'd hurt myself. I set fire to my flat. So eventually, like, I went into hospital for a year. Came out and my three kids had all changed, they were not my babies anymore. So I put them up for adoption, where they'd been, they'd like be better off being adopted than having me drunk every day, did not do no housework, I couldn't look after them. Do you know what

> I mean? You can love a child, but it doesn't mean that you're doing the best for that child. (...) I came out and I went straight back on the drink. In a matter of a couple of days, two days, three days. I was back drinking heavily, taking a lot of pills. So me and big Danny split up. Stayed on me own for about two years.

Two years later she had a fourth child by a partner whom she left several times because of his violence. They split up for good and she had a fifth child from a casual relationship. In four of her five pregnancies she had not taken any contraceptives and the other pregnancy happened when she was on the coil. Her four previous relationships had failed because she resented the fathers' violence, their jealousy, and their lack of commitment. Neither of the fathers was in contact with their children, nor did they pay maintenance. However, she also wanted to keep the children to herself, particularly the last two, after she had given up the first three for adoption. She seemed resigned to the adoptions and this seemed to have had the effect that she enjoyed being a full-time mother of the last two:

> And at the end of the day, I've given up three kids to adoption, what I wanted, and with the two little ones I've got, there's no space in my life to share my life with anybody except my two babies. That's the way it goes with me, you know.

Social Services threatened to take away her fourth child if she did not overcome her alcohol addiction. She managed to do this with a lot of support from a social worker, a psychiatrist, family and friends. However, because of her depression she had been in a psychiatric hospital twice since her last child was born, and she had therapy sessions three times a week. She had cut herself off from many of her friends because she was embarrassed about her behaviour when drunk or depressed. Hence, she felt quite isolated and lonely. However, her younger stepsister supported her by staying at her house when she was getting depressed. She blamed the alcoholism on her negative experiences with men:

> Depression, I've had that as long as I can ever remember. The drink was about, I was getting in and out of relationships, I was having kids, and the men did not want to know. The relationship kept failing. In the end I thought it was something wrong with me, why I was meeting these men, these men were just turning out to be right gits, by hitting me all the time, beating me up. Just not being there, but wanting me to do everything for them and they do not want to do nothing for me and my kids. That is a lot of like different things, like which mounted up for me to hit the drink.

Her children had asthma and did not like the smell of smoke but she continued to smoke because:

> If I tried stopping me cigarettes, then I'd be back on the drink. I'd need something for me, not for anybody else. Like the drink was for me, it wasn't to share with my kids. You know, and it's the same as the cigarettes. Cigarettes are yours; they're not to share with your children.

After Michele had her first child she used to do some casual work in a pub where her son could sleep in the buggy by the pub kitchen. She also had no means of paying back £675 owed to a loan shark from whom she initially borrowed £500.

> I've took my little boy like up to Social Security with me. And he's seen kids running round with, they've got holes in their jeans, holes in their t-shirt, you know, and their coats are torn, you know. And the babies, like my little one, he's saying, are them people poor? And I've said, well, yeh, they are. He's said, but we're poor but we do not go round like tramps. And I say no, only cause I get myself in debt. That lady probably do not owe nobody nothing, where Mummy does, you know. Fine. Like Christmas. I asked him what did he want for Christmas off Father Christmas. A bike. He had his heart set all year on a bike. Christmas morning, how could I tell him like Father Christmas wasn't bringing his bike? You know. So, one way I had to get the money. I would have got the money one way or another for his bike, no matter what it cost me; he would have got his bike.

She had no inclination to work because she knew that she would not be able to command a sufficient salary, and because she recognized that nobody would employ her considering her current mental instability. She did not want to train at anything nor be in paid employment because she could hardly cope with the housework and looking after her children. Michele regretted having had her first three children while she was so young. She was almost relieved to be a single mother because she did not want to repeat past experiences: 'you ain't got to share the kids with a man. There's no man to holler and shout at the children and tell them what to do.' She does feel stigmatized by the public though but is quite defensive about it at the same time:

> Well they say so much about single parents, it's like we're the scum of the, like the earth sometimes. Like you hear so many people, like even going out, well look at her, look she's got two kids from two different men. (...) I'm not ashamed of that. I do not feel, well, I should be. Least I know I try and do the best for my kids.

During the interview Michele came across as very 'matter of fact' about her life, with a very independent mind, and hence an unlikely struggler. However, she shared all the values in the Struggler category apart from the dissatisfaction with full-time mothering. She seemed to be satisfied with being a mother after her first three children were adopted. However, she found it difficult to cope with her day-to-day situation because of her mental instability and her debts:

> If the kids want something, clothes, and I know there's no way I can afford it, then I'll get really depressed, I will cry a lot, I do not sleep, I won't eat. I'd feel that, if I was eating that the food that I'd be putting in my mouth would be coming off their feet. That being that extra few quid to put towards a pair of shoes for them. So, yeh, I go like really bad.

Michele felt lonely and isolated but, unlike Mary, she was grateful for the support from a Social Services nurse and from her younger sister and she did not feel stigmatized about receiving Income Support. She knew she needed Income Support to survive:

> I've no conscience about receiving Income Support. I've got to be fed and my kids' got to be fed. So we've got to have money from somewhere. If it's from the State or if someone was going to put an envelope in my letterbox every week.

Michele did not divert all responsibility for her situation to others, but she blamed her previous relationships for her alcohol problem. Like Mary, she felt paralysed and could hardly cope with her day-to-day life: 'You know, we just, for me mentally I just take one day at a time. I couldn't think of what I'm going to do in two weeks time because I can not remember what I've done two weeks ago.' Michele was also a struggler because state benefits were essential to her but were still not enough because of her debts and her inability to budget. She was not in paid work nor in further education because she found her current situation difficult enough to manage. She is a coper in two aspects though. First, because she was actually satisfied with being a full-time mother, particularly since she gave her first three children up for adoption. Secondly, although she felt quite lonely and isolated, she also appreciated the therapy sessions she had three times a week as well as the support from her younger sister.

In this study, there were just two struggler type cases but the following chapters show that there are women on the border between coper and struggler as well as between coper and pioneer.

Chapter 10

Borderliners

Borderline cases are cases that do not fit neatly into any of the three categories. They highlight the limitations of type categories but also clarify type category characteristics. Moreover, they show that type categories are dynamic and not fixed and stagnant. In other words, lone mothers can move between categories over time but can also bear characteristics of more than one type at the same time.

A mother is both a coper and a pioneer or a borderline coper/pioneer if she meets three to four criteria of either the pioneer or the coper category. A borderline coper/struggler also has only three to four values in the struggler or coper category each. Of 70 mothers interviewed, there was no evidence of a 'triple' borderline coper/pioneer/struggler case, or an even split across all categories.

Borderline cases between coper and struggler

Connie

I met Connie in the waiting corridors of the Katzenhain state benefit department where we arranged the interview for later. I visited her in her un-modernized one bedroom ground floor flat on a medium sized council estate. She lived here with her mother, her two children and two cats. We talked on her balcony while her two children (seven and three years old) and her mother were watching TV in the lounge.

Connie was 25 years old and was raised by her working-class lone mother in East Berlin. She had five siblings and did not know who her father was. Her family remained her main social network to this day. Connie left full-time education after ten years. When she was 17 years old she became pregnant by chance which made her leave her apprenticeship to become a farm worker. Connie and her partner moved to East Berlin to escape the gossip and the prejudices in the country but they separated soon after her daughter was born and her partner moved back to the country. A year later she found another partner who moved in with her and who became the father of her second child. She only realized that she was pregnant when it was too late for an abortion. Her partner was unemployed and used to drink quite a lot. They had many arguments and he moved out before their child was one year old. Connie's children had no contact with their fathers.

Connie and her two children slept in one room and her mother lived in the second smaller room. In the winter they used to move into her mother's flat as it gets very cold in Berlin and her mother's flat was easier to heat. However, her mother could no longer afford the flat and moved in with her. Connie had not applied to get a larger flat as she thought she would have needed to earn more to pay the rent once she was in paid employment. Before reunification she felt it was easier to live as a single mother. She would have received subsidies and did not have to pay for nursery care or public transport.

Connie could rely on her family for some financial support. Connie had little enthusiasm for paid employment because as an untrained labourer she could not command a good wage: 'I do not want to lie but I find, when I get some money for doing nothing, then I want to get more money for going to work. I won't go to work for the same money.' The state benefit office expected her to apply for ten jobs a month but she found that difficult. During the last seven years she had had temporary jobs in hotels and in factories.

> You have to go where you are needed and then you end up with a commute of two hours. I've done that but after all, I have two children. I want to be with them too. My mother does the drop offs and in the evening when I come home they are in bed already. It doesn't have to be like that.

Ideally, she would have liked to commute for no more than one hour each way and earn £700 per month after tax, perhaps as a kitchen help or as a chambermaid. However, she doubted that someone would employ her because of her children. By law, she was allowed to take up to 20 days off a year to look after her children when they were ill. However, later in the interview she said that she could not really imagine working because she was not used to it:

> I do not want to work by all means. I haven't really been working before, apart from the two years in the apprenticeship. I am lethargic most of the time. I am more or less used to always staying at home and you can get used to it. While other people get used to going to work I get used to staying at home.

Her day-to-day schedule looked like this:

> Get up at 6.30, At eight o'clock the big one has to be taken to school. Then it's tidying up, shopping, sometimes playing with the boy. Often he's already playing by himself. At lunchtime he'll get a tin of food. Sometimes we cook, like a chicken drumstick or something. Otherwise it's pasta. I tend to watch the soaps and series all day.

Connie had a boyfriend who lived with his parents but sometimes stayed with her overnight on her balcony and helped her out a little financially. As a single mother she appreciated that the fathers could not tell her how to raise her children. However, she blamed reunification for her difficult financial situation:

> The wall should be up again. Then, everything was easier. The state was more child-friendly. You did not have to pay for this and that. You got subsidies and stuff that you do not get anymore nowadays. Nowadays, it is very difficult to live without money. (…) There are also more lone mothers because of reunification. Our men do not get the jobs anymore and you spend all day together and then you start fighting. Women have children to look after at home while the men – when they have no work - then they basically go

drinking. Then the real fights start. The foreigners should also leave again and not take our men's jobs.

Connie was a coper because she perceived some aspects of her situation as meaningful, manageable and comprehensible. She felt ambivalent about being with the children. She wanted to be with them but she also stated that she could not relate to them and regretted that she had had her children early. Connie could not do without state benefits but she still had debts and could not budget despite relying on occasional financial support from her family and boyfriend. She was not ambivalent about receiving state benefits because she made external factors responsible for her situation, such as reunification and asylum seekers.

Her family constituted her only support network but she did not feel isolated. She knew she was caught in the poverty trap and that employers would not employ her because of her children. As a struggler she was phlegmatic and passive and felt that her current situation was enough to get through. To help her cope better and to make her feel more relaxed Connie drank about six beers during the day but she denied that she was an alcoholic. She had no plans to increase her skill set and no plans for the future. Instead, she lived from day to day: 'I take everything as it comes. I do not think about this very much. I try to cope with what just happens to me.' Hence, in three out of seven variables she fits into the coper category while the other four show that Connie is a struggler too.

Susanne

I met Susanne through a friend of hers who contacted me through my classified newspaper advert. Susanne, 36, and her son, four, lived just south of the city centre in the western part of Berlin, in her one bedroom flat in a purpose-built block in a central lower middle-class area with a few parks.

Susanne came from a town in West Germany and she had one brother. Her parents, a toolmaker and an accounts clerk, separated when she was 18. After she completed her GCSE's she trained to become a nursery nurse and then a hairdresser. She married when she was 19 and moved to Berlin with her husband. She found employment as a sales assistant in a stationery shop. Although she had always wanted children her husband wanted to have some security and savings first. She separated from her husband seven years later and retrained as an office clerk, after which her son was born soon when she was 32.

Although she became pregnant by accident she was quite happy about it, because initially she thought her partner of two years would be supportive. However, he was unable to commit to the relationship and they had already separated by the time of her pregnancy. He did not have to pay maintenance as long as he continued being a mature student. She had also had her child for another reason: 'I thought, I am getting older too. Who knows whether I find the ideal partner with whom I can raise children together. I might as well go ahead and do it now.'

When her son was born she found it easy to manage financially but when her Childrearing Benefit ran out after two years it became difficult to live on a reduced budget. She was physically exhausted because her son would not sleep through the night and it was hard to find suitable childcare for him. He finally got a place in Kindergarten when he was two and a half although both mother and son took a long time to get used to being separated from each other. She put herself under pressure to find employment and this was encouraged by her advisor from the state benefit department. After unsuccessful attempts to secure employment she did a nine months training course in office communication/computers. For one year she had been unsuccessful in trying to find flexible part-time employment. She felt that she was too inexperienced and not flexible enough to even respond to many job advertisements:

> Every time I see a job advert I am shocked when I read about the expectations and minimum requirements employers have: you have to be perfect and flexible. I haven't got them. I am not flexible and I am not perfect. So I still keep on applying for jobs.

Susanne was embarrassed about receiving state and unemployment benefit and she preferred not to tell people. She saw herself as unemployed as opposed to being a full-time mother and she sent about three job applications out each week. She received two job offers but she could not take them up because she could not find any childcare for Saturdays nor negotiate flexible hours.

> I am totally dissatisfied with my life. Thankfully, because of my therapies I can be happy once in a while. When I can tell myself: other people are much worse off than me. Being unemployed makes me dissatisfied, having little money makes me unhappy. And then I get into a phase where I think: Good that there is nobody else. I can not imagine having a partner, somebody expecting things of me. It's up and down with me really.

She had little support and could not rely on friends to help out with looking after her son and there was no contact with his father. She had little contact with her mother who never seemed to have encouraged her nor showed her love. She felt others had prejudices against her and thought she would have been better off without a child:

> Work is such an important part of our lives. I think it has moved up to first place. If you do not work you slide down the social prestige scale. And that kills me really. I am convinced, if I had not had my child I would feel better. I am sure of that. I would have had a job in sales. When you are independent and without responsibilities you can do all sorts of things.

Through having a child she realized how needy she was herself emotionally and how difficult she found raising her child. She had moments where she thought she had to give up her son, where she did not think that she was good for him anymore. The main theme in the interview was that she was very dissatisfied with her life. She suffered because she could not fulfil society's expectations to be a mother and to be in paid work. She wanted to conform to the norms of society, including pleasing her friends and family whom she could not really rely on. She was torn between the demands of the Job Centre who pressured her into paid employment and her childcare inflexibilities.

Ideally, she wanted to combine mothering with working part-time but she was unable to find well-paid and flexible work because the labour market discriminated against her as a mother. She continued to look for paid work and bridged unemployment with education while easing deprivation with casual work. However, she was embarrassed about receiving state benefits and tended not to tell anyone. She had difficulties coping and she suffered from depression, but she managed to keep applying for jobs and planned to work in an office in the near future. For Susanne, four aspects of her life were manageable, meaningful and comprehensible. But in three variables she was clearly a struggler.

Melody

Melody was 23 years old, Afro-Caribbean, and lived in Northington with her five-year-old son. I met her when I handed out letters in front of post offices on a Monday morning. I visited her in her one bedroom flat on a large estate.

Melody was born into a working-class family. Her dad was a bus driver and her mother a receptionist. Her parents separated when she was little and she did not get on with her step dad, a mechanic. After school she used to stay in after-school care. Her mother was religious and so strict with her that she would not let her go out with her friends. Melody was laughed about at school and she became so depressed that she threw herself out of the window to commit suicide. She was in a coma in hospital and still suffered from epileptic fits.

She left school at 16 but stayed with her mother and three other half brothers and one sister in their three bedroom house. Melody started to work in a shoe shop where she made some friends and became involved in smoking dope. After a while she did not put all the money into the till for the shoes she sold. She was caught for not accounting for all the money and got sacked. She ran away from home and moved into a hostel to wait for a council flat to come up. Once she had her own flat she went to college where she met her boyfriend. She left college and her casual cleaning job when she became pregnant at 18:

> When I found out I was scared and I did not know what to do. I realized when I had him I needed some help. I realized I needed my mum. Went to my mum, knocked on the door: I have my little boy here. Would you like to see him? She did not want to see me. I saw her in the street. Said: hello mum. She doesn't want to know me. She just walked away. She was angry with the fact that I fell pregnant, plus me running away made it even worse. I was really upset and I was really getting down and depressed about it. My son's father, ended up being in prison and that. It was his mum that I had to rely on in giving me things, and giving me money and that because I was not working at the time.

After six months her mother relented and they were back in touch and went to church together. However, she continued to feel excluded from the family while craving for their recognition. The father of her baby sometimes stayed with her at her flat but it was a fairly violent relationship:

> When he did stay, we were just having arguments. He wasn't helping me. He was just going to sleep, coming in late, going to sleep and then waking up, watching telly and then

> he was out. He wasn't helping me in the house or nothing. He wasn't doing nothing for me. And that's when I started realising it wasn't worth it. ... When he hit me, he slapped me in the face and pushed me down and everything. I fell onto the bed and onto the floor and my son came in and goes: Mum, mum, he was like really screaming around me and that's the thing that really hurt me. He just left. He did not even worry about his son. While we were here, we were having arguments again. I kept telling my son, go in his room. Telling him to go outside or something when it was starting but it just wasn't right. It was something, you know, my son would hear. He'd hear all the noise and know what's going on again.

To make ends meet she got married to an African immigrant to get him into Britain. From the money she bought a TV, chair and the settee which got smashed by her partner when he found out about it.

> We used to have arguments and he hit me a couple of times when he was upset. He used to smoke as well and drugs and everything. I used to smoke as well but it was only like cannabis. He just smoked the harder stuff. He found out that I got married for money. And when he found out he was really mad because I did not tell. So what he had done, one day, I went out of the house and he ripped out my settee, cut them up, smashed my telly, smashed my stereo. Like really messed up everything up in the house. When I came home I was really devastated (…) So what happens is he got put in prison again. He was doing some robberies and that. So I felt pleased about that, so I had my freedom. I could walk the streets and whatever and not worry about looking behind my shoulders to see if he was there.

To buy new furniture, Melody had a couple of temporary jobs, one in a mailing company and one in a department store, which she really enjoyed. She went to college to learn typing, English and computing, mainly to bridge unemployment. In the meantime she was registered with a recruitment agency for a part-time job in retail. She was embarrassed about not having a job and living off state benefits:

> All I used to do is sit at home, take my son to nursery. Go and lie down in bed, or just sit and watch telly or go out shopping to the market, come back home. It's not nice. With just one I feel embarrassed, for people to know and see that I am not working or nothing. Because I like people to think me working or something, or recognize me working in a suit or something. I hate for people to see that I am not working. ... I'd rather be working than sitting at home. Because I feel bad about my son as well. Because sometimes when he is at school, I feel embarrassed when the teacher will ask the kids: What's your parents doing, or whatever. And he'll turn around, and he can not really say, my mum is working or whatever.

Financially, she found it difficult to cope. She was in arrears with rent and water. Her son's father was out of prison again but had not been in contact with his son although she left messages for him: 'He has just left his son in a lurch. He says he going to buy him things and until now I haven't seen him buy nothing.'

Melody was a coper as well as a struggler. She wanted to be in paid work to be a role model for her son instead of being a full-time mother but she had no alternative. She was embarrassed about receiving state benefits and still struggled financially and was in debt. Melody also felt stigmatized and excluded, especially by her family.

However, she was registered with a recruitment agency to find work in the retail sector. She enrolled on some college courses to increase her employment chances. She was quite pragmatic about her future in that she registered with agencies and she went to college to improve her job prospects.

Short biographies of coper/strugglers

Sabina, 34, came from West Berlin from a working-class family and had one child who went to primary school. After her GCSE's she trained to become an office clerk and used to work full-time until recently, apart from taking two years maternity leave. Her partner and her only separated when their daughter was four-years old but were still in contact with each other. Sabina was really dissatisfied with being at home and resented the fact that it was the mothers who had to look after children after a separation. She would have much rather been in paid employment and had been looking for office jobs unsuccessfully. She took part in training courses to enhance her chances of employment. Her parents were dead and she felt lonely with her child. Not only did she not like being on state support and felt embarrassed about it, after all these years she could not live on it and had run up debts. Sabina had plans for the future though and she was determined to find a job although she was discriminated against by employers who feared that she would be the one staying at home with her sick child.

Meral, 21, was Turkish and lived in Hundedorf, West Berlin. Having grown up in Turkey and Berlin, she was torn between her working-class, traditional Turkish parents and her German friends and environment. She escaped parental violence and moved in and out of sheltered housing as well as various educational courses. She had no educational qualifications and little work experience. When she became pregnant unintentionally she could not face a third abortion. Her negative views of men were confirmed when her German partner left her for someone else once he was released from prison. Social Services wrote a 'bad' report about her, took her child away from her and placed him with foster parents where her one-year-old son lived during the week. She found it difficult to hand over her child after the weekend and felt very ambivalent about it.

State benefits were absolutely vital to her and she had managed alright with the income so far. She wanted to have something to 'offer' to her child when he was older and was pragmatic about her future. She was caught in the poverty trap and she applied for various apprenticeships to improve her chances of employment. The Job Centre assisted her in finding an apprenticeship in sales as well as a computer training course. Although she had two friends she could rely on she felt isolated and had no support from her parents and siblings.

Denise, 39, white, was from a suburb in South London and had two children. Born into a middle-class family she hinted that her childhood was not a happy one. She left private education with 'A' levels and worked as a professional Arabic dancer and as a secretary for 12 years. Her first partner was unfaithful and the father of her second, one-year-old child, lived in another country. She had been happy to be pregnant both times and initially she had lived with her mother, which was quite liberating: 'If I wanted to go out in the evening whether to work as a dancer or go to a party, my mum had her. It was very very easy. I was free even though I had a child.' This ended when her mother got Alzheimers and was sent into a nursing home. From then on she found her situation difficult to deal with and could not imagine being in paid employment as her life without support was difficult enough: 'I do not think it's really possible for someone to work and have no support.'

She also felt quite isolated. A few months after the birth of her son she was hospitalized for depression. This helped her to get the council to pay for a childminder for her son and gave her some time to recuperate so that she could enjoy being a mother again. She felt ambivalent about receiving state support and had difficulties coping financially. She had debts through occasionally borrowing money from friends. She was not resigned to her situation and had made plans for the future. She was about to study for her 'A' levels in Biology so that once her son started school in two years she planned to study to become a physiotherapist.

Taiwo, 25, was born in London but grew up in Sierra Leone. After her GCSE's she worked as a housekeeper in a hotel. Her parents died early and she was disappointed in her friends because they had not been there when she needed them. She had a five-year-old child from a relationship with a man who became abusive, was very controlling and who had left her since. Once her child was born she gained more vocational qualifications because it facilitated mothering and improved her employment prospects. She was unsatisfied being a full-time mother, felt ambivalent about state benefits but blamed the lack of appropriate jobs for her dependence.

Taiwo desperately wanted an office job and kept applying for work every day. However, she could not find any jobs she was trained to do: 'I do not want to sit around all day. I want to prove the skills I got and use my ability.' She found it difficult to live on state benefits and now had debts to pay back too. She really disliked being a single mother on state benefits: 'It just makes your life miserable and sad. You can not talk with someone, you have little money and it is difficult to get a job because child minders are expensive.'

Sabine, 21, lived in a suburb of East Berlin with her four-year-old child. She had experienced sexual abuse by her stepfather and felt excluded and let down by her mother, a laboratory worker. She grew up in mental hospitals and care homes and had been seeing a psychiatrist for many years. She became pregnant from a casual relationship and did not have an abortion because she wanted to make her boyfriend pay for the pain he had caused her. After the birth she lived in a mother-and-child home but was kicked out. She then found another flat and recently finished her apprenticeship as a 'cemetery gardener'.

After her apprenticeship she became unemployed but she is still on the look out for new jobs. She perceived state benefits to be only a temporary situation and wanted a job to pay off her debts. She was not satisfied being at home and being a mother. She used to watch a lot of TV while her child was in full-time childcare. She was very lonely and had few friends. For the future, she planned to make friends (she was already answering contact adverts in the local papers), she planned to find a job and to work on her mental health together with the psychiatrist.

Borderline cases between coper and pioneer

Laura

Laura, 26, responded to my advert in London's classified newspaper Loot. She lived with her three-year-old son on the outskirts of London in a house that she rented privately. She grew up in a working-class family with her brother. Her step dad was a printer and her mother was a school play leader. They divorced when she was 13 years old and her mother remarried. She had had some emotional problems after she traced her biological father. Laura found out that she came from a very large family that often had trouble with the police. When she was 16, she 'went off the rails and got in trouble with the police quite a bit.' She left school with no qualifications and had many different jobs. She moved in with her boyfriend and his parents when she was 15 and the council found her a flat after she was brought into hospital when her partner beat her up.

She was given a 12 months suspended sentence for cheque forgery which served as a catalyst for her to get a 'proper job'. Despite her criminal record she managed to get a job as a criminal investigator in which she repossessed cars, credit cards and houses.

> I just loved the job and I fell right into it and within four weeks of starting it I had a letter from the managing director about how well I was doing and giving me extra areas and extra money and extra this and extra that. I was thinking, like ooh, this is my vocation in life and I've found it. I was there nearly two years so I mean it was a long time for me to work anywhere 'cause I get bored so easily and then I got pregnant and never went back.

She became pregnant from a casual relationship and stopped that well paid work while she was having a difficult pregnancy. After she gave birth to a stillborn baby she 'was so depressed and so doolally, I did not even reply to their letters you know and I was really out of order but I just couldn't help it.' From then on she desperately wanted a baby even though she had never been in a long-term relationship. She worked as a waitress in a strip club and smuggled Kurdish women and children into Britain in the boot of her car. It was illegal but she thought she was helping them:

> Now I think about it gives me the horrors to think that I did but, you know, we thought we were saving these people (…) But I do not know where the money went, it was just spent on going out and having a good time. But then I found I was pregnant anyway so that changed me completely.

She was caught but her sentence was suspended again. By the time she found out she was pregnant she was no longer in a relationship with the father of her son, a market trader: 'I wanted someone to love me. I felt I needed it and it would sort my life out and straighten me out completely.' Becoming pregnant acted as a catalyst because when she was pregnant she 'stopped smoking, stopped doing drugs.

I stopped going out. I stopped drinking. I stopped swearing. I changed a lot. (…) I thought to myself that I would be a perfect mum.'

She felt very strongly about not doing drugs anymore because she believed that smoking cannabis had caused her to feel depressed. After the baby was born she did not leave the house very often and was often alone as she had broken off the contact with her old friends. Only when she moved into a 'nicer' neighbourhood and simultaneously left an unloving relationship did she start making new friends at mother and toddler groups. 'I've gone there and met more people and it's just really really worked out lovely and I'm like the happiest now I've ever been in my whole life.'

Her family were very supportive, financially as well, and she described her mother as her best friend who she could confide in. Her mother would have liked for her to meet somebody and joked that the taxes she paid went towards Laura's state benefits.

Her son's father was not registered on the birth certificate, was not in contact with them and gave no financial support. To top up her benefits, and to be able to buy her son presents, she worked in a cab office once a fortnight. Her mother usually looked after her son during that time. She felt that she could live quite comfortably on Income Support and the £15 extra each week. 'I think that it's more than enough, well it's more than enough for me. We eat very well.'

Once her child goes to nursery school she would like to work in childcare and was applying for GCSE courses to improve her employability. She was very happy with her house that she found herself. It was fairly new, was on a private estate and had a garden. She sold all her possessions and furniture to raise the money for the £1000 deposit for the house. Her daily routine was:

> Get up about 7.15.7.30 make breakfast for Jordan and me. Watch a bit of telly in the morning. Go and get bathed and ready by about ten o'clock. Go out to walk around the shops or we go to the park or we go to visit my mum or might just do some housework. About 12.30 have lunch, sandwiches or beans on toast or something. In the afternoon we go to the park.

She was satisfied being a single mother because of the freedom and independence: 'Your whole time is spent with the child and not having to look after somebody else - to cook and feed and wash and iron and everything for a man you know.' All her previous relationships were based on an unequal footing: 'I've only been in relationships where I've done everything. I've done all the running. I've done all the paying out and done all the cooking all the cleaning all everything.' Laura seemed a very determined person with a positive outlook:

> I think everything can be overcome. Every problem there is in your life can be overcome if you put your mind to it I think. If you're a strong enough person you do not just let life pass you by you know overcoming anything that stands in your way. Whatever it is, I do not intend to let anything keep me down nor knock me down. I intend to get back up and get what I want really.

At the same time though, she felt discriminated against and was embarrassed about receiving state benefits but she was also determined to put her child first: 'He always comes first, easily.' She enjoyed staying at home with her son but was planning to enter education in one year's time:

> Worrying about what other people think, yeah that does bother me, but it doesn't cause any problems. I do not intend to be on benefit for the rest of my life. I do not intend to just get what I can.

Laura was as happy as she had ever been in her life. She had a positive outlook and saw the future bringing up her child well. She experienced two catalysts that transformed her life. The first was when she became a criminal investigator. She was again thrown off balance when her first child was stillborn but a second child acted as a second catalyst and made her stop criminal activities, taking drugs, change her friends and become a highly satisfied mother. She was not in work by choice but wanted to enter education to up her chances in the labour market. Nonetheless, she was also a coper because she was embarrassed about receiving state benefits, and she worked cash in hand to cope better financially. A social network was important to her and she could rely on her mother. The transformation into a good mother was an achievement that gave Laura confidence and motivation.

Manuela

Manuela had four children. Her four children were eleven, nine, six and one-year-old. She lived in an unmodernized 2 bedroom ground floor flat in Katzenhain in a four storey purpose-built street property. It was built at the end of the last century and still had coal brick ovens. I met her at the state benefit department in Katzenhain.

Her mother died from cancer when she was two years old. At first she lived in an orphanage but lived with her father once he married and had three more children. The relationship between Manuela and her stepmother wasn't good and she only began to feel part of the family when her father divorced and remarried a woman who brought three sons into the family, each of them from a different father. Her father was a lorry driver and her second stepmother was a cleaner. After the East German equivalent of GCSE's (10te Klasse) she enrolled into technical college and then completed an apprenticeship in the post room at a tax office. Later, she also worked at a travel agency and for the then state owned telephone directory enquiries.

When she was 20 she had her first child, a son from a long-term relationship. Her daughter was born two years later. She broke off this relationship because her partner was working at a factory all the time and was no help with the children. Five years later she had a third child from another relationship with a metal worker, and shortly after she had a fourth child by a third partner, a builder. Both relationships did not work: the former was too young and noncommittal and the latter was considered too lazy. The father of the first two children had no contact with his children but the others had. The third father also paid maintenance and saw his daughter every second weekend. The father of her fourth child also saw his daughter on a regular basis.

She now had a partner who had his own flat nearby and she often stayed with him overnight, once her children were asleep in her flat. He accepted her and her children and got on with all of them but she did not want him to move in with them just yet. After years of having been unemployed he had just found work as a builder and did not want to have to support a big family too. Her children liked him very much and called him daddy. Her parents were also quite supportive although her stepmother had hoped that Manuela would not copy her and have many children by different fathers.

Manuela had always wanted to have many children and she was proud of the fact that she had managed to gain educational and vocational qualifications first. She was very happy about every single child but did not want to have any more and so had a sterilization.

> I always meant to finish school, then an apprenticeship, wanted my own flat, and then I wanted children. And I have done it in this order. I had always wanted many children. And now I have four.

After each of her three children, she returned to work after the Baby year, the statutory maternity leave in former East Germany. She never experienced difficulties in returning to her workplace and in finding a nursery place for any of her first three children. She enjoyed her job working in an animal food factory which was physically challenging but also well paid. After reunification she was made redundant but she managed to find a job working for the housing department at her local authority. However, after she had had her fourth child she decided to ask for the full three-year Childrearing Leave and to leave her job. She felt that people looked down on her when she had to take leave when one of her children fell ill. As it happened, her first son had a learning disability, attention deficit disorder and food allergies.

After reunification she felt bewildered by the new system of having to apply for everything and by not automatically becoming part of a state programme. It also became more difficult to find nursery care. A friend advised her on the benefits she was entitled to and Manuela had only good words to say about her advisor at the state benefit office. But she also thoroughly enjoyed not being in paid employment, being a housewife as she called it. She rented a caravan in the country and spent every school holiday and weekends at the campsite, a short train journey away, with her children. This was also where she had many friends who supported her and complimented her on coping so well. She was part of a group of 15 couples that met once a week to socialize and to help each other out. They had a babysitter exchange for example. This was a leftover from the way friendships and networks worked before reunification:

> We are still trying to help each other. You know, this neighbourhood network that hardly anyone is familiar with nowadays. Even if this sounds stereotypical; the West Germans should learn from us.

Despite her support network she felt discriminated against and used one example when she used the underground with her four children: ‘People looked at us in the tube and there was one remark: Do not you have another hobby?’ She felt that people looked down at her because she received state benefits and her children were not dressed in branded clothing although she tried to conform and to dress them in more expensive clothes.

At the time of the interview Manuela was retraining as a secretary and learning word processing. She wanted to finish her retraining programme to earn her own money before she would consider marrying her partner. However, both were also aware that they would receive less benefits and fewer tax breaks. She did not think that financially she would be better off in paid employment as she not only received state benefits but also other grants and subsidies for heating and clothing. For the future, she did not rate her chances very high as she thought employers would discriminate against her as a lone mother of four children who had the right to stay at home when the children became ill. However, for now she was happy not to be in paid employment.

She managed financially: 'I can not afford the big things but I can live off that.' She did bemoan the fact that she could not afford many activities for her children because in former East Germany they had either been free or relatively cheap so that everyone could be part of society.

Manuela was a coper and a pioneer. She was a full-time mother by choice. She said about herself: 'I am full of life and have a positive outlook. I am never going to resign to a situation I find myself in.' She did not feel threatened by social services but felt cared for by them and actively co-operated with them. She was very proud of the fact that she managed to raise four children and she felt supported when her friends also complimented her on coping so well. But she was a coper because she sought approval from her friends and relied on them. She felt ambivalent about state benefits but she managed to live on them. She was not in work by choice and enjoyed her word processing course.

Burcu

I met Burcu in the waiting corridors in Hundedorf in West Berlin. She had three children (five years, two years and six months) and lived in a two bedroom flat in a high-rise block of flats on a large housing estate.

Her parents had migrated from Turkey to Berlin and worked in factories. When Burcu was 11 months old her parents sent her brother and her back to Turkey to live with their aunt. For seven years she and her brother moved back and forth between Berlin and Turkey, first going to boarding school in Turkey then finishing primary school in Berlin. She got the German equivalent of GCSE level education and although she wanted to go to college she decided against it. Her family needed some financial support as her father had to retire early for health reasons. Furthermore, her father was very traditional and did not want his daughter in further education. Burcu had to look after the house and her three siblings while her mother was working.

Her family were just too strict and when she turned 18 she moved out to move in with her partner, a Kurd from Iraq. They had a son in the same year. He was also quite traditional and hit her when he became jealous. She was not impressed with the treatment she had from the police: 'When I got hit and went to the police they said: You must know what your men are like. Why do you get yourself a Turkish man?

And after that, I did not bother to go to the police anymore.' When her son was one year old she managed to escape to a refuge.

After the separation she started to socialize but soon felt quite lonely and heartbroken about another man. She had suffered from depression before and this time she tried to kill herself. She also found it very difficult to look after her son and sent him into a home for one year. While her first child was in a home she started to work as a security guard for the American military base. Nevertheless, after one year she had had enough:

> It was hard work. It sends you doolally. You are standing there, in winter the cold and the heat in summer. And shift work and overtime. That wasn't very nice. I did not think it was worth it, to do this sort of thing despite the fact that it was good money. You do not have to think, doing this type of work.

In the meantime she became pregnant from a casual relationship with an Afro-Caribbean American soldier who she did not stay in contact with. She moved into sheltered housing as part of a Mother-Child project and lived there for two years. Here, she started other apprenticeships but she did not like the work enough to leave her two children in a nursery for long days. She had a third child from a partner she was still with, six months later. He was an asylum seeker from an African country and lived near to where he was doing an apprenticeship as a carpenter and she did not want her partner to move in with them.

A social worker from a national charity helped her to get the flat she lived in. The area was considered 'rough' but she liked it because of its many playgrounds. It was also close to many buses and shops and the nursery. With three children now, she would have liked a bigger flat.

The fathers of her children did not pay any maintenance and only her current partner was in contact with their children. Her children liked her new boyfriend and started to call him daddy but Burcu defined herself as a lone mother as she alone was responsible for her children.

Her mother had become more supportive now but kept on telling people that Burcu was divorced. Her father found it difficult to accept that each of his grandchildren had a different father, that she was not married and that one father was Kurdish as to him, all Kurds were terrorists. 'With another family there would have been a quick marriage. But I am not willing to change my life only to make the family happy.' She had a few friends who were also lone mothers but she saw her siblings most often.

Burcu liked sending her children to nursery, where they learned and made friends. Eventually, probably when her last born was about two years old, she contemplated part-time employment, perhaps to become an office clerk. She knew though that employers would be prejudiced against her because she would need to stay at home when the children became ill. Burcu actually liked being pregnant and liked being a mother of young children:

> I like being pregnant and I like having babies, especially when things get difficult or when children get bigger and expect more of me. That's not so good. But I really like being pregnant and did not think about abortion. I couldn't do that. Once I am pregnant I am occupied. I do not know, then I have something for myself somehow. I do not know how

> you can explain this. It a bit like a substitute, an Ersatz. Others overeat, go mad and I like being pregnant. I do not want a fourth child right now but I think whoever can cope with three children, can cope with four too.

State benefits were considered a wage for her mothering despite the fact that she experienced resentment. She knew her rights and she did ask for them:

> The woman at the benefit office doesn't like me and when I told her about the third pregnancy she said: Oh, no, Not that, not again. You should know about contraception by now. And she did not give me the pregnancy allowance that I was entitled to. I had to complain and went to her manager. She wasn't very happy about that and said: You know your rights, that you do know do not you. They have no idea what I have been through.

State benefits also made Burcu feel independent. She was proud about the fact that she did not rely on the fathers, that she could manage with her income and she had become very conscientious, she did not go out socializing anymore and budgeted carefully.

Burcu made the most out of her situation and state benefits were a facilitator for autonomy and independence. She liked being pregnant and having young children even though it may have been an escape, a substitute. She knew her rights and how to find support and she fought for them. She was not in paid work out of choice and because, strictly speaking, she was still on maternity leave and would not consider employment until her youngest was at least two years old. She had not considered further education.

However, she was also a coper. Her social network mattered to her and she relied on the help of her family. Burcu wanted to be accepted by her family but not at all costs. She did not succumb to her parents' pressure to marry and move to Turkey. She viewed her relative deprivation as manageable and budgeted carefully. Like other copers she had a pragmatic outlook on the future. She contemplated having a fourth child and knew that it would be difficult to find part-time employment with young children.

Short biographies of coper/pioneers

Chris, 32, Afro-Caribbean, lived in a suburb in North London with her daughter. She was adopted into a working-class family and used state benefits to become a professional songwriter - she wanted to concentrate on this instead of being in paid employment too. Hence, full-time mothering was viewed as temporary. She had experienced abuse as a child as well as a string of 'bad' relationships. Her life was 'not really about getting a job, paying the gas bill or getting a job to buy my daughter some new shoes.' Becoming a Christian made her feel more secure and gave her more self-esteem partly through a good social network too. She did not feel financially deprived and money was not that important to her: 'you got a roof over your head, you've go a TV, you got a hi-fi, generally you are living quite well, whether you realize it or not.' However, she still lacked self-esteem and would have liked more success in her career. She was also pragmatic. If she did not get a recording contract in the near future she was going to enter education to improve her employment chances.

Lorna, 26, Afro-Caribbean lived in Northington and came from a working-class family with a good family support system which she valued. She coped well with the situation because she felt that in her Afro-Caribbean culture women were stronger than men. She was aware of her rights and how to 'manipulate' the system and managed well on housing and state benefits through careful budgeting. She had a pragmatic outlook. She chose not to be in paid employment so that she could be with her child. Instead, state benefits enabled her to be in higher education that also facilitated mothering. Higher educational qualifications, she felt, would make up for racial discrimination and improve her living standard eventually. Nonetheless, she felt that being a black lone mother was hard.

Christina, 37, white, from West Berlin was born into a middle-class family and had left university without a degree. Her self-identity was that of a professional mother who 'takes time out for herself'. She chose not to be in paid employment and she was not in education. She was optimistic about the future and her ability to find work in art education. Financially she coped well because she did regular casual work. Nonetheless, she felt ambivalent about state benefits and felt discriminated against by family members and friends. At least, she was glad to have good friends.

Heide, 34, white, lived in West Berlin and was on Childrearing Leave from her job as an accountant. She had become pregnant by accident and had had her child because she viewed it as probably her last chance because of her age although she did not love the father who was noncommittal anyway. Motherhood was also viewed as a career break and state benefits were deemed a wage for mothering. She could live on it because she received the Childrearing Benefit. She was not in work by choice for now but she would return to her place of work on a part-time basis in the near future. She could rely on her social network and had not thought about further education. Ideally, she would have liked to conform to a modernized male breadwinner contract, more precisely, a working husband, two children and part-time work.

Julia, 25, white, lived in Katzenhain and used state benefits for her ambitions to be a good mother and to be in education. Higher educational qualifications would help her to find well paid part-time work that fitted within school hours in the near future. For now, she chose not to be in paid work. She had friends and relied on support from the father of her twins. Through his support and gifts she managed alright financially while on state benefits. She contemplated moving back in with her partner who regularly looked after their two daughters. Julia and her partner hid their separation from their friends and neighbours because she was afraid of being stigmatized.

Dora, 25, white, lived in Katzenhain, knew 'how to work the system' and had even supported her former partner in the past with state benefits and casual work. Now she could live well off state benefits because she did some casual work. Benefits facilitated her ambition to pursue her art. She was not in paid employment because of this despite the fact that the Job Centre pressurized her to look for it. She actively created her biography within state benefits as a mother and as an artist. She was also a pragmatist as she had applied to train as a physiotherapist. As a physiotherapist she could 'pay the rent' and view art as a hobby in the future. Friends were very important to her and although she thought that men were 'pathetic' she had the desire to be provided for too.

Chapter 11

Going it Alone? Concluding Discussion

This chapter returns to the questions the research sought to address. First, how do lone mothers negotiate their lives as mothers and as dependants? Secondly, can state-dependent lone motherhood be experienced as a liberating experience? Thirdly, to what extent can the thesis of individualization explain the experience of state-dependent lone mothers? The chapter then considers some social policy implications which could increase lone mothers' choices. Recommendations with regard to paid employment, education and state benefits derive from specific suggestions made by interviewees and from conclusions drawn from the findings.

How do lone mothers negotiate their lives as mothers and dependants?

The analysis of in-depth-interviews with 70 mothers maps out the diversity and dynamics of state-dependent lone motherhood and demonstrates that lone mothers are neither a homogenous nor a static group. The research findings suggest that constraints are not the overriding influence in the lives of these women and the shaping of self-identity is not merely a reaction to structural circumstances. 'Poor' lone mothers are able to negotiate their life satisfactorily despite certain constraints such as state benefit dependency and mothering alone. State-dependent mothering may be seen as a source of pride and power and not necessarily as a source of oppression. Hence, state-dependent lone motherhood can be 'promising' as well as 'threatening', as the concept of individualization predicts.

The analysis of specific social policies and state benefits of the East and West German and British welfare states have revealed country specific differences. These can be traced to the ideological and historical development of the respective welfare states. For example, different cultural developments in East and West Germany are discussed (see chapter 4). In Germany, lone mothers are treated differently according to the age of the child. Mothers with small children are financially rewarded for staying at home while mothers with older children are financially punished and expected to be in educational or vocational training or in paid employment. Nonetheless, policies do not accommodate full-time employment and so, lone mothers remain in some form of dependency. In Britain, state benefits do not change with the age of the child and social policies that encourage lone mothers into paid employment have yet to prove themselves. Hence, lone motherhood can be considered a residual social category in social policy. These mothers are neither positioned as workers nor carers but as dependants in both, the reunited Germany and more so in Britain.

Although lone mothers can be 'defamiliarised' - that is to gain autonomy from a marriage or partnership - means tested benefits are not comparable with the security full-time paid employment provides. For these reasons, we can also speak of a 'limited' individualization.

How lone mothers negotiate their lives as mothers is inseparable from their views on paid employment. Most mothers interviewed were in paid employment prior to having children, are planning to go back to paid employment eventually and view their dependence on state benefits as only temporary. One reason for being out of employment are gendered moral rationalities that influence views on good mothering. Nonetheless, this concept under-emphasizes individual agency, altruism and self-interest in mothering. I have not found one mother who could not enter paid employment because her social network would not support her decision (see chapter 3).

This research has enabled the identification of 'socially-acceptable' and 'socially-objectionable' reasons for being out of employment. In addition to the labour market and the number and age of their children, London lone mothers tend to give socially acceptable reasons such as the cost of childcare and high rents while Berlin lone mothers problematize inflexible childcare, the lack of flexible work and employer discrimination. Many lone mothers in this study have a strong desire for education for personal and professional reasons. The research argues that lone mothers may use socially-acceptable reasons to justify their full-time mothering orientation and situation or to cover up socially-objectionable reasons such as wanting to be a professional mother of a child that already goes to school or lack of confidence (see chapter 5).

The concept of individualization is useful for explaining that mothering is not a fixed traditional role but that there are several possibilities that are negotiated in a do-it-yourself biography. Everyone is obliged to create their own biography within their different constraints as there are no more universal certainties and no more fixed models of life. Nonetheless, new distinctive patterns and processes could be deciphered and several concepts of how mothers negotiated their lives as mothers emerged from the data.

First, the research identified the 'professional mother' who commits herself to her child and who views childrearing as a profession as well as self-realization, more explicitly as a career break or as a time to reconsider personal and professional goals. Here, motherhood becomes a profession in the desire to further the development of the child as well as giving a complete new self-identity. Moreover, state benefits acts as an enabler, a choice (see chapter 5).

Secondly, the 'serial mother' has several children with different fathers. Reasons for this appeared to be the search for intimacy, love, stability and security. Pregnancy was considered as improving self-worth and giving birth was often seen as the only achievement currently possible. These types of mothers were distinguishable from others because here full-time mothering was both the main interest and the supplier of self-identity. Thirdly, there were the mothers who pursued education for professional or personal reasons. Education also bridged unemployment and accommodated mothering.

The main focus of the book lies in the creation and application of type categories. The 'pioneer', 'coper' and the 'struggler' types are based on lone mothers' coping strategies, identity and confidence. While pioneers felt self-fulfilled, copers viewed their situation as temporary and improvable. A couple of strugglers felt overwhelmed by constraints and perceived themselves to have no choices. Their do-it-yourself biography had turned into a breakdown biography. This book has also shown that lone mothers' lives are complex and dynamic and moreover, they are transitory and not fixed but changeable. Mothers who have characteristics of two different categories are categorised as 'borderliners'.

Pioneers are an 'ideal fit' with the concept of individualization as they possess the traits that are most useful in today's society. Pioneers are able to organise, initiate and to adapt to changes in a do-it-yourself biography. For copers and strugglers, their situation was the problematic result of modernization, a symptom of the increased difficulties in conforming with the traditional nuclear family or finding flexible well-paid work. They aspired to the traditional male breadwinner/ female homemaker or a modernized version of this, where the mother would work part-time. The coper and the struggler thus live a temporary lifestyle that is found problematic. This would mean that the British social problem discourse has its place in lone mother research. However, state-dependent lone mothers do not fit into a so called 'dependency culture' or 'welfarization' that focuses on a life-long state dependency. For the vast majority, entering motherhood was the reason for entry into state dependency, not unemployment. Lone mothers envisaged that state benefits may be substituted by a male breadwinner and/or paid employment income in the future.

Type categorization in Berlin and London

The women interviewed in West Berlin were concentrated along the coper continuum as most found it difficult to find a flexible job or appropriate childcare and felt stigmatized (see table A.1). They struggled financially when they no longer received the Childrearing Benefit. Moreover, in some cases the Job Centre pressured them into finding paid employment while, paradoxically, social institutions encouraged mothers to place childrearing above participation in the labour market. The women interviewed in West Berlin also tended to be from a working-class background while the East Berlin mothers tended to be from a middle-class background and were younger too. Type categorization may be related to mothers' specific gendered moral rationalities. The women in East Berlin were more satisfied with their lives than West Berlin mothers because they tended to concentrate on their own education or mothering, did not feel stigmatized and most did not report childcare problems. This view may be a leftover from their socialist East German past, which provided childcare, did not discriminate against lone mothers and encouraged women in education and paid work (see chapter 4). At the same time, lone mothers in East Berlin may have been more self-actualized because of their higher educational qualifications and norms and values that stemmed from their upbringing in East Germany before reunification.

In London, individualization may possibly be related to low expectations as lone mothers perceived barriers to paid employment. This may be connected with the fact that the mothers interviewed there came from a working-class background and had few educational qualifications and work experience. Giddens (1991, 86) may be correct in assuming that in some circumstances of poverty, the hold of tradition has perhaps become even more thoroughly disintegrated than elsewhere and the creative construction of lifestyles may become a particularly characteristic feature. In other words, state-dependent lone mothers in London may have had a more flexible approach to their biographies than lone mothers in West Berlin.

Pioneers were only found among East Berlin and London mothers. The mothers interviewed in East Berlin appeared to have more in common with London lone mothers than with West Berlin lone mothers. London mothers' ideological notions of 'satisfaction' have to be considered as it could be that British women rate it highly and this disposition makes them perceive their lives as more meaningful, comprehensible and manageable. Alternatively, London and East Berlin mothers may have constructed their identity differently from West Berlin mothers by emphasising their strength rather than their weaknesses. However, it seems entirely plausible that lone mothers in London have figured out strategies to increase their own feeling of self-worth by entering education or by professionalizing motherhood to compensate for the fact that they are not well regarded in society.

Two London mothers were categorized as strugglers as they felt overwhelmed by constraints and perceived themselves to have no choices. This may be partly informed by mental health issues and domestic violence experiences. Giddens (1992) suggests the importance of social circumstances in childhood that create the necessary psychological conditions for trust in others. The interviews appear to support this but suggest that further research is warranted (see chapter 9). The two strugglers may have been most 'at risk' of life-long state dependency. State dependency here was not a result of lone motherhood but also of other inter-related problems such as depression, drug dependency, homelessness and state-dependent parents. Other research confirms that life-long unemployment tends to run in families (Brannen 1998, 81). Instead of welfare-to-work programmes, psycho-social care in the community may be more suitable to improve the situation of these strugglers.

Can state-dependent lone motherhood be experienced as a liberating experience?

This book has shown that state benefit lone motherhood can be a liberating experience, but seldom is. In this study, few mothers are pioneers and the majority are centred around the coper type category and a couple of mothers are strugglers.

This research indicates that structural factors alone do not predict the perception of state-dependent lone motherhood as a 'self-realization'. However, they may well facilitate them because gender has to be qualified by race, class and ethnicity (Okin 1995, 274). Statistical significance is not suggested here but looking at possible relationships between social class and type categorization helps to systematize new developments in lone motherhood. While individualization may not be limited to certain social classes this research gives an indication that class matters. For future research it may be valuable to look into the continued relevance of social class and the concept of individualization (see chapter 3).

In this study, middle-class lone mothers were more distributed around the pioneer or pioneer/coper type categories. Working-class lone mothers centred around the coper or adjacent border categories (see table A. 2). The mothers in the pioneer type category were also all white, the oldest and the best educated of all the mothers interviewed. They only ever had one child and tended to have a long employment record and a relatively short record of receiving state benefits. One woman with five children was the exception. The two struggler types were both white and had no educational qualifications as well as young children. Both have experienced state dependency prior to the birth of their children.

It seems that middle-class women may be able to perceive state benefits more positively because they are better equipped in using the welfare state as a 'tool' to suit their lifestyle. Their confidence may be facilitated by educational qualifications and work experience. The pioneers and the coper/pioneers have adapted to their situation and seek their own satisfaction strategically by using those parts of the formal institutional structure that are advantageous, and finding ways around the rules and regulations that limit them. However, the women who use state benefits as a tool to live out their idea of individualization pay a high price. Their caring work is unrecognized, they are poor, alone with their children and are disadvantaged in comparison to people with a continuous employment record.

Lone mothers' perception of their situation improved when they thought of state benefits as enabling. Some mothers preferred state payments over living with the father of the children because the state is more reliable and they valued the certainty and relative security of state benefits. It makes regular, fixed payments, it is not violent and it does not disappoint expectations over the division of domestic and caring labour because it refuses to take any role in it. For example, middle-class East Berlin women used state benefits to enter education for their personal and professional development. Here, state benefits have become a resource for the active creation of an individual's biography. In other words, state benefits have been transformed from a constraint into a choice, in people's perceptions. London and East Berlin lone mothers who are concentrated around the pioneer or borderline type because typical constraints happen to overlap with their priorities to actively negotiate their biography.

The East Berlin lone mothers in the pioneer category welcomed the freedom to choose full-time mothering, an artistic career and education over having to be in paid employment. Before reunification, East Germany's bureaucratic state collective system promoted female employment to promote gender equality. Mothers combined mothering and paid employment and this was facilitated by child friendly policies, comprehensive childcare and other subsidies. However, there were also East Berlin mothers who felt compelled to take over the role of a full-time mother because of decreasing labour market opportunities. In other words, both the concept of a 'New Modernity' and of a 'retraditionalization' have their place (see chapter 4).

State-dependent lone motherhood can be experienced as a liberating experience when the lone mother is flexible and embraces change rather than being afraid of it. She may not have the means to determine their life but she takes the fragmentation of their biography in their stride and welcomes the opportunity to 'collect experiences' as Bauman (1996, 18) has described it. In comparison, the coper or struggler type may not use state benefits and lone motherhood to collect experiences but views them as temporary, as she has a psychological need for ontological security and prefers a stable view of the world and herself.

In order to become a pioneer, it is necessary to view ones own situation as an opportunity to construct biographies in non-traditional ways. This fits into the concept of individualization. Here, typical constraints such as state dependency and living alone may even be viewed as enabling. The pioneer re-evaluates the meaning of state benefit dependency by treating it as a legitimate source of income for looking after her child full-time or as a grant for furthering her education or her artistic career. Her self-identity proved most successful in coping with the stigma attached with state dependence and with relative deprivation. She experienced her situation as a part of a growing diversity in family life which mirrors other shifts and changes in wider society and not as an individual misfortune. Perhaps she is spearheading a lifestyle that makes us rethink the value modern societies have given to paid work.

Rethinking paid work

It was one aim of this book has been to understand the lives of state-dependent lone mothers without an agenda that valorises paid work and devalues domestic and caring work. Paid employment has long been seen as the route to responsibility and respectability for men. But in the 20th century, apart from the war effort of the 1940s, it is partly a result of second wave feminism that most women have come to see employment, rather than child-rearing and domestic responsibilities, as the route to self-fulfilment and citizenship, and as their duty and responsibility (Power 2005). This is also the underlying logic of the British and to an extent the German governments.

Instead, this research suggests that feminism, rather than focus its energy on paid work, should focus on re-evaluating unpaid work. Many mothers in this study have already made this re-evaluation because their concept of good mothering involves caring for their child themselves. Some have done it more successfully than others who may be more concerned about being stigmatized. State-dependent lone motherhood may offer an alternative refuge from the working world, where it is imperative to behave responsibly, and emotions are generally considered a nuisance. If domestic and caring work is as highly regarded as paid work and can lead to full citizenship, then both become providers of self-worth and more women as well as men may want to do it.

Hence, not to participate in paid employment can be interpreted as both traditional and emancipatory. British feminists are now also critical about paid work as the promoter of gendered equality. Crompton and Le Feuvre (1996, 437) conclude that 'the world of work still remains a sphere in which relations of male domination and female subordination are maintained and reproduced.' Other feminist research also demonstrates that paid work is plagued by gendered inequality (Bruegel and Perrons 1996, 2; Ginn et al 1996, 167; Macran et al 1996). For example, the pay gap indicates that women are not treated equal to men in the labour market (Thomas and Klett-Davies 1995). Lone mothers in particular have difficulty fitting into a masculine model of employment of continuous and full-time work. Lone mothers' weaker position in the labour market is characterized by their low status and low pay which is re-enforced by the part-time hours and the sectors lone mothers work in (see chapter 2). This research has shown that there are perceived and experienced barriers to paid employment such as employment discrimination, lack of well-paid part-time work and the lack of comprehensive and public childcare (see chapter 5).

The poverty trap is a major barrier, as paid employment may not necessarily improve lone mothers' economic and social situation and this may be related to their educational and vocational qualifications. However, even well qualified full-time working lone mothers in the Swedish welfare state must rely on social assistance to supplement their income. In other words, even if lone mothers work, they remain dependent. Therefore, Western governments have exaggerated paid work as a guarantee for social inclusion and as the only form of work of value to society (Lister 2000, 40). While the research presented here is not idealising the private sphere it does challenge the boundaries of the public and the private spheres that so obviously work against the interests of women.

It is not enough to promote social policies that support full-time parenting and/or paid work. Instead, there is a need for significant cultural change that increases the value of unpaid work for everyone and develops a new concept of social inclusion that combines the pursuit of social justice with a recognition of and respect for pluralistic diversity (Stewart 2000, 10). The research supports Lister's (2000, 42) proposal that strategies to promote social inclusion are to be located 'within a broader analysis of inequality and polarization both inside and outside the labour market.' The model of citizenship has to be rethought to incorporate the claims of diverse groups without sacrificing its universalistic principles. Here, education can be a key weapon in the attack on social exclusion as well as central to promoting equality of opportunity (Lister 2000, 46). Moreover, not only mothering but also voluntary activities can be seen as strengthening 'social capital'. The research concurs with Lister (2000, 51) in that social exclusion 'has to be tackled at both the material and the symbolic level and across a range of dimensions of inequalities'. This book refrains from assumptions about 'what is good for women' and it does not essentialise women as nurturers, but argues for 'choice' and for 'caring' to become more of a feature.

The research recommends social policies that are open to diversity, that accommodate difference and give women choices, to work full-time, to look after their children full-time and to combine the two during their life course. It is based on lone mothers' complete choice on what they want to do. It is the government's responsibility to ensure that all lone parents can maintain a decent standard of living and good opportunities for career progression regardless of the choices they make regarding work and parenting.

There are additional reasons for giving people the choice of paid work. As a result of the development of the post-industrial economy, well paid and secure employment cannot be taken for granted anymore. In capitalist and post-industrialist societies, secure full employment may have become a utopian thought (Beck 1998a, 13; Bowring 1999, 69; Sennett 1998). Bauman (2000, 77) uses the term 'Zwei Drittel

Gesellschaft' (two-third-society) to explain that only two thirds of society are needed to satisfy market demand. 'Soon one third will be enough, leaving the rest of men and women without employment, making them economically useless and socially redundant.' (Bauman 2000, 77). In other words, there is just not enough work for everybody, although critics view this as highly speculative (Giddens 1987, 291). On this basis, mothers and fathers who would prefer to look after their children full-time or part-time should be given a choice. However, as long as paid employment is viewed as the key to social integration, prejudices about the non-working population are being re-enforced as state benefit dependency is connected with moral failure and social stigma. This together with a strategy that is predicated on the paid work ethic contributes to the devaluation of mothering, that is the unpaid work of reproduction and care, mostly conducted by women.

The idea that inclusion in the labour force cannot be the one and only precondition for integration into society is not new. Offe (1994a and 1994b), Beck (1997, 51 and 1998, 13) and Lister (2000) have suggested a citizen's income or a basic income scheme, 'under which every citizen would receive a tax-free income with no strings attached.' (Lister 2000, 49). Here, individual income is not dependent on paid employment but on citizenship. It is able to acknowledge all types of work - such as caring, domestic, community and voluntary work – and is able to include all types of citizens, including state-dependent lone mothers. A similar version is Giddens's (1987, 295) 'time policy' that regards being 'out of work' as a gain rather than as a loss for the individual.

Pioneers and the pioneer/copers in the borderline category are ahead of the cultural developments as they have already started re-conceptualizing state benefits to fit their biography. They have rethought citizenship in the sense that they treat state benefits as a citizen's income. In other words, they already live this utopian idea to an extent. State benefits are also being used to finance artistic careers or to enter education, which is viewed as a key weapon against an inequality of opportunities. Although the pioneer type is in a minority, this book has thoroughly investigated it because it highlights new central and theoretically relevant patterns: 'Minorities can be forerunners and new majorities do not necessarily lead to changes that can be described as reflexively modern.' (Beck, Bonß and Lau 2003, 33). Nonetheless, the next section concentrates in more detail on the more tangible social policies that emerged from the data.

Social policy implications

Implementing appropriate social policies alone might not create more pioneers. This study has shown that the pioneer appears to cope better because she perceives her current life stage as meaningful, comprehensible and manageable in what some might regard as a 'precarious' situation. It implies that mothers' changes in attitudes – by adopting a non-consumerist attitude or a professional mother orientation – increase lone mothers' confidence and identity. In addition, comprehensive social policies would increase self-image and the living standard of most lone mothers and also that of their children.

Strugglers and copers and especially the women in the border categories coper/struggler feel constrained. Women in the borderline categories may be most receptive to social policies as there are factors that stop them moving into a more 'desirable' type category. Also, the borderline categories are especially relevant for social policy as they show the dynamics and the transitions of the women between the categories. The factors that stop women in the border categories from moving into another category are the availability, quality and cost of childcare, lack of interesting and well-paid part-time and full-time work, employer discrimination, lack of educational qualifications, depression, health, low self-esteem, debts and the lack of knowledge of benefits available to them. The type categories also show that different types of lone mothers have various orientations and different needs with regards to education for example.

This investigation makes an argument for choice as state-dependent lone mothers are a dynamic and heterogeneous group. Some lone mothers respondents, especially the coper/strugglers, want to be in employment but cannot find suitable work while others prefer to be full-time mothers temporarily and others invest in their education. By listening to lone mothers' experiences we can understand the mechanisms of how social policy in practice works and simultaneously learn how mothers create meaning and make sense of their situation. For social policies to be effective, they have to try to develop supportive and flexible legislative frameworks which do recognize the varying ways in which people take decisions and the following sections of the chapter explores the ideas that came up as a part of the data analysis.

Paid employment

While paid employment provides lone mothers with increased life chances it is questionable whether they will be able to break free from dependency. Chapter four highlighted that in Britain, the state of the economy is much more relevant to women's labour market integration than welfare-to-work programmes.

In Germany, the two-year Childrearing Benefit and a three-year Childrearing Leave – now Parent Time – primarily encourages mothering. Nonetheless, fathers are now encouraged to take at least part of that leave and mothers can stay connected with the labour market because they are allowed to work up to 30 hours a week within this leave. However, employers have shown an outright prejudice against mothers with children who want to work because first, they feel that mothers should look after their children instead and secondly, they consider a mother less reliable because she is entitled to sick leave to look after her children. Here, the German anti-discrimination law needs to be enforced stricter.

European work place regulations that allow parents to reduce their hours of work are already in place. These have to be compatible with parents' domestic life and not in the evening, at night and at weekends. If these conditions were to become a legal right, then employees may no longer have to trade flexibility with lower pay and men may be tempted to reduce their hours too. Employers are said to also benefit from reduced sickness absence and improved retention rates as well as increased productivity, morale and commitment (Hogarth et al 2000).

For these work place regulations to be successful, childcare has to be developed. In Britain, the Labour government has gone some way to accepting responsibility and developed tax credits. It implemented the National Childcare Strategy aimed at reducing child poverty by increasing the number of childcare facilities and by making this free for all three-year olds. This is similar to Germany, where every three-year old has a right to a part-time nursery place. Instead of focussing on childcare as a vehicle to enable lone mothers to go to work, this research recommends emphasis on high-quality care as a vehicle for closing the educational achievement gap between rich and poor pupils. The emphasis needs to be on high quality childcare that does not harm the psychological development of a young child. This suggestion is a result of finding that particularly in Germany, there is the persistent psychological assumption that the first years are the most important in a child's life where the mother belongs to the child and not in paid employment. Nonetheless, some mothers may still prefer to look after their children full-time and this choice needs to be accommodated too by formalizing their un-paid work.

Childrearing

It emerged from the data that some of those interviewed, in particular the pioneers, already treat state transfers as a legitimate source of income for caring for their child full-time. If this wage was more formalized, it could increase every lone mothers' self-worth and reward women's unpaid domestic and caring work for raising the next generation of future tax payers. For example, the German Parent Time could be increased and paid instead of both Childrearing Benefit and state benefits.

Of course, there are downsides to this. The longer lone mothers are out of work, the more disadvantaged they are at re-entry level. This could partly be combated by educational and vocational training. Mothers with qualifications can expect to move progressively towards financial self-sufficiency but this brings us to the second point. Caring policies may reinforce gender divisions as they are mostly taken up by women. Social policies that encourage fathers to take up parental leave may not be enough to change deep-rooted gendered behaviour but may well accommodate pioneering families that initiate cultural change. However, pioneering families together with policies that make the labour market more attractive to women and caring work more attractive to men, may well accelerate massive cultural change.

Existing policies such as the Child Support Agency in Britain have not greatly contributed in increasing fathers' financial responsibilities and have not attempted to influence their caring abilities. This research recommends to define the citizenship concept in such a way that it redistributes the caring duties. If men and women are to share them equally they will experience the same consequences and this will pave a new way for organizing paid and unpaid work. In this respect, a less extreme but more democratic and tangible policy could be to instruct the Job Centre to advise whole families rather than just the father or just the mother. A balance between caring and paid work may be established through the consideration of a person's lifetime development. As a result, lone fathers or shared custody will perhaps become more common because it will be no longer taken for granted that the children stay with their mother. Fathers or step-fathers could also be encouraged to care for children by not cutting fathers nor lone mothers' state benefits when they move in together. This research has found that some lone mothers refrain from moving in with their male partner because of the detrimental effect it has on their own state benefits. Here, benefits could be recalculated to encourage 'living-together' rather than 'living-together-apart'. This would also translate into the increased availability of public housing stock.

Education

Education fulfils various functions and has several meanings. Some lone mothers chose to be in education for their professional or personal development while others use it to bridge unemployment. Colleges and universities are often perceived to be more interesting, less time-consuming and therefore more accommodating towards mothering than paid employment. By entering education, state dependence is not regarded as a personal failure but more positively as enabling. This in turn leads to the confidence of applying for jobs. Obviously, there is a risk that once these mothers come out of education, employers may perceive them as too old and too expensive as well as over-qualified and under-experienced. But for that there are already equal opportunities policies in place. On the other hand, the children of those parents will need less childcare and qualifications may improve mothers' likelihood to become gradually economically independent. Chapter four has shown that the time on state benefits is reduced for mothers with higher educational qualifications as they can enter decently paid employment that tends to be interesting. Hence, investment in education reduces future public expenditure in state benefits.

Again, lone mothers are a heterogeneous group with different needs that may be difficult for social policy to facilitate. Some mothers require specific training to increase their chances of being employed in a specific job. While some want to achieve basic qualifications, other mothers pursue A levels or a degree to find self-fulfilment and financial independence in their future employment or in their personal life. Nonetheless, they have in common that they need state benefits and childcare.

Most mothers' lives can be enhanced by social policies, employers and workplace regulations that improve the accessibility to education, paid work and childcare. It seems that women fare best when benefits are distributed on the principles of citizenship and care, particularly when they are combined with the practical possibility of employment, as is the case in Sweden. Although these policies may not immediately advance gendered equality they nonetheless increase the opportunities for women's individualization.

To what extent can the thesis of individualization explain the experience of state-dependent lone mothers?

The thesis of individualization can explain some aspects of the experience of lone mothers. This study has shown that lone mothers are dynamic and diverse and this is reflected in the perception of state dependency. State dependency reflects the world of modernity as a whole as it entails danger and new opportunity (Giddens

1991, 12). State dependency entails danger because of its association with poverty and stigmatization but it can also be an opportunity for full-time motherhood and personal and professional reorientation.

The interviews that were conducted for this study have shown that lone mothers are being reshaped by the forces of individualization and democratization, but it remains to be established how much change there has been in this direction and what is driving it. State-dependent lone motherhood is also expression of continuity and lack of freedom. This study throws up the a new line of enquiry that has been to a degree discussed by Crompton (2005) and Smart and Shipman (2004). To what extent are lone mothers' lives still linked to 'old' constraints such as social class, gender, ethnicity and other structural factors?

Individualization suggests that lone motherhood is a result of improving women's choices through their increasing economic independence and social change. It is true that the welfare state furthers the process of individualization and is not limited to the higher social classes as critics have made out (see chapter 3). However, class and other traditional constraints seem to matter much more than the thesis of individualization gives them credit for. For example, never-married and state-dependent lone mothers tend to be working-class, particularly in Britain and this may indicate a polarization of life forms. While the type categorization developed in this research shows that state benefits can enable mothers from various backgrounds to become pioneers it nonetheless indicates a relationship with social class that warrants further research. Bauman states: 'all of us are doomed to the life of choices, but not all of us have the means to be choosers' (1998, 86).

Lone mothers' individualization is not only limited but there is also considerable variation in the way state-benefit-dependent lone mothers live their lives, with different degrees of limited individualization. In late modernity, difference, exclusion and marginalization are continuously being reproduced. First, lone mothers may have been given the freedom *from* an unequal relationship but their freedom *to* have a relationship based on equality is limited. Secondly, lone mothers may have given the freedom from being dependent on a male breadwinner by being able to receive state benefits instead but their freedom *to* secure their livelihood through paid work is limited while the accreditation of unpaid work is limited too. Thirdly, women may have the freedom *to* participate in public life but as mothers they are expected to nurture in the private sphere and to compensate for the results of modernization by providing a 'safe haven'. Mothers are expected to 'devote' themselves to the children and 'sacrifice' their individualization at least in parts. Therefore, traditional constraints still have a hold on individual's lives as well as social and gendered inequality. This is what this research means by limited individualization.

Individualization has been criticized for depicting a vision of a family that is culturally monochrome and where whole cultures move into certain directions of detraditionalization, sharing the same values and practices (see chapter 3). This study has also found that individualization does not happen in a culturally monochrome way and that cultural backgrounds are an important factor in type categorization. Some lone mothers are in the coper or struggler category because they have difficulties in negotiating two different cultures successfully, as in the case of the Turkish mothers in Berlin and the Greek mothers in London who grew up in two different cultures.

The same can be said about mothers whose children have fathers from a different ethnic background. Here, cultural norms and expectations do not overlap and make life less manageable, comprehensible and meaningful.

As a result of modernization, mothers' educational qualifications may have improved but their labour market choices have not. Motherhood and paid employment are difficult to combine because of a masculine model of employment, coupled with the lack of childcare provision and a lack of fathers' involvement in childcare. Lone mothers on state benefits suffer from the withdrawal or curtailment of established rights as a result of the contraction of national welfare systems. Therefore, this research argues that individualization has so far been more beneficial to men than to women and that lone mothers' individualization is limited also because of the persistence of social inequality.

The concept of individualization could almost be construed as serving an ideological purpose in shaping perspectives about life. For example, single mothers may think that they have equality and choice but ignore the ways in which gender and class continue to structure opportunities. Individualization can almost be thought of as disempowering those whose lives are more structurally constraint than others (Brannen and Nilsen 2005, 424). Individualization is misleading insofar as it suggests an 'individual consciousness' which can be described as a form of blindness to those social conditions and processes on which individuals have little control. In fact, human beings recognize that there are phenomena that impinge on people's lives that are beyond individual control.

The interviews are evidence for a limited detraditionalization – or a modernized traditionalization - as many mothers seek a modernized male breadwinner model with increased equalities but not a role reversal. Many mothers would like to be provided for and be with a breadwinner who is committed and responsible. Some women have separated because their partners were not traditional enough because they did not fulfil the role as a committed and responsible carer and provider. It seems also that too much is expected of the family because it has become an institution laden with concepts of love, harmony and happiness that give it mythical dimensions. This is in line with the thesis of individualization. State benefits can be experienced as a substitute without the stresses of negotiating a relationship. In theory, these women have an 'idea' of gendered equality but this does not translate into the desire to work full-time and be financially independent while the children are still young. Therefore, the concept of individualization is wrong to assume that first, women want to escape patriarchal structures while ignoring their contribution to them and secondly, women put financial independence before caring for their children. However, Beck and Beck-Gernsheim would argue that a negotiation of roles alone is already a result of the process of individualization and it presents the dilemma between the consequences of the detraditionalization and traditionalization, and between self-fulfilment and family obligations.

The book also suggests that we should not assume a divide between self-fulfilment and family obligation. In this study, pioneers, copers and strugglers placed enormous importance on family ties and obligations to their children. Rather than perceiving this as evidence for their limited individualisation it shows that their lives are always relational and never individualistic. This is independent of their type categorization as a pioneer or a struggler. In other words, self-fulfilled pioneers still identify themselves as mothers who care for their children. Instead of individualisation, that valorises self-actualisation though paid-work and an individualistic experience, we can talk of a *different* individualisation for these women.

While the concept of individualization is not suited to explain the relationship experiences of lone mothers, it is useful for describing the process of negotiation. The interviews show that lone mothers negotiate their roles. Lone mothers seem to take a reflexive, individual and pragmatic approach to their biography that combines traditional and emancipatory roles. Full-time mothering can be interpreted as traditional or modern or both. Perhaps we should accept the simultaneous existence of detraditionalization and traditionalization and their mutual implication rather than thinking of them in oppositional terms (Adam 1996, 135). It is also no longer clear cut what constitutes traditional nor modern behaviour because everything has to be negotiated. For example, the resistance to paid employment may be evaluated as an escape from some aspects of public patriarchy, such as the masculine model of employment. Paradoxically, this 'radical feminist' viewpoint can also be informed by the traditional view of the female homemaker and carer. Therefore, women negotiate their lives within both traditional views and non-traditional views. However, even a personal commitment to full-time mothering may not hinder a women from supporting other mothers who are in employment. The liberal thinking according to the motto 'each to their own' may be the strongest evidence for the demise of tradition that is part of the individualization thesis.

The individualization thesis highlights that actions are now open to different interpretations. For example, some mothers may be resigned to mothering in the private sphere because they cannot find suitable employment while others professionalize it. Women with lack of educational qualifications and work experience may perceive full-time mothering as an alternative career and prefer it to a low-skilled and low-paid job that would give little satisfaction. Other women may welcome state-dependent full-time mothering as a career break and a break away from a former identity as a worker. This break can be supported by Bauman (1996) who has argued that in the post-modern era people are incessant seekers of experiences to escape binding identities. He evokes the image of the tourist as appropriate to life-strategies for identity building.

Individualization explains changing family patterns because it encapsulates the biographical uncertainties and dilemmas. It shows that the family is changing but not disappearing and that we have to broaden our understanding of it. Moreover, the individualization concept emphasizes that lifestyles are not viewed as predictable but are constructed as a do-it-yourself biography. This research has developed this concept further and shown that how a lone mother negotiates her situation depends on the individual's perception of choices, not just 'practical action'. State-dependent lone mothers experience more than just constraints and do more than fulfil a role as a carer. Lone motherhood is not just a question of material resources and it is simplifying to distinguish mothers into either 'lone mothers by choice' or 'lone mothers in poverty' because both and more has become evident in this study.

The interviews with lone mothers show that there is no longer a clear line between tradition and its demise, between the advantaged and the disadvantaged. Boundaries cease to be givens and state dependency can be viewed as a liberating as well as a comforting experience. These experiences extend beyond nation states and lone mothers in the German and the British welfare state. However, while many premises have changed, freedom and equality is shaped by social institutions and some premises of the first modernity stay coercive, such as class, ethnicity and gender. It is the mother who lives with the children and middle-class mothers with higher qualifications are able to command higher wages. Beck and Beck-Gernsheim know that inequalities do not disappear but they emphasize that instead they are redefined in terms of an individualization of social risks, in terms of psychological dispositions. Social classes have been pushed into the background with the individual having find their own rules. This study has documented how individuals find these rules.

My categorization shows mothers in the pioneer type category incorporate most character traits that are relevant for succeeding in today's society according to the concept of individualization. They perceive their lives on state benefits as most meaningful, comprehensible and manageable. It appears that pioneers are not only mothers who realize their choices but mothers who are able to change their identity to sustain a positive self-image within their constraints. Pioneers are women who are able to reinterpret their situation to create a more satisfying alternative identity – that of a professional lone mother on state benefits. Therefore, the research has focussed not on the realization of choice but has categorised mothers who embrace change in a positive way and who are flexible with their identities, as long as it does not impinge on their relationship with their children. Pioneers collect experiences as part of a reflexive biography and as an opportunity for renewed narrative movement in identity building. They have initiative, ability and are not easily discouraged and are self-realized.

It seems that pioneers go it alone. They use the situation to make it suit their needs and wishes and value the time spent out of paid employment. They are spearheading a new lifestyle and lead a life contrary to policies in the UK and to an extent in Germany which currently prioritize paid work. This book has shown how lone mothers could be enabled to follow the lead of pioneers in our society so that they do not have to go it alone.

Appendix

The Berlin and the London Interviewees

It was my criteria that lone mothers had to be never-married, state-dependent, not in paid employment and with young, mostly pre-school children. I interviewed 70 lone mothers dependent on state benefits in London throughout a three-year period from 1996 to 1998. Of 35 from Berlin, 19 interviewees lived in East Berlin and 16 lived in West Berlin.

Lone mothers were between 18 and 44 years old but their age average varies slightly. In this research, lone mothers in the London group were oldest with 30 years on average and they also had the oldest children. In Berlin, the average age was 28. These age distributions compared well with national statistics .

The majority of lone mothers had one child only. Lone mothers in London tended to have more children than lone mothers in the Berlin group (1.66 and 1.34 children respectively). Mothers in London were slightly older than in Berlin and this may explain why they had not only more but also older children. The children in London were older too with 41 per cent being of school age in contrast to Berlin where the proportion of school aged children was only 29 per cent.

London lone mothers were more likely to come from an working-class background than lone mothers in Berlin (29/35 and 21/35). Most Berlin lone mothers also possessed at least basic educational qualifications in comparison to London lone mothers. Only four mothers had no educational qualifications in Berlin. In keeping with national statistics, almost a third of single lone mothers in London had no educational qualification (10/35). Perhaps partly because of their lack of qualifications and the number and age of children, the London mothers had the shortest work experience before their pregnancy.

The proportion of ethnic minorities in deprived parts of large cities is higher than elsewhere in the country and so was the number of ethnic minority lone mothers in London (13/35). Other research found that West Indian women are five times more likely than whites to be lone mothers (Rowlingson and McKay 1998, 48). Almost half (6/14) of the ethnic minorities in London were Afro-Caribbean, and the remainder African (3/14) or came from mixed parentage (4/14). It was surprising to find out about the ethnic mix of lone mothers' children. Of all first born children almost half had two ethnicities (19/35). For example, eight white lone mothers had a child from fathers who are Afro-Caribbean, African, Greek, Turkish or from another other country. In Berlin, all but two Turkish mothers from West Berlin were white and had German citizenship. The 19 lone mothers who lived in East Berlin grew up in the former socialist German Democratic Republic (GDR), mostly in East Berlin, and were all white.

The lone mothers I have interviewed in East Berlin were different from the lone mothers in West Berlin in some other aspects too. Lone mothers in West Berlin were more equally distributed across all age groups and had the least as well as the youngest children. They tended to come from a working-class background (13/16), left school with a basic level of education and had the longest paid employment record of all. In comparison, lone mothers in East Berlin were the youngest group. They also tended to have one child only that was still pre-school age. East Berlin lone mothers came from a more middle-class background (11/19) and most had left school with the basic level of education. This could have been a result of the social acceptance of lone parenthood in former East Germany.

When comparing and contrasting the Berlin and the London interviewees it appears that London mothers came from a working-class background and had the least educational and vocational qualifications and least work experience. They were also the oldest group with the most children, although their youngest children were still below school age. The West Berlin lone mothers were not that dissimilar to the London lone mothers with regards to class background but the vast majority in West Berlin had at least the basic level of educational qualifications and substantial work experience, with fewer and younger children.

Table A.1 Type categorization according to location

	London		Berlin		East Berlin		West Berlin	
	n	%	n	%	N	%	n	%
Pioneer	4	11	4	11	4	21	0	0
Coper/Pioneer	13	37	11	31	7	37	4	25
Coper	13	37	14	31	6	32	8	50
Coper/struggler	3	9	6	26	2	11	4	25
Struggler	2	6	0	0	0	0	0	0
Total	35	100*	35	100	19	100	16	100

**Percentages may not add up to 100% due to rounding*

Table A.2 Lone mothers' class background and type category*

	Working Class		Middle Class		Total	
	N	%	N	%	N	%
Pioneer	3	6	5	23	8	11
Pioneer/Coper	15	31	9	41	24	34
Coper	20	42	7	32	27	34
Coper/Struggler	8	17	1	5	9	17
Struggler	2	4	-	-	2	3
Total	48	100**	22	100	70	100

**The distinction between working-class and middle-class is made based on the 'highest' profession of either lone mothers' mother or father since few lone mothers have a professional occupation.*

***Percentages may not add up to 100% due to rounding.*

Bibliography

Abbott, P. and Wallace, C. (1997), *An Introduction to Sociology – Feminist Perspectives*, 2nd edition. (London: Routledge).

Adam, B. (1996), 'Detraditionalization and the certainty of uncertain futures', in P. Heelas et al. (eds.).

Albelda, R., Himmelweit, S. and Humphries, J. (eds.) (2005), *Dilemmas of Lone Motherhood* (New York: Routledge).

Andreß, H.-J. (2001), 'Die wirtschaftliche Lage Alleinerziehender', in Bundesministerium für Familie, Senioren, Frauen und Jugend (ed.).

Annesley, C. (2002), 'Reconfiguring women's social citizenship in Germany: The right to Sozialhilfe; the responsibility to work', *German Politics* 11:1, 81-96.

Antonovsky, A. (1987), *Unravelling the Mystery of Health* (San Francisco: Jossey-Bass Inc.).

— (ed.) (1990), *The Sociology of Health and Health Care in Israel* (New Brunswick: Transaction Publishers).

Antonovsky, A. and Sourani, T. (1990), 'Family sense of coherence and family adaptation', in A. Antonovsky (ed.).

Archer, M. S. (1995), *Realist Social Theory: the Morphogenetic Approach* (Cambridge: Cambridge University Press).

— (1996), 'Social integration and system integration developing the distinction', *Sociology* 30:2, 679-99.

Askonas, P. and Stewart, A. (eds.) (2000), *Social Inclusion – Possibilities and Tensions* (Basingstoke: Macmillan).

Baily, L. (1999), 'Refracted selves? A study of changes in self-identity in the transition to motherhood', *Sociology* 34:2, 335-52.

Baldwin, S. and Falkingham, J. (eds.) (1994), *Social Security and Social Change: New Challenges to the Beveridge Model* (New York: Harvester Wheatsheaf).

Barlow, A., Duncan, S. and James, G. (2002), 'New Labour, the rationality mistake and family policy in Britain', in A. Carling et al. (eds.).

Barnes, B. (2000), *Understanding Agency – Social Theory and Responsible Action* (London: Sage).

Barrett, M. and McIntosh, M. (1991), *The Anti-social Family*, 2nd Edition. (London: Verso).

Bartholomew, R., Hinnert, A. and Sidaway, J. (1992), 'Lone parents and the labour market: evidence from the Labour Force Survey', *Employment Gazette,* November, 559-77.

Bauman, Z. (1996), 'From pilgrim to tourist – or a short history of identity', in S. Hall and Du Gay (eds.).

— (1998), *Globalization* (Cambridge: Polity Press).

— (2000), 'What it means 'to be excluded': living to stay apart – or together?', in P. Askonas and A. Stewart (eds.).

— (2001), *The Individualized Society* (Cambridge: Polity Press).
Beck, U. (1992), *Risk Society: Towards a New Modernity* (London: Sage).
— (1997), 'Capitalism without work', *Dissent*, Winter, 51-56.
— (1998a), 'Das große Los – arbeitslos – Ein Berliner Manifest proklamiert: Freizeit macht froh', *Süddeutsche Zeitung*, 19. June, 13.
— (1998b), *Democracy without Enemies* (Cambridge: Polity Press).
Beck, U. and Beck-Gernsheim, E. (1993), 'Nicht Autonomie sondern Bastelbiographie. Anmerkungen zur Individualisierungsdiskussion am Beispiel des Aufsatzes von Günter Burkart', *Zeitschrift für Soziologie* 22:3, 178-87.
— (1994), 'Individualisierung in modernen Gesellschaften – Perspektiven und Kontroversen einer subjektorientierten Soziologie', in U. Beck and E. Beck-Gernsheim (eds.).
— (eds.) (1994), *Riskante Freiheiten* (Frankfurt am Main: Suhrkamp).
— (1995), *The Normal Chaos of Love* (Cambridge: Polity Press).
— (1996), 'Individualisation and 'precarious freedoms': perspectives and controversies of a subject-oriented sociology', in P. Heelas et al. (eds.).
— (2002), *Individualization* (London: Sage).
Beck, U., Bonß, W. and Lau, C. (2003), 'The theory of reflexive modernization: problematic, hypotheses and research programme', *Theory, Culture and Society* 20:2, 1–34.
Becker-Schmidt, R. (1987), 'Frauen und Deklassierung. Geschlecht und Klasse', in U. Beer (ed.).
Beck-Gernsheim, E. (1994), 'Auf dem Weg in die postfamiliare Familie – von der Notgemeinschaft zur Wahlverwandtschaft', in U. Beck and E. Beck-Gernsheim (eds.).
— (2002), *Reinventing the Family: in Search of Lifestyles* (Cambridge: Polity Press).
Beer, U. (ed.) (1987), *Klasse Geschlecht. Feministische Gesellschaftsanalyse und Wissenschaftskritik* (Bielefeld: Kleine Verlag).
Behrend, H. (1995), 'East German women and the Wende', *The European Journal of Women's Studies* 2, 237-55.
Bell, A., Finch, N., La Valle, I. Sainsbury, R. and Skinner, C. (2005), *A Question of Balance: Lone Parents, Childcare and Work,* Department of Work and Pensions, Research Report 230. (Leeds: Corporate Document Services).
Bellers, A. (1992), *Politik für die Familie – Eine Vergleichende Analyse familienpolitischer Maßnahmen auf Bundes-, Landes- und kommunaler Ebene in der Bundesrepublik Deutschland,* Band 78. (Münster: Lit Verlag).
Berthoud, D. (2003), 'Lone parents and jobs – Can the 70 per cent target be met?', in D. Thurley (ed.).
Bertram, H., Hradil, G. and Kleinhenz, G. (eds.) (1996), *Sozialer und demographischer Wandel in den neuen Bundesländern* (Obladen: Leske und Budrich).
Bien, W. (ed.) (1996), *Familie an der Schwelle zum neuen Jahrtausend* (Opladen: Leske and Budrich).
Bleses, P. (2003), 'Der Umbau geht weiter – Lohnarbeit und Familien in der rot-gruenen Sozialpolitik', *Zeitschrift für Sozialreform* 49, 557– 83.

Blossfeld, H.-P. (ed.) (1995), *The New Role of Women – Family Formation in Modern Societies* (Boulder: Westview Press).

Blossfeld, H.-P. and Rohwer, G. (1995), 'West Germany', in H.-P. Blossfeld (ed.).

Bowring, F. (1999), 'Job scarcity: the perverted form of a potential blessing', *Sociology* 33:1, 69-84.

Bradshaw, J. (1998), 'International comparisons of support for lone parents', in R. Ford and J. Millar (eds.).

Bradshaw, J., Stimson, C., Skinner, C. and Williams, J. (1999), *Absent Fathers?* (London: Routledge).

Brand, D. and Hammer, V. (eds.) (2002), *Balanceakt Alleinerziehend. Lebenslagen, Lebensformen, Erwerbsarbeit* (Wiesbaden: Westdeutscher Verlag).

Brannen, J. (1994), 'Sociological definitions of the family: employment relationships in the United Kingdom', in M.-T. Letablier and L. Hantrais (eds.).

— (1999), 'Reconsidering children and childhood: sociological and policy perspectives', in E.B. Silva and C. Smart (eds.).

Brannen, J. and Nilsen, A. (2005), 'Individualisation, choice and structure: a discussion of current trends in sociological analysis', *The Sociological Review* 53:3, 412-28.

Braun, M., Scott, J. and Alwin, D. F. (1994), 'Economic necessity or self-actualisation? Attitudes towards women's labour force participation in East and West Germany', *European Sociological Review* 10:1, 29-47.

Bruegel, I. and Perrons, D. (1996), *Deregulation and woman's employment: the diverse experiences of women in Britain*, Gender Institute, Discussion Paper 2. (London: London School of Economics).

Bruttel, O. and Sol, E. (2006), 'Work First as a European Model? Evidence from Germany and the Netherlands', *Policy and Politics* 34:1, 69-89.

Bryman, A. and Burgess, R.G. (eds.) (1994), *Analysing Qualitative Data* (London: Routledge).

Bryson, A., Ford, R. and White, M. (1997), *Making Work Pay – Lone Mothers, Employment and Well Being* (York: Joseph Rowntree Foundation).

Bryson, C., Kazimirski, A. and Southwood, H. (2006), *Childcare and Early Years Provision: A Study of Parents' Use, Views and Experience*, Department of Education and Skills, Research Report 723. (London: National Centre for Social Research).

<http://www.dfes.gov.uk/research/data/uploadfiles/RR723.pdf> accessed 10 July 2006.

Bütow, B. and Stecker, H. (eds.) (1994), *EigenArtige Ostfrauen – Frauenemanzipation in der DDR und den neuen Bundesländern* (Bielefeld: Kleine Verlag).

Bundesforschungsanstalt für Landeskunde und Raumordnung (ed.) (1994), *Wohnsituation Alleinerziehender II* (Bonn: Bundesforschungsanstalt für Landeskunde und Raumordnung).

Bundesministerium für Familien, Senioren, Frauen und Jugend (1998), *Die neue Beistandschaft* (Bonn: Bundesministerium für Familien, Senioren, Frauen und Jugend).

— (ed.) (2001), *Alleinerziehen in Deutschland: Resourcen und Risiken einer Lebensformen* (Berlin: Langelüddecke).

— (2006), 'Bosch-Studie - Unternehmen Familie bestaetigt Entscheidungen in Familienpolitik', *Pressemitteilung,* 31 March.

Burkhart, G. (1998), 'Individualisierung und Elternschaft. Eine empirische Überprüfung der Individualisierungsthese am Beispiel USA und ein Systematisierungsvorschlag', in J. Friedrichs (ed.).

Campbell, C. (1996), 'Detraditionalization, character and the limits to agency', in P. Heelas et al. (eds.).

Carling, A., Duncan, S. and Edwards, R. (eds.) (2002), *Analysing Families – Morality and Rationality in Policy and Practice* (London: Routledge).

Casebourne, J. and Britton, L. (2004), *Lone Parents, Health and Work,* Department for Work and Pensions, Research Report 214. (Leeds: Corporate Document Services).

Chamberlayne, D. (1993), 'Women and the state: changes in roles and rights in France, West Germany, Italy and Britain, 1970 – 1990', in J. Lewis (ed.).

Chancellor of the Exchequer (1998), *Pre-Budget Report,* November. (London: HMSO).

Cheal, D. (1991), *Family and the State of Theory* (Hemel Hampstead: Harvester Wheatsheaf).

Chodorow, N. (1978), *The Reproduction of Mothering: Psychoanalysis and the Sociology of Gender* (Berkley: University of California University Press).

Clarke, J. and Langan, M. (1993a), 'The British welfare state: foundation and modernisation', in A. Cochrane and J. Clarke (eds.).

— (1993b), 'Restructuring welfare: the British welfare regime in the 1980s', in A. Cochrane and J. Clarke (eds.).

Clasen, J. and Freeman, R. (1994), *Social Policy in Germany* (Hemel Hampstead: Harvester Wheatsheaf).

Cochrane, A. and Clarke J. (eds.) (1993), *Comparing Welfare States – Britain in International Context* (London: Sage).

Crompton, R. (2005), *Class and the Family,* Department of Sociology, GeNet Working Paper 9. (London: City University), <http://www.genet.ac.uk/workpapers/GeNet2005p9.pdf> accessed on 10 July 2006.

Crompton, R. and Le Feuvre, N. (1996), 'Paid employment and the changing system of gender relations: a cross-national comparison', *Sociology* 30:3, 427-45.

Crow, G. (2002), 'Families, moralities and social change', in A. Carling et al. (eds.).

Daly, M. (1996), *The Gender Division of Welfare: the British and German Welfare States Compared,* PhD thesis. (Florence: European University Institute).

— (2005), 'Changing family life in Europe: Significance for state and society', *European Societies* 7:3, 379-98.

Dathe, D. (1996), 'Zur Einkommenslage ausgewählter Haushaltstypen in den neuen Bundesländern', in H. Bertram et al. (eds.).

Daune-Richard, A. M. (1998), 'How does the 'societal effect' shape the use of part-time work in France, the UK and Sweden?', in J. O'Reilly and C. Fagan (eds.).

Deacon, B. (1993), 'Developments in East European social policy', in C. Jones (ed.).

Dennis, N. and Erdos, G. (1992), *Families Without Fatherhood* (London: Institute of Economic Affairs Health and Welfare Unit).

Department for Work and Pensions (2005), *Delivering PSA Targets – Target 4a* (Leeds: Corporate Document Services). <http://www.dwp.gov.uk/publications/dwp/2005/dr05/targets/target4a.asp> accessed on 10 July 2006.

Dienel, C. (ed.) (2005), *Abwanderung, Geburtenrückgang und Regionale Entwicklung* (Wiesbaden: VS Verlag).

DiQuinzio, P. (1999), *The Impossibility of Motherhood: Feminism, Individualism and the Problem of Mothering* (New York: Routledge).

Drauschke, P. and Stolzenburg, M. (1994a), 'Alleinerziehende Frauen in Berlin Ost - Sie wohnen wie immer - nur anders', in Bundesforschungsanstalt für Landeskunde und Raumordnung (ed.).

— (1994b), *Zur Situation alleinerziehender Frauen in Berlin Ost auf dem Arbeitsmarkt - Sozialreport 1* (Gelsenkirchen: Sozialwissenschaftliches Forschungszentrum).

Duncan, S. (2000), *New Labour's 'Rationality and Morality Mistakes' – and Some Alternatives*, ESRC Research Group on Care, Values and the Future of Welfare, Workshop Paper 11. (Leeds: University of Leeds).

— (2002), 'Policy discourses on 'reconciling work and life' in the EU', *Social Policy and Society* 1:4, 305-14.

— (2006), 'Mothers' work-life balance: individualized preferences or cultural construction?', in D. Perrons et al. (eds.).

Duncan, S. and Edwards, R. (eds.) (1997), *Single Mothers In an International Context: Mothers or Workers?* (London: UCL Press).

— (1999), *Lone Mothers, Paid Work and Gendered Moral Rationalities* (London: MacMillan).

Duncan, S. and Pfau-Effinger, B. (eds.) (2000), *Gender, Economy and Culture in the European Union* (London: Routledge).

Edwards, R. and Duncan, S. (1996), 'Rational economic man or lone mothers in context? The uptake of paid work', in E. B. Silva (ed.).

Ellermann, H. and Klatt, K. (1995), *Bundesdeutsche Hausfrau? – Nie im Leben* (Berlin: Hoho Verlag Christine Hoffmann).

Ely, M. (1999), 'The importance of estimates and confidence intervals rather than p values', *Sociology* 33:1, 185-90.

Engels, F. (1990), *Der Ursprung der Familie, des Privateigentums und des Staats*, 7th edition. (Berlin: Dietz Verlag).

Engstler, H. (1998), *Die Familie im Spiegel der amtlichen Statistik* (Berlin: Bundesministerium für Familie, Senioren, Frauen und Jugend).

Engstler, H. and Menning, S. (2003), *Die Familie im Spiegel der amtlichen Statistik* (Berlin: Bundesministerium für Familie, Senioren, Frauen und Jugend), <http://www.bmfsfj.de/Kategorien/Publikationen/Publikationen,did=3122.html> accessed on 10 July 2006.

Erler, W. (2004), 'Single parents in Germany: The career of a topic in social research and policy', in S. Hübner-Funk (ed.).

Esping-Andersen, G. (1990), *The Three Worlds of Welfare Capitalism* (Cambridge: Polity Press).

— (1999), *Social Foundations of Post-industrial Economies* (Oxford: Oxford University Press).

Evans, M., McKnight, A. and Namazie, C. (2002), *New Deal for Lone Parents: First Synthesis Report of the National Evaluation*, Department for Work and Pensions, Research Report 116. (Leeds: Corporate Document Services).

Evans, M., Eyre, J., Millar, J. and Sarre, S. (2003), *New Deal for Lone Parents: Second Synthesis Report of the National Evaluation*, Department for Work and Pensions, Research Report 163. (Leeds: Corporate Document Services).

Evans, M., Harkness, S. and Ortiz, R. (2004), *Lone Parents Cycling Between Work and Benefits,* Department for Work and Pensions, Research Report 217. (Leeds: Corporate Document Services).

Evans, P. M. (1992), 'Targeting single mothers for employment: comparisons from the United States, Britain and Canada', *Social Services Review* 66:3, 378-98.

Everingham, C. (1994), *Motherhood and Modernity* (Buckingham: Open University Press).

Ferri, E. and Smith, K. (1996), *Parenting in the 1990s* (London: Family Policy Studies Centre).

Ferris, J. and Page, R. (eds.) (1994), *Social Policy in Transition* (Avebury: Aldershot).

Finch, J. (1989), *Family Obligations and Social Change* (Cambridge: Polity Press).

Finlayson, L. and Marsh, A. (1998), 'Lone parents on the margins of work', in R. Ford and J. Millar (eds.).

Finlayson, L., Ford, R., Marsh, A., McKay, A. and Mukherjee, A. (2000),*The British Lone Parent Cohort 1991-1998*, Department of Social Security, Report 25. (Leeds: Corporate Document Services).

Folbre, N. (1994), *Who Pays for the Kids? Gender and the Structures of Constraints* (New York: Routledge).

Ford, R. (1996), *Childcare in the Balance: How Lone Parents Make Decisions About Work* (London: Policy Studies Institute).

—(1998), 'Lone mothers' decisions whether or not to work: childcare in the balance', in R. Ford and J. Millar (eds.).

Ford, R. and Millar, J. (eds.) (1998), *Private Lives and Public Responses – Lone Parenthood and Future Policy in the UK* (London: Policy Studies Institute).

Friedrichs, J. (ed.) (1998), *Die Individualisierungsthese* (Opladen: Leske and Budrich).

Frise, M. and Stahlberg, J. (1992), *Allein mit Kind - Alleinerziehende Mütter und Väter* (München: Piper).

Gardner, S. (1998), 'Mothers to get full rights to pensions', *Sunday Times*, Money Section, 6. September.

Gauthier, A. H. (1996), *The State and the Family – a Comparative Analysis of Family Policies in Industrialised Countries* (Oxford: Clarendon Press).

General Household Survey (2006), 'Tables from the 2004/2005 General Household Survey', <http://www.statistics.gov.uk/ghs/> accessed on 10 July 2006.

Giddens, A. (1987), *Social Theory and Modern Sociology* (Stanford: Stanford University Press).

—(1991), *Modernity and Self-Identity* (Cambridge: Polity Press).

—(1992), *The Transformation of Intimacy: Sexuality, Love and Eroticism in Modern Societies* (Cambridge: Polity Press).

— (1997), *Sociology*, 3rd edition. (Cambridge: Polity Press).

— (1998), *The Third Way: the Renewal of Social Democracy* (Cambridge: Polity Press).

Giddings, L., Dingeldey, I. and Ulbricht, S. (2005), 'The commodification of lone mothers' labour: a comparison of US and German Policies', in R. Albelda et al. (eds.).

Gillies, V. (2005), 'Raising the 'meritocracy'? Parenting and the individualization of social class, *Sociology* 39:5, 835-53.

Ginn, J., Arber, S., Brannen, J. et al. (1996), 'Feminist fallacies: a reply to Hakim on women's employment', *British Journal of Sociology* 17:1, 167-74.

Ginsburg, N. (1992), *Divisions of Welfare – a Critical Introduction to Comparative Social Policy* (London: Sage).

Glaser, B. G. and Strauss, A. L. (1967), *The Discovery of Grounded Theory: Strategies for Qualitative Research* (Chicago: Aldine).

Gonzáles López, M. and Solsona Pairó, M. (2000), 'Households and families', in S. Duncan and B. Pfau-Effinger (eds.).

Großmann, H. and Huth, S. (1996), 'Sozialhilfeabhängigkeit Alleinerziehender als Folge gesellschaftlichen Umbruchs', in H. Bertram et al. (eds.).

Gutschmidt, G. (1994), *Single mit Kind, Alleinerziehen – wie es die anderen machen* (Freiburg: Herder Verlag).

— (1997), 'Die Mütterfalle', *Emma* Jan/Feb, 88-91.

Habermas, J. (1985), *Theorie des kommunikativen Handelns* 2, 3rd edition. (Frankfurt a.M.: Suhrkamp).

Hakim, C. (1997), 'Predicting work-lifestyles in the 21st century: preference theory', paper presented to the workshop on 'Towards a gendered political economy', University of Sheffield, 17-18 September.

— (2000), *Work-Lifestyle Choices in the 21st Century – Preference Theory* (Oxford: Oxford University Press).

Hall, S. and Du Gay, P. (eds.) (1996), *Questions of Cultural Identity* (London: Sage).

Hammer, V. (2005), 'Lebensform Alleinerziehende', Online-Texte der *Evangelischen Akademie Bad Woll,* <www.ev-academie-boll.de> accessed on 10 July 2006.

Hank, K., Tillmann, K. and Wagner, G. (2001), *Ausserhäusliche Kinderbetreuung in stdeutschland vor und nach der Wiedervereinigung. Ein Vergleich mit Westdeutschland in den Jahren 1990-1999,* Working Paper 2001-003. (Rostock: Max-Planck-Institute).

Hantrais, L. (1994), 'Comparing family policy in Britain, France and Germany', *Journal of Social Policy* 23:2, 135-60.

Harrop, A. and Moss, P. (1995), 'Trends in parental employment', *Work, Employment and Society* 9:3, 424-44.

Haskey, J. (1993), 'Lone parents and married parents with dependent children in Great Britain: a comparison of their occupation and social class profiles', *Population Trends* 72, 34-44.

— (1995), 'Trends in marriage and cohabitation: the decline in marriage and the changing patterns of living in partnerships', *Population Trends* 80, 8-15.

— (1998), 'One-parent families and their dependent children in Great Britain', in R. Ford and J. Millar (eds.).

— (2002), 'One-parent families – and the dependent children living in them – in Great Britain', *Population Trends* 109, 46-57.

Heelas, P., Lash, S. and Morris, P. (eds.) (1996), *Detraditionalization: Critical Reflections on Authority and Identity* (Oxford: Blackwell).

Heiliger, A. (1993), *Alleinerziehen als Befreiung* (Pfaffenweiler: Centaurus-Verlagsgesellschaft).

— (1994), 'Alleinerziehen als emanzipatorische Chance für Frauen', in R. Simsa (ed.).

Henze, G. and Klar, C. (1996), 'Einstellungen zur Erwerbstätigkeit und Vereinbarkeit mit der Familie', in W. Bien (ed.).

Höpflinger, F. and Erni-Scheuwly, D. (eds.) (1989), *Werteinstellungen, Lebensformen im Wandel und Lebenslagen junger Frauen* (Bern: Haupt).

Hoff, A. (2001), 'How do individuals mobilise support in emergencies', *Marie Curie Research Annals 2*, November. <http://www.mariecurie.org/annals/volume2/hoff.doc> accessed on 10 July 2006.

Hoffmann-Nowotny, H.-J. (1989), 'Die Zukunft der Beziehungsformen – Die Beziehungsformen der Zukunft', in F. Höpflinger and D. Erni-Scheuwly (eds.).

Hogarth, T., Hasluck, C., Pierre, G., Winterbotham, M. and Vivian, D. (2000), *Work-Life Balance: Baseline study of work-life balance practices in Great Britain,* Institute for Employment Research (Warwick: University of Warwick).

Hoyle, R. H., Harris, M. J. and Judd, C. M. (2002), *Research Methods in Social Relations,* 7th edition. (Stamford: Wadsworth).

Hübner-Funk, S. (ed.) (2004), *Research in Progress: Selected Studies of the German Youth Institute,* German Youth Institute, DJI International Series 1 (München: DJI International Series 1).

Humphrey, R. (ed.) (1996), *Families Behind the Headlines* (Newcastle: University of Newcastle upon Tyne).

Huth, S., Großmann, H. and Schallhöfer, P. (1996), 'Alleinerziehend in Ost und West, eine familiale Lebensform mit Risiken', *Leviathan* 24:3, 412-31.

Irwin, S. (2000), *Conceptualising Social Change: Family, Work and the Changing Pattern of Social Reproduction*, ESRC Research Group on Care, Values and the Future of Welfare, Workshop Paper 7a. (Leeds: University of Leeds).

Jahoda, M., Lazarsfeld, P.-F. and Zeisel, H. (1971), *Marienthal – The Sociography of an Unemployed Community* (Chicago: Aldine Atherton).

Jamieson, L. (1999), 'Intimacy transformed? A critical look at the 'pure' relationship', *Sociology* 33:3, 477-94.

Jones, C. (ed.) (1993), *New Perspectives on the Welfare State in Europe* (London: Routledge).

Joshi, H. (1990), 'Obstacles and opportunities for lone parents as breadwinners in Great Britain', in Organisation for Economic Co-operation and Development (OECD) (ed.).

Junge, M. (2002), *Individualisierung* (Frankfurt: Campus Verlag).

Kameraman, S. B. and Kahn, A. J. (1988), *Mothers Alone – Strategies for a Time of Change* (Dover: Auburn House Publishing Company).

Kaufmann, F.– X. (1995), *Zukunft der Familie im vereinten Deutschland: Gesellschaftliche und politische Bedingungen* (München: Beck).

Keiser, S. (1997), *Ostdeutsche Frauen zwischen Individualisierung und Re-traditionalisierung – Ein Generationenvergleich* (Hamburg: Verlag Dr. Kovac).

Keränen, M. (1997), *Social Problems in Different Contexts*, Gender Institute, Discussion Paper 4. (London: London School of Economics).

Kiernan, K. E., Lewis, J. and Land, H. (1998), *Lone Motherhood in Twentieth-century Britain: from Footnote to Front Page* (New York: Clarendon Press).

Kjeldstad, R. and Ronsen, M. (2005), 'Welfare use, business cycles, and employment dynamics among lone parents in Norway', in R. Albelda et al. (eds.).

Klett-Davies, M. (1997), 'Single mothers in Germany: supported mothers who work', in S. Duncan and R. Edwards (eds.).

— (2005), 'The diversity of state benefit dependent lone mothers: The use of type categories as an analytical tool', *Sociological Research Online* 10:1, <http://www.socresonline.org.uk/10/1/2.html> accessed on 10 July 2006.

Knight, G. and Thomas, A. (2006), *LPWFI and Review Meetings – Administrative Data Analyses and Qualitative Evidence: Final Report*, Department of Work and Pensions, Research Report 315. (Leeds: Corporate Document Services).

Kolinsky, E. and Nickel, H. (eds.) (2003), *Reinventing Gender: Women in Eastern Germany Since Unification* (Portland: Frank Cass).

Koppetsch, C. and Maier, M. S. (1998), 'Individualisierung ohne Gleichheit? Zur aktuellen Lage des Geschlechterverhältnisses', in J. Friedrichs (ed.).

Kosmann, M., Neubauer, J., Schultz, A. and Wunderlich, H. (2003), *Alleinerziehende im Sozialhilfebezug – Risiken und Chances im Leben zwischen Familie und Erwerbstaetigkeit*, Endbericht. (Bochum: Zentrum für interdisziplinäre Ruhrgebietsforschung).

Land, H. (1994), 'The demise of the male breadwinner – in practice but not in theory: a challenge for social security systems', in S. Baldwin and J. Falkingham (eds.).

Lawler, S. (1999), 'Children need but mothers only want: the power of 'Needs Talk' in the constitution of childhood', in J. Seymour and P. Bagguley (eds.).

Lehmann, P. and Wirtz, C. (2004), 'Household formation in the EU – Lone parents', *Statistics in Focus – Population and Social Conditions* 3:5, 1-7.

Leibfried, S. (1993), 'Towards a European welfare state? On integrating poverty regimes into the European Community', in C. Jones (ed.).

Leisering, L. (1998), 'Sozialstaat und Individualisierung', in J. Friedrichs (ed.).

Leisering, L. and Leibfried, S. (1999), *Time and Poverty in Western Welfare States: United Germany in Perspective* (Cambridge: Cambridge University Press).

Letablier, M.-T. and Hantrais, L. (eds.) (1994), *The Family-Employment Relationship*, Cross-National Research Group, Fourth Series. (Loughborough: University of Technology).

Lewis, J. (ed.) (1993), *Women and Social Policies in Europe* (Aldershot: Edward Elgar).

— (ed.) (1997), *Lone Mothers in European Welfare State Regimes* (London: Jessica Kingsley).

— (2001), *The End of Marriage? Individualism and Intimate Relations* (Cheltenham: Edward Elgar Publishing).

— (2002), 'Gender and Welfare State Change', *European Societies* 4:4, 331-57.

Liebecke, H. (1994), 'Heiraten, irgendwann schon... – Alleinerziehen im Osten', in B. Bütow and H. Stecker (eds.).

Lister, R. (1994), 'She has other duties – women, citizenship and social security', in S. Baldwin and J. Falkingham (eds.).

— (2000), 'Strategies for social inclusion: promoting social cohesion or social justice?', in P. Askonas and A. Stewart (eds.).

Macran, S., Joshi, H. and Dex, S. (1996), 'Employment after childbearing: a survival analysis', *Work, Employment and Society* 10:2, 273-96.

Mädje, E. and Neusüß, C. (1994a), *Frauen im Sozialstaat: Subjektive Deutungen, Orientierungen und staatliches Handeln am Beispiel alleinerziehender Sozialhilfeempfängerinnen*, Dissertation. (Berlin: Freie Universität Berlin).

— (1994b), 'Lone mothers on welfare in West Berlin: disadvantaged citizens or women avoiding patriarchy?', *Environment and Planning A* 26, 1419-33.

Mählmann, M. (1998), *Alleinerziehen als Folge gesellschaftlicher Umbrüche*', Dissertation. (Bremen: Hochschule Bremen).

Maleck-Lewy, E. (1995), 'Between self-determination and state supervision: women and the abortion law in post-unification Germany', *Social Politics* Spring, 62-75.

Marsh, A. and Vegeris, S. (2004), *The British Lone Parent Cohort and Their Children 1999-2001,* Department of Work and Pensions, Research Report 209. (Leeds: Cooperative Document Services).

McKay, S. and Marsh, A. (1994), *Lone Parents and Work – the Effects of Benefits and Maintenance*, Department of Social Security, Research Report 25. (London: HMSO).

Maynard, M. and Purvis, J. (eds.) (1994), *Researching Women's Lives from a Feminist Perspective* (London: Taylor and Francis).

Meyer, S. and Schulze, E. (1989), *Balancen des Glücks – Neue Lebensformen: Paare ohne Trauschein, Alleinerziehende und Singles* (München: Beck).

Meyer, T. (1996), 'Ausgerechnet jetzt. Über die Einführung des Rechtsanspruches auf einen Kindergartenplatz in der Krise des Sozialstaates', *Diskurs* 2, 62-67.

Miles, M. and Huberman, A. (1994), *Qualitative Data Analysis: An Expanded Sourcebook* (Thousand Oaks: Sage).

Millar, J. (1994), 'Lone parents and Social Security policy in the UK', in S. Baldwin and J. Falkingham (eds.).

— (1996), 'Mothers, workers, wives – policy approaches to supporting lone mothers in comparative perspective', in E. B. Silva (ed.).

— (1998), 'Policy and changing family forms: placing lone parenthood in context', paper presented to the seminar 'Current European Research on lone mothers', Göteborg University, April.

Millar, J. and Ridge, T. (2001), *Families, poverty, work and care*, Department for Work and Pensions, Research Report 153. (Leeds: Corporate Document Services).

Miller, T. (2005), *Making Sense of Motherhood – A Narrative Approach* (Cambridge: Cambridge University Press).

Moore, H. (1994), *A Passion for Difference: Essays on Anthropology and Gender* (Cambridge: Polity Press).

Morgan, D. (2002), 'Sociological perspectives on the family', in A. Carling et al. (eds.).

Morgan, P. (1995), *Farewell to the Family? Public Policy and Family Breakdown in Britain and the USA* (London: Institute of Economic Affairs, Health and Welfare Unit).

Müller, U. (1989), 'Warum gibt es keine emanzipatorische Utopie des Mutterseins?', in B. Schön (ed.).

Mulroy, E. A. (1995), *The New Uprooted: Single Mothers in Urban Life* (Westport: Auburn House).

Murray, C. (1990), *The Emerging British Underclass* (London: Institute of Economic Affairs, Health and Welfare Unit).

— (1994), *Underclass: The Crisis Deepens* (London: Institute of Economic Affairs, Health and Welfare Unit).

Napp-Peters, A. (1983), 'Geschlechtsrollenstereotypen und ihr Einfluß auf Einstellungen zur Ein-Elternteil-Situation', *Kölner Zeitschrift für Soziologie und Sozialpsychologie* 35, 321-34.

— (1987), *Ein-Elternteil-Familien - soziale Randgruppe oder neues familiales Selbstverständnis?* (Weinheim: Juventa Verlag).

Nave-Herz, R. (1992a), 'Ledige Mutterschaft: Eine alternative Lebensform?', *Zeitschrift für Sozialisationsforschung und Erziehungssoziologie* 6, 219-232.

— (1992b), *Frauen zwischen Tradition und Moderne* (Bielefeld: Kleine Verlag).

— (1994), *Familie Heute - Wandel der Familienstrukturen und Folgen für die Erziehung* (Darmstadt: Wissenschaftliche Buchgesellschaft).

Nave-Herz, R. and Krüger, D. (1992), *Ein-Eltern-Familien - eine empirische Studie zur Lebenssituation und Lebensplanung alleinerziehender Mütter und Väter* (Bielefeld: Kleine Verlag).

Nestmann, F. and Stiehler, S. (1998), *Wie allein sind Alleinerziehende? Soziale Beziehungen alleinerziehender Frauen und Männer in Ost und West* (Opladen: Leske und Budrich).

Niepel, G. (1994a), *Alleinerziehende - Abschied von einem Klischee* (Opladen: Leske and Budrich).

— (1994b), *Soziale Netze und soziale Unterstützung alleinerziehender Frauen: Eine empirische Studie* (Opladen: Leske and Budrich).

Noble, M., Smith, G., Cheung, S.Y., De Moor, D., Smith, T. and Whitlock, S. (1998), *Lone Mothers Moving in and out of Benefits*, Joseph Rowntree Foundation, Work and Opportunity Series 4. (York: Joseph Rowntree Foundation).

Notz, G. (1994), 'Frauenemanzipation und Frauenrealität in Ost und West', in B. Bütow and H. Stecker (eds.).

Nussbaum, M.C and Glover, J. (eds.) (1995), *Women, Culture and Development: a Study of Human Capabilities* (Oxford: Clarendon Press).

Oakley, A. (1974), *The Sociology of Housework* (London: Robertson).

— (1992), *Social Support and Motherhood: the Natural History of a Research Project* (Oxford: Blackwell).

OECD (ed.) (1990), *Lone Parent Families - the Economic Challenge* (Montreal: OECD).

Offe, C. (1994a), 'A non-productivist design for social policies', in J. Ferris and R. Page (eds.).

— (1994b), 'Vollbeschäftigung? Zur Kritik einer falsch gestellten Frage', *Gerwerkschaftliche Montashefte* 45:12, 796-806.

Okin, S. M. (1995), 'Inequalities between the sexes in different cultural contexts', in M. C. Nussbaum and J. Glover (eds.).

O'Reilly, J. and Fagan, C. (eds.) (1998), *Part-Time Prospects* (London: Routledge).

Ostner, I. (1993), 'Slow motion: women, work and the family in Germany', in J. Lewis (ed.).

Ott, N. (2001), 'Die sozialpolitische Situation von Alleinerziehenden und spezifische Belastungen', in Bundesministerium für Familie, Senioren, Frauen und Jugend (ed.).

Parsons, T. (1971), *The System of Modern Societies* (Englewood Cliffs: Prentice-Hall).

Perrons, D. (1998), 'Flexible employment and the reconciliation of work and family life', paper presented to the ESRC Seminar Series 'Parenting, Motherhood and Paid Work', University of Bradford, 16–17 September.

Perrons, D., Fagan, C., McDowell, L., Ray, K. and Ward, K. (eds.) (2006), *Gender Divisions and Working Time in the New Economy* (Cheltenham: Edwards Elgar Publishing).

Pfau-Effinger, B. (1994), 'The gender contract and part-time paid work by women - Finland and Germany compared', *Environment and Planning A* 26, 1355-76.

— (1998), 'Gender cultures and the gender arrangement – a theoretical framework for cross-national gender research', *Innovation* 11:2, 147-62.

— (2005), 'Welfare state policies and the development of care arrangements', *European Societies* 7:2, 321-47.

Pfau-Effinger, B. and Geissler, B. (2002), 'Cultural change and family policies in East and West-Germany', in A. Carling et al. (eds.).

Phizacklea, A. and Wolkowitz, C. (1995), *Homeworking Women: Gender, Racism and Class at Work* (London: Sage).

Phoenix, A. (1994), 'Practicing feminist research: the intersection of gender and "race" in the research process', in M. Maynard and J. Purvis (eds.).

— (1996), 'Social constructions of lone motherhood – a case of competing discourses', in E. B. Silva (ed.).

Pinl, C. (2003), 'Uralt, aber immer noch ruestig: der deutsche Ernaehrer', *Aus Politik und Zeitgeschichte* 44, 6-8.

Quack, S. and Maier, F. (1994), 'From state socialism to market economy - women's employment in East Germany', *Environment and Planning A* 26, 1257-76.

Rerrich, M. S. (1994), 'Zusammenfügen, was auseinanderstrebt: Zur familialen Lebensführung von Berufstätigen', in U. Beck and E. Beck-Gernsheim (eds.).

Reuter, W. (ed.) (2004), *Germany on the Road to Normalcy* (London: Palgrave/ MacMillan).

Reynolds, T. (1998), 'African-Caribbean mothering, paid work and identity', paper presented to the ESRC Seminar Series 'Parenting, Motherhood and Paid Work', University of Bradford, 16–17 September.

— (2002), 'Re-analysing the Black family', in A. Carling et al. (eds.).

Ribbens, J. (1994), *Mothers and Their Children: a Feminist Sociology of Childrearing* (London: Sage).

— (1998), 'Hearing my feeling voice? An autobiographical discussion of motherhood', in J. Ribbens and R. Edwards (eds.).

Ribbens, J. and Edwards, R. (eds.) (1998), *Feminist Dilemmas in Qualitative Research* (London: Sage).

Ribbens-McCarthy, J., Edwards, R. and Gillies, V. (2003), *Making Families: Moral Tales of Parenting and Step-parenting* (Durham: Sociology Press).

Rich, A. (1977), *Of Women Born: Motherhood as Experience and Institution* (London: Virago).

Ridge, T. (2004), 'Supporting children? The impact of child support policies on children's wellbeing in the UK and Australia', *Journal of Social Policy* 34:1, 121-42.

Rose, N. (1996), 'Authority and the genealogy of subjectivity', in P. Heelas et al. (eds.).

Rosenfeld, R., Trappe, H. and Gornick, J. (2004), 'Gender and work in Germany: Before and after reunification', *Annual Review of Sociology* 30, 103-124.

Rowlingson, K. and McKay, S. (1998), *The Growth of Lone Parenthood – Diversity and Dynamics* (London: Policy Studies Institute).

Rowlingson, K. and McKay, S. (2005), 'Lone motherhood and socio-economic disadvantage: insights from quantitative and qualitative evidence', *Sociological Review* 53:1, 30-60.

Rubery, J. (1998), 'Part-time work: a threat to labour standards?', in J. O'Reilly and C. Fagan (eds.).

Ruddick, S. (1980), 'Maternal thinking', *Feminist Studies* 6:2, 342-67.

Ruspini, E. (1998), *Living on the Poverty Line: Lone Mothers in Belgium, Germany, Italy, Sweden and Great Britain*, Mannheim Centre for European Social Research, Working Paper 28. <http://econpapers.repec.org/paper/erpmzesxx/p0044.htm> accessed on 10 July 2006.

Sackmann, R. (2000), 'Living through the myths – gender, values, attitudes and practices', in S. Duncan and B. Pfau-Effinger (eds.).

Sainsbury, D. (1996), *Gender, Equality and Welfare States* (Cambridge: Cambridge University Press).

Sayer, A. (1992), *Method in Social Science – A Realist Approach*, 2nd edition. (London: Routledge).

Schenk, S. (2003), 'Employment opportunities and labour market exclusion: towards a new pattern of gender stratification?', in E. Kolinsky and H. Nickel (eds.).

Schilling, C. (1997), 'The under-socialised conception of the embodied agent in modern sociology', *Sociology* 31:4, 737-54.

Schneider, N., Krüger, D., Lasch, V., Limmer, R. and Matthias-Bleck, H. (2001), A*lleinerziehen. Vielfalt und Dynamik einer Lebensform* (Weinheim: Juventa Verlag).

Schön, B. (ed.) (1989), *Emanzipation und Mutterschaft* (Weinheim: Juventa Verlag).

Schröter, U. (1996), 'Ostdeutsche Frauen zwischen Verlieren und Gewinnen', in H. Bertram et al. (eds.).

Schülein, J. A. (1994), 'Zur Entwicklung des familären Zusammenslebens: Von der Überlebensgruppe zur individualisierten Beziehungsgemeinschaft', in R. Simsa (ed.).

Schülein, J. A. and Simsa, R. (1994), 'Zur Diskriminierung von Einelternfamilien in Gesellschaft und Forschung', in R. Simsa (ed.).

Schütze, Y. (1991), *Die gute Mutter – Zur Geschichte des normativen Musters, Mutterliebe'* (Bielefeld: Kleine Verlag).

Seeleib-Kaiser, M. (2004), 'Continuity or change: Red-Green social policy after sixteen years of Christian Democratic rule', in W. Reuter (ed.).

Sennett, R. (1998), *The Corrosion of Character: the Personal Consequences of Work in the New Capitalism* (New York: Norton).

Sevenhuijsen, S. (2002), 'A third way? Moralities, ethics and families: An approach through the ethic of care', in A. Carling et al. (eds.).

Seymour, J. and Bagguley, P. (eds.) (1999), *Relating Intimacies – Power and Resistance* (Basingstoke: MacMillan Press).

Silva, E. B. (ed.) (1996), *Good Enough Mothering – Feminist Perspectives on Lone Motherhood* (London: Routledge).

Silva, E. B. and Smart, C. (eds.) (1999), *The New Family* (London: Sage).

Simsa, R. (ed.) (1994), *Kein Herr im Haus (*Frankfurt a.M.: Fischer).

Sinha, R. (1998), *The Cultural Adjustment of Asian Lone Mothers Living in London* (London: Ashgate).

Smart, C. (ed.) (1993), *Regulating Womanhood: Historical Essays on Marriage, Motherhood and Sexuality* (London: Routledge).

Smart, C. and Shipman, B. (2004), 'Visions in monochrome: families, marriage and the individualization thesis', *The British Journal of Sociology* 55:4, 491-509.

Smart, C. and Neale, B. (1999), *Family Fragments?* (Cambridge: Polity Press).

Sorensen, A. and Trappe, H. (1995), 'The persistence of gender inequality in earnings in the German Democratic Republic', *American Sociological Review* 60:June, 398-406.

Southwark Council (1996), *The Southwark Poverty Profile – Indicators of Poverty and Deprivation in Southwark* (London: Southwark Regeneration and Environment Department).

Speak, S. (2000), 'Barriers to lone parent's employment', *Local Economy* 15:1, 32-44.

Spensky, C. (1993), 'Producers of legitimacy – homes for unmarried mothers in the 1950s', in C. Smart (ed.).

Staat, M. and Wagenhals, G. (1993), *The labour supply of lone mothers in the Federal Republic of Germany*, Diskussionsbeitrag 82. (Stuttgart: Universität Hohenheim).

— (1994), 'The labour supply of German single mothers: a bivariate probit model', *Vierteljahrshefte zur Wirtschaftsordnung* 1:2, 113-118.

Stanley, L. and Wise, S. (1993), *Breaking Out Again – Feminist Ontology and Epistemology*, (New York: Routledge).

Statistisches Bundesamt (2006), *Unpublished Tables from Mikrozensus Data* (Wiesbaden: Statistisches Bundesamt).

Stewart, A. (2000), 'Social inclusion: an introduction', in P. Askonas and A. Stewart (eds.) (2000).

Strohmeier, K. P. (1993), 'Pluralisierung und Polarisierung der Lebensformen in Deutschland', *Aus Politik und Zeitgeschichte* 17, 11-22.

Strohmeier, K. and Kersting, V. (2003), 'Segregierte Armut in der Stadtgesellschaft', *Informationen zur Raumentwicklung* 3:4, 231-35.

Sullivan, M. (1996), *The Development of the British Welfare State* (London: Harvester Wheatsheaf).

Szypkowski, B. (1997), *Die Kontinuität der guten Mutter* (Pfaffenweiler: Centaurus-Verlagsgesellschaft).

The Economist (2002), 'Cost-of-Living Index', *The Economist, 24 January.*

Thomas, H. and Klett-Davies, M. (1995), *Equal Pay for Work of Equal Value*, Department of Sociology, Goldsmiths' College (London: University of London).

Thurley, D. (ed.) (2003), *Working to Target: Can Policies Deliver Paid Work for Seven in Ten Lone Parents?* (London: One Parent Families).

Veil, M. (2003), 'Kinderbetreuungskulturen in Europa: Schweden, Frankreick, Deutschland', *Aus Politik und Zeitgeschichte* 44, 12-22.

Vetter, H., Richter, G. and Seil, K. (eds.) (2002), *Lebenslage Alleinerziehen – Theoretische Modelle und International Perspektiven* (München: Rainer Hamp Verlag).

Wagner, S. (1999), *Familien und Soziale Ungleichheit – Deutschland und Großbritannien im Vergleich* (München: tuduv Verlag).

Walby, S. (1990), *Theorising Patriarchy* (Oxford: Blackwell).

Walker, J. (1996), 'Changing families', in R. Humphrey (ed.).

Walther, U.J. (1992), *Wohnsituation Alleinerziehender*, Materialien zur Raumentwicklung 43. (Bonn: Bundesforschungsanstalt für Landeskunde und Raumordnung).

Walling, A. (2005), 'Families and work', *Labour Market Trends*, July, 275-283.

Whyte, W. F. (1984), *Learning from the Field – A Guide from Experience* (London: Sage).

Williams, F. (1993), 'Gender, 'race' and class in British welfare policy', in A. Cochrane and J. Clarke (eds.).

Wilson, M. (1993), 'The German welfare state: a conservative regime in crisis', in A. Cochrane and J. Clarke (eds.).

Winterborn, M. (1990), 'Single mother', *New Statesman and Society*, 26 January, 10-11.

Yin, R. K. (2003), *Case Study Research – Design and Methods* (London: Sage).

Zulauf, M. (1997), 'Mother and baby hostels: A viable option for young single mothers?', *Research, Policy and Planning* 15:1, 13-18.

Index